Bibliographical Guide
to
Self-Disclosure Literature:
1956-1976

Bibliographical Guide
to
Self-Disclosure Literature:
1956-1976

by

Carolyn Moss

Whitston Publishing Company
Troy, New York
1977

Library of Congress Catalog Card Number 77-89643

ISBN 0-87875-132-7

Printed in the United States of America

To my father, my husband, and my son:
Bonnie King, Sidney Moss, and Mark Kressenberg

PREFACE

The *Bibliographical Guide to Self-Disclosure Literature: 1956-1976* is divided into eight sections, as follows:

A. MAJOR REVIEWS OF SELF-DISCLOSURE LITERATURE
B. METHODOLOGY
C. DISCLOSER DIMENSIONS
D. DISCLOSEE (RECIPIENT OR TARGET OF DISCLOSURE) DIMENSIONS
E. INTERPERSONAL DIMENSIONS
F. SITUATIONAL DIMENSIONS: STRUCTURAL AND ENVIRON-MENTAL
G. MODIFICATION OF SELF-DISCLOSING BEHAVIOR: PRE-TRAINING, TRAINING, AND CONDITIONING
H. SELF-DISCLOSURE IN SPECIAL POPULATIONS

Six of these sections (A, B, C, D, E, H) are divided into topics. For example, Section B (METHODOLOGY) is divided into three topics, as follows:

B1. Parameters of Construct of Self-Disclosure
B2. Measures of Self-Disclosure
B3. Methodological Issues

Two of these topics (B1 and B2) are, in turn, divided into subtopics. For example, B1 (Parameters of Construct of Self-Disclosure) is divided into eight subtopics:

B1.1 Definition of self-disclosure
B1.2 Mode of disclosure: communication channel
B1.3 Stimulus for disclosure: solicited, volunteered, and reciprocated
B1.4 Concreteness of language
B1.5 Content of disclosure
B1.6 Vocalic communication
B1.7 Duration, length, and frequency of disclosure
B1.8 Interpersonal dimensions of disclosure

Some of these subtopics are also subdivided. For example, B1.1 (Definition of self-disclosure) is subdivided as follows:

B1.1.1 Facilitative self-disclosure
B1.1.2 Congruency, genuineness, authenticity

THE RUBRICS OF EVERY SECTION, TOPIC, AND SUBTOPIC
REPRESENT A SHORTHAND ANNOTATION OF ALL ENTRIES.

Within each section, topic, and subtopic, bibliographical entries are arranged in alphabetical order, according to the last name of the author or (if more than one) the last name of the first author. Additional entries by the same author or authors are arranged chronologically.[1]

An entry may occur more than once if a study touches upon more than one section, topic, or subtopic. For example, Jourard's "Self-Disclosure Scores and Grades in Nursing College" is entered three times, once under the topic H3 (College Students), again under the subtopic C3.9 (Performance and achievement), and still again under the sub-subtopic, B2.1.3 (Jourard self-disclosure questionnaires).

The rubrics under which this representative reference occurs can be found in two ways: by consulting the Table of Contents or the Subject Index. The Table of Contents provides a full outline of the *Guide;* the Subject Index alphabetically lists rubrics used in the *Guide.* An Author Index is also provided; it lists the name of every author cited, whether first or joint author.

In addition to the bibliographies and reviews listed in Section A, the following works issued from January 1956 to January 1977 were consulted:

Bibliographic Annual in Speech Communication
Books in Print
Current Index to Journals in Education
Dissertation Abstracts International
Educational Documents Index
Psychological Abstracts
Resources in Education
Social Science Index

Too, works in manuscript and master's theses were cited when their existence was known.

---

[1]Only one departure has been made from the bibliographical style of the *Publication Manual of the American Psychological Association,* second edition: the first names of authors were also used, rather than merely the initials, whenever those names were known.

Though the greatest diligence has been exercised in collecting, analyzing, and classifying the works cited in the *Guide,* there is always the likelihood that some errors and omissions have occurred. Judging from the testimony of other bibliographers, such a likelihood is inevitable. Fortunately, whatever inadvertencies have occurred can be corrected in future editions, if readers will be good enough to send their additions and corrections to the author via the publisher.

In the meantime the *Guide,* as it is the first full-scale bibliography of self-disclosure literature, should prove valuable as a reference tool. It is hoped that, with its topical framework, the *Guide* will also prove valuable in suggesting possibilities for future research in the field.

I wish to take this opportunity to thank Alan M. Cohn, Head of the Humanities Library of Southern Illinois University, Carbondale, for being so helpful in this enterprise. I also wish to express appreciation of my husband, Sidney Moss, for encouraging me at every turn.

TABLE OF CONTENTS

A. MAJOR REVIEWS OF SELF-DISCLOSURE LITERATURE

A1. *Annotated Bibliographies*

Breed, George and Jourard, Sidney M. *Research in self-disclosure: An annotated bibliography.* Unpublished manuscript. University of South Dakota, 1970.

A2. *General Reviews*

Cozby, Paul C. Self-disclosure: A literature review. *Psychological Bulletin,* 1973, *79,* 73-91.

Goodstein, Leonard D. and Reinecker, Virginia M. Factors affecting self-disclosure: A review of the literature. In Brendan A. Maher (Ed.), *Progress in experimental personality research* (Vol. 7). New York: Academic Press, 1974.

A3. *Selective Reviews*

Allen, Jon G. Implications of research in self-disclosure for group psychotherapy. *International Journal of Group Psychotherapy,* 1973, *23,* 306-321.

Pearce, W. Barnett and Sharp, Stewart M. Self-disclosing communication. *Journal of Communication.* 1973, *23,* 409-425.

Sinha, Virendra. Self-disclosure: Its clinical importance. *Indian Journal of Clinical Psychology,* 1974, *1,* 81-83.

Strassberg, Donald S.; Roback, Howard B.; D'Antonio, M.; and Gabel, Harris. Self-disclosure: A critical and selective review of the clinical literature. *Comprehensive Psychiatry,* in press.

B. METHODOLOGY

B1. *Parameters of Construct of Self-Disclosure*

B1.1 *Definition of self-disclosure*

Allen, Jon G. When does exchanging personal information constitute self-disclosure? *Psychological Reports,* 1974, *35,* 195-198.

Benner, Harold J. *Self-disclosure as a construct.* Unpublished doctoral dissertation, Michigan State University, 1968. *Dissertation Abstracts International,* 1969, *30* (1-A), 162.

Chaikin, Alan L. and Derlega, Valerian J. *Self-disclosure.* Morristown, New Jersey: General Learning Press, 1974.

Chelune, Gordon J. Self-disclosure: An elaboration of its basic dimensions. *Psychological Reports,* 1975, *36,* 79-95.

Culbert, Samuel A. The interpersonal process of self-disclosure: It takes two to see one. *Explorations in Applied Behavioral Science,* 1967, *3,* 2-31.

Derlega, Valerian J. and Chaikin, Alan L. *Sharing intimacy: What we reveal to others and why.* Englewood Cliffs, New Jersey: Prentice-Hall, Inc., 1975.

Egan, Gerald. *Encounter: Group processes for interpersonal growth.* Belmont, California: Brooks/Cole Publishing Company, 1970.

Egan, Gerald. *Face to face: The small group experience and interpersonal growth.* Belmont, California: Brooks/Cole Publishing Company, 1973.

3

Gilbert, Shirley J. and Whiteneck, Gale G. Toward a multidimensional approach to the study of self-disclosure. *Human Communication Research*, 1976, *2*, 347-355.

Goodstein, Leonard D. and Reinecker, Virginia M. Factors affecting self-disclosure: A review of the literature. In Brendan A. Maher (Ed.), *Progress in experimental personality research* (Vol. 7). New York: Academic Press, 1974.

Haggerty, P. A. *The concept of self-disclosure.* Unpublished master's thesis, Ohio State University, 1964.

Jourard, Sidney M. A study of self-disclosure. *Scientific American,* 1958, *198,* 77-82.

Jourard, Sidney M. Healthy personality and self-disclosure. *Mental Hygiene,* 1959, *43,* 499-507.

Jourard, Sidney M. *Personal adjustment: An approach through the study of healthy personality.* New York: Macmillan, 1964. (a) [revised and expanded edition, *Healthy personality: An approach from the viewpoint of humanistic psychology.* New York: Macmillan, 1974.]

Jourard, Sidney M. *The transparent self.* Princeton, New Jersey: D. Van Nostrand Company, 1964. (b)

Jourard, Sidney M. *Disclosing man to himself.* Princeton, New Jersey: D. Van Nostrand Company, 1968.

Jourard, Sidney M. The beginnings of self-disclosure. *Voices: The Art and Science of Psychotherapy,* 1970, *6,* 42-51.

Jourard, Sidney M. *Self-disclosure: An experimental analysis of the transparent self.* New York: Wiley-Interscience, 1971.

Jourard, Sidney M. and Lasakow, Paul. Some factors in self-disclosure. *Journal of Abnormal Social Psychology,* 1958, *56,* 91-98.

Luft, Joseph. *Of human interaction.* Palo Alto: National Press Books, 1969.

Luft, Joseph. The Johari window and self-disclosure. In Gerald Egan (Ed.), *Encounter groups: Basic readings.* Belmont, California: Brooks/Cole Publishing Company, 1971.

Moss, Carolyn J. *Effects of leader behavior in personal growth groups: Self-disclosure and experiencing.* Unpublished doctoral dissertation, Southern Illinois University, Carbondale, 1975. *Dissertation Abstracts International,* 1976, *36* (12-B), 6361.

Pearce, W. Barnett and Sharp, Stewart M. Self-disclosing communication. *Journal of Communication,* 1973, *23,* 409-425.

Plog, Stanley C. The disclosure of self in the United States and Germany. *Journal of Social Psychology,* 1965, *65,* 193-203.

Polansky, Norman A. The concept of verbal accessibility. *Smith College Studies in Social Work,* 1965, *36,* 1-46.

Powell, John. *Why am I afraid to tell you who I am?* Chicago: Peacock, 1969.

Rickers-Ovsiankina, Maria A. Social accessibility in three age groups. *Psychological Reports,* 1956, *2,* 283-294.

Rickers-Ovsiankina, Maria A. Cross-cultural study of social accessibility. *Acta Psychologica,* 1961, *19,* 872-873.

Rickers-Ovsiankina, Maria A. and Kusmin, Arnold. Individual differences in social accessibility. *Psychological Reports,* 1958, *4,* 391-406.

Wenburg, John R. and Wilmot, William W. *The personal communication process.* New York: Wiley, 1973.

B1.1.1   *Facilitative self-disclosure*

Carkhuff, Robert R. Toward a comprehensive model of facilitative inter-personal processes. *Journal of Counseling Psychology,* 1967, *14,* 67-72.

Carkhuff, Robert R. *Helping and human relations: A primer for lay and professional helpers* (2 vols.). New York: Holt, Rinehart and Winston, Inc., 1969.

B1.1.2   *Congruency, genuineness, authenticity (see also B1.8.2 Honesty and accuracy)*

Bayne, Rowan. Does the JSDQ measure authenticity? *Journal of Humanistic Psychology,* 1974, *14,* 79-86.

Jourard, Sidney M. Healthy personality and self-disclosure. *Mental Hygiene*, 1959, *43*, 499-507.

Jourard, Sidney M. *Personal adjustment: An approach through the study of healthy personality.* New York: Macmillan, 1964. (a) [revised and expanded edition], *Healthy personality: An approach from the viewpoint of humanistic psychology.* New York: Macmillan, 1974.

Jourard, Sidney M. *The transparent self.* Princeton, New Jersey: D. Van Nostrand Company, 1964. (b) [Revised ed., 1971]

Jourard, Sidney M. Counseling for authenticity. In Carlton E. Beck (Ed.), *Guidelines for guidance.* Dubuque, Iowa: William C. Brown, 1966.

Jourard, Sidney M. *Disclosing man to himself.* Princeton, New Jersey: D. Van Nostrand Company, 1968.

Rogers, Carl R. The necessary and sufficient conditions of therapeutic personality change. *Journal of Consulting Psychology,* 1957, *21*, 95-103.

Rogers, Carl R. The interpersonal relationship: The core of guidance. *Harvard Education Review,* 1962, *32*, 416-429.

Rogers, Carl R. The therapeutic relationship: Recent theory and research. *Australian Journal of Psychology,* 1965, *17*, 95-108.

Rogers, Carl R.; Gendlin, Eugene T.; Kiesler, Donald J.; and Truax, Charles B. (Eds.). *The therapeutic relationship and its impact: A study of psychotherapy with schizophrenics.* Madison: University of Wisconsin Press, 1967.

Truax, Charles B. Self-disclosure, genuineness, and the interpersonal relationship. *Counselor Education and Supervision,* 1971, *10*, 351-354.

B1.2 *Mode of disclosure: communication channel*

Culbert, Samuel A. The interpersonal process of self-disclosure: It takes two to see one. *Explorations in Applied Behavioral Science,* 1967, *3*, 2-31.

Gabbert, Larry C. *Interviewee self-disclosure as a function of two forms of interviewer disclosure.* Unpublished doctoral disserta-

tion, State University of New York, Albany, 1975. *Dissertation
Abstracts International*, 1976, *36* (11-A), 7205.

Gadaleto, Angelo I. *Differential effects of fidelity in client pretraining
on client anxiety, self-disclosure, satisfaction, and outcome.*
Unpublished doctoral dissertation, University of Virginia, 1976.
Dissertation Abstracts International, 1976, *37* (5-B), 2503.

Hick, Kenneth W.; Mitchell, Terence R.; Bell, Cecil H.; and Carter,
William B. Determinants of interpersonal disclosure: Some competitive tests. *Personality and Social Psychology Bulletin*, 1975, *1*,
620-623.

Janofsky, Annelies I. *A study of affective self-references in telephone
vs. face-to-face interviews.* Unpublished doctoral dissertation,
University of Oregon, 1970. *Dissertation Abstracts International*,
1971, *31* (10-B), 6258.

Janofsky, Annelies I. Affective self-disclosure in telephone vs. face-to-
face interviews. *Journal of Humanistic Psychology*, 1971, *11*, 93-
103.

Millard, Edward R. *The effects of writing assignments upon rational
thinking and level of self-disclosure in group counseling.* Unpublished doctoral dissertation, Fordham University, 1976. *Dissertation Abstracts International*, 1976, *37* (2-A), 813.

Moore, Dana L. *The effects of a model presented in two different
media upon two measures of self-disclosure.* Unpublished doctoral
dissertation, West Virginia University, 1976. *Dissertation Abstracts
International*, 1976 *37* (4-B), 1918.

Shapiro, Jeffrey G. Agreement between channels of communication
in interviews. *Journal of Consulting Psychology*, 1966, *30*, 535-
538.

Shapiro, Jeffrey G. Variability in the communication of affect. *Journal of Social Psychology*, 1968, *76*, 181-188.

B1.3 *Stimulus for the disclosure: solicited, volunteered, and reciprocated*

Allen, Jon G. When does exchanging personal information constitute
self-disclosure? *Psychological Reports*, 1974, *35*, 195-198.

Culbert, Samuel A. The interpersonal process of self-disclosure: It takes two to see one. *Explorations in Applied Behavioral Science,* 1967, *3,* 2-31.

Isaza, J.; Suchman, David; and Epting, Franz. *Elicited and provided self-disclosures.* Unpublished manuscript. University of Florida, 1970. [see A1. Breed and Jourard, 1970, pp. 8-9.]

Kaplan, Kalman J.; Firestone, Ira J.; Degnore, Roberta; and Moore, Michael. Gradiants of attraction as a function of disclosure probe intimacy and setting formality: On distinguishing attitude oscillation from attitude change—study one. *Journal of Personality and Social Psychology,* 1974, *30,* 638-646.

Moss, Carolyn J. *Effects of leader behavior in personal growth groups: Self-disclosure and experiencing.* Unpublished doctoral dissertation, Southern Illinois University, Carbondale, 1975. *Dissertation Abstracts International,* 1976, *36* (12-B), 6361.

Moss, Carolyn J. and Harren, Vincent A. Effects of leader disclosure on member disclosure in personal growth groups. *Small Group Behavior,* in press.

Pearce, W. Barnett and Sharp, Stewart M. Self-disclosing communication. *Journal of Communication,* 1973, *23,* 409-425.

Sermat, Vello and Smyth, Michael. Content analysis of verbal communication in the development of a relationship: Conditions influencing self-disclosure. *Journal of Personality and Social Psychology,* 1973, *26,* 332-346.

B1.4 *Concreteness of the language*

Carkhuff, Robert R. *Helping and human relations: A primer for lay and professional helpers* (2 vols.). New York: Holt, Rinehart, and Winston, Inc., 1969.

Moss, Carolyn J. *Effects of leader behavior in personal growth groups: Self-disclosure and experiencing.* Unpublished doctoral dissertation, Southern Illinois University, Carbondale, 1975. *Dissertation Abstracts International,* 1976, *36* (12-B), 6361.

Moss, Carolyn J. and Harren, Vincent A. Effects of leader disclosure on member disclosure in personal growth groups. *Small Group Behavior,* in press.

Stone, Gerald L. and Jackson, Ted. Internal-external control as a determinant of the effectiveness of modeling and instructions. *Journal of Counseling Psychology*, 1975, *22*, 294-298.

Truax, Charles B. and Carkhuff, Robert R. Concreteness: A neglected variable in psychotherapy. *Journal of Clinical Psychology*, 1964, *20*, 264-267.

West, Lloyd W. and Boutillier, Robert H. Increasing concreteness of expression of counsellees through observation learning. *Canadian Journal of Behavioral Science*, 1972, *4*, 364-370.

B1.5 *Content of disclosure*

B1.5.1 *Topic and area of the self revealed*

Burhenne, Dianne and Mirels, Herbert L. Self-disclosure in self-descriptive essays. *Journal of Consulting and Clinical Psychology*, 1970, *35*, 409-413.

Culbert, Samuel A. The interpersonal process of self-disclosure: It takes two to see one. *Explorations in Applied Behavioral Science*, 1967, *3*, 2-31.

Daher, Douglas M. *Types of self-disclosure content, similarity and interpersonal attraction.* Unpublished doctoral dissertation, University of Notre Dame, 1975. *Dissertation Abstracts*, 1975, *36* (6-B), 3118.

Daher, Douglas M. and Banikiotes, Paul G. Interpersonal attraction and rewarding aspects of disclosure content and level. *Journal of Personality and Social Psychology*, 1976, *33*, 492-496.

Fitzgerald, Maureen P. *Relationship between expressed self-esteem, assumed similarity, and self-disclosure.* Unpublished doctoral dissertation, Fordham University, 1961. *Dissertation Abstracts International*, 1962, *22* (12), 4402.

Fitzgerald, Maureen P. Self-disclosure and expressed self-esteem, social distance and areas of the self-revealed. *Journal of Social Psychology*, 1963, *56*, 405-412.

Friedman, Robert. *Eye-contact and self-disclosure.* Unpublished honors paper, University of Florida, 1968. [see 21 item questionnaire in Sidney M. Jourard, *Self-disclosure: An experimental analysis of the transparent self.* New York: Wiley-Interscience, 1971, Appendix 12, p. 215]

Giannandrea, Vincenzo and Murphy, Kevin C. Similarity self-disclosure and return for a second interview. *Journal of Counseling Psychology,* 1973, *20,* 545-548.

Gitter, A. George; Antonellis, Richard; and Cohen, Steven. *Candor of communication about self* (CRC Report No. 69). Boston: Boston University, 1975.

Goodstein, Leonard D. and Reinecker, Virginia M. Factors affecting self-disclosure: A review of the literature. In Brendan A. Maher (Ed.), *Progress in experimental personality research* (Vol. 7). New York: Academic Press, 1974.

Horner, Beverly M. *The effect of counselor similarity self-disclosure on clients with differing role expectations.* Unpublished doctoral dissertation, University of Iowa, 1974. *Dissertation Abstracts International,* 1975, *35* (7-A), 4158.

Jourard, Sidney M. A study of self-disclosure. *Scientific American,* 1958, *198,* 77-82.

Jourard, Sidney M. Self-disclosure and other-cathexis. *Journal of Abnormal Social Psychology,* 1959, *59,* 428-431. [15 item questionnaire]

Jourard, Sidney M. Self-disclosure scores and grades in nursing college. *Journal of Applied Psychology,* 1961, *45,* 244-247. (a) [25 item questionnaire]

Jourard, Sidney M. Self-disclosure patterns in British and American college females. *Journal of Social Psychology,* 1961, *54,* 315-320. (b)

Jourard, Sidney M. The effects of experimenters' self-disclosure on subjects' behavior. In Charles D. Spielberger (Ed.), *Current topics in clinical and community psychology* (Vol. 1). New York: Academic Press, 1969.

Jourard, Sidney M. *Self-disclosure: An experimental analysis of the transparent self.* New York: Wiley-Interscience, 1971. [all the questionnaires]

Jourard, Sidney M. and Lasakow, Paul. Some factors in self-disclosure. *Journal of Abnormal Social Psychology,* 1958, *56,* 91-98.

Ksionzky, Sheldon M. *Some determinants of breadth and depth of self-disclosure.* Unpublished doctoral dissertation, University of California, Los Angeles, 1974. *Dissertation Abstracts International,* 1975, *35* (10-B), 5117.

Levinger, George and Senn, David J. Disclosure of feelings in marriage. *Merrill-Palmer Quarterly,* 1967, *13,* 237-249.

Murphy, Kevin C. and Strong, Stanley R. Some effects of similarity self-disclosure. *Journal of Counseling Psychology,* 1972, *19,* 121-124.

Norton, Robert; Feldman, Charles; and Tafoya, Dennis. Risk parameters across types of secrets. *Journal of Counseling Psychology,* 1974, *21,* 450-454.

Pedersen, Darhl M. and Breglio, Vincent J. Personality correlates of actual self-disclosure. *Psychological Reports,* 1968, *22,* 495-501.

Plog, Stanley C. The disclosure of self in the United States and Germany. *Journal of Social Psychology,* 1965, *65,* 193-203. [40 item willingness-to-disclose questionnaire]

Polansky, Norman A.; Weiss, Erwin S.; and Blum, Arthur. Children's verbal accessibility as a function of content and personality. *American Journal of Orthopsychiatry,* 1961, *31,* 153-169.

Rickers-Ovsiankina, Maria A. Social accessibility in three age groups. *Psychological Reports,* 1956, *2,* 283-294. [25 item inventory]

Rickers-Ovsiankina, Maria A. and Kusmin, Arnold. Individual differences in social accessibility. *Psychological Reports,* 1958, *4,* 391-406. (50 item inventory)

Stehura, Eugene F. *The relationship between the experiencing scale and focusing method regarding the counselor in the clinical interview.* Unpublished doctoral dissertation, Illinois Institute of Technology, 1973. *Dissertation Abstracts International,* 1974, *35* (2-B), 1065.

Taylor, Dalmas A. and Altman, Irwin. *Intimacy-scaled stimuli for use in studies of interpersonal relationships.* Naval Medical Research Institute Report No. 9, Contract Number MF 022.01.-03-1002, Bethesda, Maryland, 1966. (Abridged version: *Psychological Reports,* 1966, *19,* 729-730) [671 items]

Tiwari, J. G. and Singh, Sultan. Self-disclosure in urban and rural students. *Journal of Psychological Researches*, 1967, *11*, 7-12.

Vondracek, Fred W. and Marshall, Marilyn J. Self-disclosure and interpersonal trust: An exploratory study. *Psychological Reports*, 1971, *28*, 235-240.

Vondracek, Sarah I. *The measurement and correlates of self-disclosure in pre-adolescents.* Unpublished doctoral dissertation, Pennsylvania State University, 1969. *Dissertation Abstracts International*, 1970, *30* (11-B), 5230.

West, Lloyd W. Sex differences in the exercise of circumspection in self-disclosure among adolescents. *Psychological Reports*, 1970, *26*, 226.

West, Lloyd W. Mapping the communication patterns of adolescents. *Canadian Counselor*, 1974, *8*, 54-65.

Worthy, Morgan; Gary, Albert L.; and Kahn, Gay M. Self-disclosure as an exchange process . *Journal of Personality and Social Psychology*, 1969, *13*, 59-63.

B1.5.2   *Privacy of the topic or importance for the discloser*

Culbert, Samuel A. The interpersonal process of self-disclosure: It takes two to see one . *Explorations in Applied Behavioral Science*, 1967, *3*, 2-31.

Isaza, Judith L. *Cross-cultural self-structure.* Unpublished doctoral dissertation, University of Florida, 1974. *Dissertation Abstracts International*, 1974, *35* (6-B), 2991.

Meares, Russell. The secret. *Psychiatry*, 1976, *39*, 258-265.

Polansky, Norman A. The concept of verbal accessibility. *Smith College Studies in Social Work*, 1965, *36*, 1-46.

Polansky, Norman A. and Brown, Sara Q. Verbal accessibility and fusion fantasy in a mountain country. *American Journal of Orthopsychiatry*, 1967, *37*, 651-660.

Rickers-Ovsiankina, Maria A. Social accessibility in three age groups. *Psychological Reports*, 1956, *2*, 283-294.

Rickers-Ovsiankina, Maria. Cross-cultural study of social accessibility. *Acta Psychologica*, 1961, *19*, 872-873.

Rickers-Ovsiankina, Maria A. and Kusmin, Arnold. Individual differences in social accesssibility. *Psychological Reports*, 1958, *4*, 391-406.

White, Roger L. *Adolescent and pubescent self-disclosure patterns: Phenomenal ratings of the privacy and importance of topics.* Unpublished doctoral dissertation, Claremont Graduate School, 1974. *Dissertation Abstracts International*, 1975, *35* (8-A), 5045.

B1.5.3   *Intimacy of the topic*

Altman, Irwin. Reciprocity of interpersonal exchange. *Journal for the Theory of Social Behavior*, 1973, *3*, 249-261.

Altman, Irwin and Haythorn, William W. Interpersonal exchange in isolation. *Sociometry*, 1965, *28*, 411-426.

Altman, Irwin and Taylor, Dalmas A. *Social penetration: The development of interpersonal relationships.* New York: Holt, Rinehart, and Winston, 1973.

Argyle, Michael. *The psychology of interpersonal behaviour.* Baltimore: Penguin, 1967.

Ayres, Joe and Ivie, Robert L. *Verbal patterns in dyadic interaction.* Paper presented at the Annual Meeting of the Western Speech Communication Association, Newport Beach, California, 1974. (ERIC Document Reproduction Service No. ED 099 919)

Brasfield, Charles R. *Intimacy of self-disclosure, availability of reaction to disclosure, and formation of interpersonal relationships.* Unpublished doctoral dissertation, University of British Columbia, Canada, 1971. *Dissertation Abstracts International*, 1972, *32,* (10-B), 6043.

Brasfield, Charles R. and Cubitt, Anne. Changes in self-disclosure behavior following an intensive "encounter" group experience. *Canadian Counselor*, 1974, *8*, 12-21.

Breed, George R. *Nonverbal communication and interpersonal attraction in dyads.* Unpublished doctoral dissertation, University of Florida, 1969. *Dissertation Abstracts International*, 1970, *31* (3-A), 1369.

Carr, Suzanne J. and Dabbs, James M. Jr. The effects of lighting, distance, and intimacy of topic on verbal and visual behavior. *Sociometry*, 1974, *37*, 592-600.

Certner, Barry C. *The exchange of self-disclosures in same-sexed and heterosexual groups of strangers.* Unpublished doctoral dissertation, University of Cincinnati, 1970. *Dissertation Abstracts International*, 1971, *31* (9-A), 4885.

Certner, Barry C. Exchange of self-disclosures in same-sexed groups of strangers. *Journal of Consulting and Clinical Psychology*, 1973, *40*, 292-297.

Chaikin, Alan L. and Derlega, Valerian J. *Self-disclosure.* Morristown, New Jersey: General Learning Press, 1974. (a)

Chaikin, Alan L. and Derlega, Valerian J. Variables affecting the appropriateness of self-disclosure. *Journal of Consulting and Clinical Psychology*, 1974, *42*, 588-593. (b)

Chaikin, Alan L.; Derlega, Valerian J.; Bayma, Benjamin; and Shaw, Jacqueline. Neuroticism and disclosure reciprocity. *Journal of Consulting and Clinical Psychology*, 1975, *43*, 13-19.

Chaikin, Alan L.; Derlega, Valerian J.; and Miller, Sarah J. Effects of room environment on self-disclosure in a counseling analogue. *Journal of Counseling Psychology*, 1976, *23*, 479-481.

Chelune, Gordon J. Self-disclosure: An elaboration of its basic dimensions. *Psychological Reports*, 1975, *36*, 79-85.

Chelune, Gordon J. *Studies in the behavioral and self-report assessment of self-disclosure.* Unpublished doctoral dissertation, University of Nevada, Reno, 1976. *Dissertation Abstracts International*, 1976, *37* (1-B), 453.

Cogan, James M. *The effect of the presence or absence of another person on the verbalizations of schizophrenics under a demand for intimate self-disclosure.* Unpublished doctoral dissertation, University of Missouri, Columbia, 1975. *Dissertation Abstracts International*, 1976, *36* (7-B), 3594.

Daher, Douglas M. *Types of self-disclosure content, similarity and interpersonal attraction.* Unpublished doctoral dissertation, University of Notre Dame, 1975. *Dissertation Abstracts International*, 1975, *36* (6-B), 3118.

Daher, Douglas M. and Banikiotes, Paul G. Interpersonal attraction and rewarding aspects of disclosure content and level. *Journal of Personality and Social Psychology*, 1976, *33*, 492-496.

Davis, John D. Self-disclosure in an acquaintance exercise: Responsibility for level of intimacy. *Journal of Personality and Social Psychology*, 1976, *33*, 787-792.

Derlega, Valerian J. *Social penetration processes: The effects of acquaintance, topic intimacy, and support on nonverbal behavior.* Unpublished doctoral dissertation, University of Maryland, 1971. *Dissertation Abstracts International*, 1972, *32* (10-B), 6025-6026.

Derlega, Valerian J. and Chaikin, Alan L. *Sharing intimacy: What we reveal to others and why.* Englewood Cliffs, New Jersey: Prentice Hall, Inc., 1975.

Derlega, Valerian J.; Chaikin, Alan L.; and Herndon, James. Demand characteristics and disclosure reciprocity. *Journal of Social Psychology*, 1975, *97*, 301-302.

Dietch, James and House, James. Affiliative conflict and individual differences in self-disclosure. *Representative Research in Social Psychology*, 1975, *6*, 69-75.

Ehrlich, Howard J. and Graeven, David B. Reciprocal self-disclosure in a dyad. *Journal of Experimental Social Psychology*, 1971, *7*, 389-400.

Ellsworth, Phoebe and Ross, Lee. Intimacy in response to direct gaze. *Journal of Experimental Social Psychology*, 1975, *11*, 592-613.

Gilbert, Shirley J. and Whiteneck, Gale G. Toward a multidimensional approach to the study of self-disclosure. *Human Communication Research*, 1976, *2*, 347-355.

Gitter, A. George; Antonellis, Richard; and Cohen, Steven. *Candor of communication about self* (CRC Report No. 69). Boston: Boston University, 1975.

Gorman, John R. *Adjustment and self-disclosing behavior of Roman Catholic priests.* Unpublished doctoral dissertation, Loyola University of Chicago, 1973. *Dissertation Abstracts International*, 1973, *34* (1-B), 413.

15

Hick, Kenneth W.; Mitchell, Terence R.; Bell, Cecil H.; and Carter, William B. Determinants of interpersonal disclosure: Some competitive tests. *Personality and Social Psychology Bulletin*, 1975, *1*, 620-623.

Hyink, Paul W. *The influence of client ego-strength, client sex and therapist sex on the frequency, depth, and focus of client self-disclosure.* Unpublished doctoral dissertation, Michigan State University, 1974. *Dissertation Abstracts International*, 1975, *35* (9-B), 4652.

Jones, Mary G. *Self-disclosure among deaf adolescents and its relationship to social sensitivity and personality.* Unpublished doctoral dissertation, The Catholic University of America, 1975. *Dissertation Abstracts International*, 1975, *36* (3-B), 1437.

Jourard, Sidney M. The effects of experimenters' self-disclosure on subjects' behavior. In Charles D. Spielberger (Ed.), *Current topics in clinical and community psychology* (Vol. 1). New York: Academic Press, 1969.

Jourard, Sidney M. *Self-disclosure: An experimental analysis of the transparent self.* New York: Wiley-Interscience, 1971.

Jourard, Sidney M. and Jaffe, Peggy E. Influence of an interviewer's disclosure on the self-disclosing behavior of interviewees. *Journal of Counseling Psychology*, 1970, *17*, 252-257.

Keiser, George J. and Altman, Irwin. Relationship of nonverbal behavior to the social penetration process. *Human Communication Research*, 1976, *2*, 147-161.

Kirshner, Barry J. *The effects of experimental manipulation of self-disclosure on group cohesiveness.* Unpublished doctoral dissertation, University of Maryland, 1976. *Dissertation Abstracts International*, 1976, *37* (6-B), 3081.

Krause, Fred. *An investigation of verbal exchanges between strangers.* Unpublished doctoral dissertation, Yeshiva University, 1969. *Dissertation Abstracts International*, 1969, *30* (3-A), 1235.

Ksionzky, Sheldon M. *Some determinants of breadth and depth of self-disclosure.* Unpublished doctoral dissertation, University of California, Los Angeles, 1974. *Dissertation Abstracts International*, 1975, *35* (10-B), 5117.

O'Hare, Christopher. *Impact of intimacy and temporal orientation of helper self-disclosure on the helping process.* Unpublished doctoral dissertation, University of California, 1975. *Dissertation Abstracts International,* 1976, *36* (7-B), 3618.

Page, Janice M. *Social penetration processes: The effects of interpersonal reward and cost factors on the stability of dyadic relationships.* Unpublished doctoral dissertation. The American University, 1969. *Dissertation Abstracts International,* 1969, *30* (4-A), 1638.

Persons, Roy W. Jr. *Interpersonal intimacy with recidivists.* Unpublished doctoral dissertation, Ohio State University, 1969. *Dissertation Abstracts International,* 1969, *30* (4-B), 1905.

Persons, Roy W. and Marks, Philip A. Self-disclosure with recidivists: Optimum interviewer-interviewee matching. *Journal of Abnormal Psychology,* 1970, *76,* 387-391.

Petzelt, John A. *Self-disclosure and interpersonal attraction: The intimacy value and attitudinal similarity of the content of disclosure.* Unpublished doctoral dissertation, Georgia State University, 1973. *Dissertation Abstracts International,* 1974, *34* (8-B), 4026.

Rubin, Zick. Lovers and other strangers: The development of intimacy in encounters and relationships. *American Scientist,* 1974, *62,* 182-190.

Rubin, Zick. Disclosing oneself to a stranger: Reciprocity and its limits. *Journal of Experimental Social Psychology,* 1975, *11,* 233-260.

Rubin, Zick. Naturalistic studies of self-disclosure. *Personality and Social Psychology Bulletin,* 1976, *2,* 260-263.

Savicki, Victor E. *Self-disclosure strategy and personal space proximity in intimacy development.* Unpublished doctoral dissertation, University of Massachusetts, 1971, *Dissertation Abstracts International,* 1971, *31* (8-B), 5008.

Sermat, Vello and Smyth, Michael. Content analysis of verbal communication in the development of a relationship: Conditions influencing self-disclosure. *Journal of Personality and Social Psychology,* 1973, *26,* 332-346.

Sherman, Richard C. and Goodson, John L. The intimacy of discussion topics: A comparison of three scaling methods. *Bulletin of the Psychonomic Society,* 1975, *6,* 581-584.

Shimkunas, Algimantas M. Demand for intimate self-disclosure and pathological verbalization in schizophrenia. *Journal of Abnormal Psychology,* 1972, *80,* 197-205.

Switkin, Linda R. *Self-disclosure as a function of sex roles, experimenter-subject distance, sex of experimenter and intimacy of topics.* Unpublished doctoral dissertation, St. Louis University, 1974. *Dissertation Abstracts International,* 1974, *35* (5-B), 2451.

Taylor, Dalmas A. *Some aspects of the development of interpersonal relationships: Social penetration processes.* ONR Technical Report, No. 1, Contract Number Nonr-2285(04), Center for Research on Social Behavior, University of Delaware, 1965.

Taylor, D   nas A. *Some aspects of the development of interpersonal relationships: Social penetration processes.* Unpublished doctoral dissertation, University of Delaware, 1966. *Dissertation Abstracts International,* 1967, *28* (4-A), 1530.

Taylor, Dalmas A. The development of interpersonal relationships: Social penetration processes. *Journal of Social Psychology,* 1968, *75,* 79-90.

Taylor, Dalmas A. *Self-disclosure as an exchange process: Reinforcement effects.* Paper presented at the Meeting of the American Psychological Association, Montreal, Canada, 1973. (ERIC Document Reproduction Service No. ED 083 521)

Taylor, Dalmas A. and Altman, Irwin. *Intimacy-scaled stimuli for use in studies of interpersonal relationships.* Naval Medical Research Institute Report, No. 9, Contract Number MF 022.01.03-1002. Bethesda, Maryland, 1966. (Abridged version: *Psychological Reports,* 1966, *19,* 729-730)

Taylor, Dalmas A. and Altman, Irwin. Self-disclosure as a function of reward-cost outcomes. *Sociometry,* 1975, *38,* 18-31.

Taylor, Dalmas A.; Altman, Irwin; and Sorrentino, Richard. Interpersonal exchange as a function of rewards and costs and situational factors: Expectancy confirmation-disconfirmation. *Journal of Experimental Social Psychology,* 1969, *5,* 324-339.

Taylor, Dalmas A.; Wheeler, Ladd; and Altman, Irwin. Self-disclosure in isolated groups. *Journal of Personality and Social Psychology*, 1973, *26*, 39-47.

Tognoli, Jerome J. *Reciprocal behavior in interpersonal information exchange.* Unpublished doctoral dissertation, University of Delaware, 1967. *Dissertation Abstracts International*, 1968, *29* (3-B), 1193.

Tognoli, Jerome J. Response matching in interpersonal information exchange. *British Journal of Social and Clinical Psychology*, 1969, *8*, 116-123.

Vondracek, Fred W. and Marshall, Marilyn J. Self-disclosure and interpersonal trust: An exploratory study. *Psychological Reports*, 1971, *28*, 235-240.

Wagner, Mary P. *Intimacy of self-disclosure and response processes as factors affecting the development of interpersonal relationships.* Unpublished doctoral dissertation, University of Minnesota, 1975. *Dissertation Abstracts International*, 1976, *36* (7-B), 3684.

Wagner, Stephen C. *The effects of pretraining and intimacy level of topic on depth of self-disclosure.* Unpublished doctoral dissertation, Ohio State University, 1976. *Dissertation Abstracts International*, 1976, *37* (6-B), 3101.

Walker, Lilly J. *Friendship patterning as affected by intimate and nonintimate self-disclosure.* Unpublished doctoral dissertation, University of North Dakota, 1972. *Dissertation Abstracts International*, 1973, *33* (7-B), 3326.

Walker, Lilly S. and Wright, Paul H. Self-disclosure in friendship. *Perceptual and Motor Skills*, 1976, *42*, 735-742.

Wheeless, Lawrence R. and Grotz, Janis. Conceptualization and measurement of reported self-disclosure. *Human Communication Research*, 1976, *2*, 338-346.

Young, Barbara A. *The effects of sex, assigned therapist or peer role, topic intimacy, and expectations of partner compatibility on dyadic communication patterns.* Unpublished doctoral dissertation, University of Southern California, 1969. *Dissertation Abstracts International*, 1969, *30* (2-B), 857.

B1.5.3 Methodology

Zoberi, Seemie. *Rapport by operant conditioning.* Unpublished doctoral dissertation, University of South Dakota, 1973. *Dissertation Abstracts International,* 1974, *34* (5-B), 2324.

B1.5.4 *Valence, social desirability of the experience: positive and negative*

Adesso, Vincent J.; Euse, Franklin J.; Hanson, Richard W.; Hendry, Derek; and Choco, Pedro. Effects of a personal growth group on positive and negative self-references. *Psychotherapy: Theory, Research and Practice,* 1974, *11,* 354-355.

Axtell, Bryan and Cole, Charles W. Repression-sensitization response mode and verbal avoidance. *Journal of Personality and Social Psychology,* 1971, *18,* 133-137.

Crowley, Thomas J. *The conditionability of positive and negative self-reference emotional affect statements in a counseling type interview.* Unpublished doctoral dissertation, University of Massachusetts, 1970. *Dissertation Abstracts International,* 1970, *31* (5-A), 2100.

Derlega, Valerian J.; Harris, Marian S. and Chaikin, Alan L. Self-disclosure reciprocity, liking and the deviant. *Journal of Experimental Social Psychology,* 1973, *9,* 277-284.

Doster, Joseph A. and Brooks, Samuel J. Interviewer disclosure modeling, information revealed, and interviewee verbal behavior. *Journal of Consulting and Clinical Psychology,* 1974, *42,* 420-426.

Gilbert, Shirley J. and Horenstein, David. The communication of self-disclosure: Level versus valence. *Human Communication Research,* 1975, *1,* 316-322.

Gilbert, Shirley J. and Whiteneck, Gale G. Toward a multidimensional approach to the study of self-disclosure. *Human Communication Research,* 1976, *2,* 347-355.

Jones, Edward E. and Archer, Richard L. Are there special effects of personalistic self-disclosure? *Journal of Experimental Social Psychology,* 1976, *12,* 180-193.

Jones, Edward E. and Gordon, Eric M. Timing of self-disclosure and its effects on personal attraction. *Journal of Personality and Social Psychology,* 1972, *24,* 358-365.

Katz, Irwin; Goldstein, Judith; Cohen, Melvin; and Stucker, Solomon. Need satisfaction, perception, and cooperative interaction in married couples. *Marriage and Family Living*, 1963, *25*, 209-214.

Kessel, Elizabeth V. *Interpersonal trust and attitude toward the expression of positive and negative affect within the T-group.* Unpublished doctoral dissertation, West Virginia University, 1971. *Dissertation Abstracts International*, 1971, *32* (4-A), 1855-1856.

Krohn, Marvin; Waldo, Gordon P.; and Chiricos, Theodore G. Self-reported delinquency: A comparison of structured interviews and self-administered checklists. *Journal of Criminal Law and Criminology*, 1974, *65*, 545-553.

Levin, Fredrica M. and Gergen, Kenneth J. Revealingness, ingratiation, and the disclosure of self. *Proceedings of the 77th Annual Convention of the American Psychological Association*, 1969, *4*, 447-448.

Levinger, George and Senn, David J. Disclosure of feelings in marriage. *Merrill-Palmer Quarterly*, 1967, *13*, 237-249.

Lieberman, Morton A.; Yalom, Irvin D.; and Miles, Matthew B. *Encounter groups: First facts.* New York: Basic Books, 1973. [expression of positive and negative affect]

Moss, Carolyn J. *Effects of leader behavior in personal growth groups: Self-disclosure and experiencing.* Unpublished doctoral dissertation, Southern Illinois University, Carbondale, 1975. *Dissertation Abstracts International*, 1976, *36* (12-B), 6361.

Moss, Carolyn J. and Harren, Vincent A. Effects of leader disclosure on member disclosure in personal growth groups. *Small Group Behavior*, in press.

Nelson-Jones, Richard and Strong, Stanley R. Positive and negative self-disclosure, timing, and personal attraction. *The British Journal of Social and Clinical Psychology*, 1976, *15*, 323-325.

Paradis, Mark H. *The effects of eye contact on positive and negative self-disclosure.* Unpublished doctoral dissertation, Washington State, 1972. *Dissertation Abstracts International*, 1972, *33* (6-B), 2795.

B1.5.4 Methodology

Shapiro, Jeffrey G. Variability in the communication of affect. *Journal of Social Psychology,* 1968, *76,* 181-188.

Shapiro, Jeffrey G.; Krauss, Herbert H.; and Truax, Charles B. Therapeutic conditions and disclosure beyond the therapeutic encounter. *Journal of Counseling Psychology,* 1969, *16,* 290-294.

Shapiro, Jeffrey G.; McCarroll, J. E.; and Fine, H. Perceived therapeutic conditions and disclosure to significant others. *Discussion Papers,* Arkansas Rehabilitation Research and Training Center, 1967, *1.* [*see* A1. Breed and Jourard, 1970, pp. 40-41]

Simon, William E. The AEPT: An adjunct in counseling. *Personnel and Guidance Journal,* 1973, *51,* 350-352.

Tolor, Alexander; Cramer, Marie; D'Amico, Denis; and O'Marra, Margaret. The effects of self-concept, trust, and imagined positive or negative self-disclosures on psychological space. *Journal of Psychology,* 1975, *89,* 9-24.

Vajner, Paul R. *The effects of different types of interviewer self-disclosure on verbal behavior and relationship in the initial interview.* Unpublished doctoral dissertation, Ohio University, 1975. *Dissertation Abstracts International,* 1976, *36* (11-B), 5821.

Wheeless, Lawrence R. Self-disclosure and interpersonal solidarity: Measurement, validation, and relationships. *Human Communication Research,* 1976, *3,* 47-61.

Wheeless, Lawrence R. and Grotz, Janis. Conceptualization and measurement of reported self-disclosure. *Human Communication Research,* 1976, *2,* 338-346.

Wortman, Camille B.; Adesman, Peter; Herman, Elliot; and Greenberg, Richard. Self-disclosure: An attributional perspective. *Journal of Personality and Social Psychology,* 1976, *33,* 184-191.

B1.5.5 *Verbal affect*

Allen, Jon G. *Adaptive function of affect in interpersonal interaction.* Unpublished doctoral dissertation, University of Rochester, 1973. *Dissertation Abstracts International,* 1973, *33* (12-B), 6069.

Cleland, Robert S. and Carnes, G. Derwood. Emotional vs. ideational emphasis during group counseling with student nurses. *Journal of Counseling Psychology,* 1965, *12,* 282-286.

Crowley, Thomas J. *The conditionability of positive and negative self-reference emotional affect statements in a counseling type interview.* Unpublished doctoral dissertation, University of Massachusetts, 1970. *Dissertation Abstracts International,* 1970, *31,* (5-A), 2100.

Crowley, Thomas J. and Ivey, Allen E. Dimensions of effective interpersonal communications: Specifying behavioral components. *Journal of Counseling Psychology,* 1970, *23,* 266-271.

Dawson, Carolyn. *Affect and self-disclosure as a function of touch in an interview between strangers.* Unpublished doctoral dissertation, Colunbia University, 1973. *Dissertation Abstracts International,* 1973, *34* (6-B), 2925.

Fuller, James B. *An investigation of self-disclosing behavior and the affective response within a T-group.* Unpublished doctoral dissertation West Virginia University, 1971. *Dissertation Abstracts International,* 1971, *32* (4-A), 1852.

Goodman, G. M. Findings from a study of emotional disclosure in psychotherapy relationships. *Counseling Center Discussion Papers,* University of Chicago, 1962, *8* (13). [*see* A1. Breed and Jourard, 1970, p. 11]

Green, Alan H. and Marlatt, G. Alan. Effects of intructions and modeling upon affective and descriptive verbalization. *Journal of Abnormal Psychology,* 1972, *80,* 189-196.

Highlen, Pamela S. *Effects of social modeling and cognitive structuring strategies on affective self-disclosure of single undergraduate college males.* Unpublished doctoral dissertation, Michigan State University, 1975. *Dissertation Abstracts International,* 1976, *36* (9-A), 5823.

Janofsky, Annelies I. *A study of affective self-references in telephone vs. face-to-face interviews.* Unpublished doctoral dissertation, University of Oregon, 1970. *Dissertation Abstracts International,* 1971, *31* (10-B), 6258.

Janofsky, Annelies I. Affective self-disclosure in telephone vs. face-to-face interviews. *Journal of Humanistic Psychology,* 1971, *11,* 93-103.

B1.5.5 Methodology

Kessel, Elizabeth V. *Interpersonal trust and attitude toward the expression of positive and negative affect within the T-group.* Unpublished doctoral dissertation, West Virginia University, 1971. *Dissertation Abstracts International,* 1971, *32* (4-A), 1855-1856.

Levinger, George and Senn, David J. Disclosure of feelings in marriage. *Merrill-Palmer Quarterly,* 1967, *13,* 237-249.

Lieberman, Morton A.; Yalom, Irvin D.; and Miles, Matthew B. *Encounter groups: First facts.* New York: Basic Books, 1973. ["expressivity"]

Mann, Joe W. *The effects of reflection and race on verbal conditioning of affective self-disclosure in black and white males.* Unpublished doctoral dissertation, Auburn University, 1972. *Dissertation Abstracts International,* 1972, *33* (6-A), 2717.

Moss, Carolyn J. *Effects of leader behavior in personal growth groups: Self-disclosure and experiencing.* Unpublished doctoral dissertation, Southern Illinois University, Carbondale, 1975. *Dissertation Abstracts International,* 1976, *36* (12-B), 6361.

Moss, Carolyn J. and Harren, Vincent A. Effects of leader disclosure on member disclosure in personal growth groups. *Small Group Behavior,* in press.

Neff, Richard. The group constellation. *Psychotherapy: Theory, Research and Practice,* 1974, *11,* 80-82.

Pearson, Richard E. *Verbal behavior in the training group setting of individuals differing in conceptual style.* New York: Syracuse University, 1966. (ERIC Document Reproduction Service No. ED 050 420)

Shapiro, Jeffrey G. Agreement between channels of communication in interviews. *Journal of Counseling Psychology,* 1966, *30,* 535-538.

Shapiro, Jeffrey G.; Krauss, Herbert H.; and Truax, Charles B. Therapeutic conditions and disclosure beyond the therapeutic encounter. *Journal of Counseling Psychology,* 1969, *16,* 290-294.

Shapiro, Jeffrey G.; McCarroll, J. E.; and Fine, H. Perceived therapeutic conditions and disclosure to significant others. *Discussion Papers,* Arkansas Rehabilitation Research and Training Center, 1967, *1.* [*see* A1. Breed and Jourard, 1970, pp. 40-41]

Shapiro, Jeffrey G. and Truax, Charles B. *Therapeutic conditions and disclosure in a normal population.* Unpublished manuscript. [*see* A1. Breed and Jourard, 1970, p. 41]

Smallwood, Ronney E. *Group modification of affective and self-disclosing verbalizations in a psychiatric population.* Unpublished doctoral dissertation, Oklahoma State University, 1975. *Dissertation Abstracts International,* 1976, *36* (11-B), 5817.

Vajner, Paul R. *The effects of different types of interviewer self-disclosure on verbal behavior and relationship in the initial interview.* Unpublished doctoral dissertation, Ohio University, 1975. *Dissertation Abstracts International,* 1976, *36* (11-B), 5821.

Voight, Nancy L. *The effects of self-management strategies as initial training and as secondary training for affective self-disclosure of undergraduate males.* Unpublished doctoral dissertation, Michigan State University, 1975. *Dissertation Abstracts International,* 1976, *36* (9-A), 5842.

B1.5.6   *Spatial/temporal focus of the disclosure: here-and-now, there-and-then*

Kangas, Jon A. Group members' self-disclosure: A function of preceding self-disclosure by leader or other group member. *Comparative Group Studies,* 1971, *2,* 65-70.

Kuppersmith, Joel H. *The relative effects of here-and-now versus there-and-then self-disclosure upon personality and cohesiveness in marathon encounter groups.* Unpublished doctoral dissertation, University of Mississippi, 1975. *Dissertation Abstracts International,* 1975, *36* (4-A), 2028.

MacDoniels, Joseph W. *Factors related to the level of open expression in small group laboratory learning experiences.* Unpublished doctoral dissertation, University of Kansas, 1972. *Dissertation Abstracts International,* 1973, *33* (11-A), 6488-6489.

Moss, Carolyn J. *Effects of leader behavior in personal growth groups: Self-disclosure and experiencing.* Unpublished doctoral dissertation, Southern Illinois University, Carbondale, 1975. *Dissertation Abstracts International,* 1976, *36* (12-B), 6361.

Moss, Carolyn J. and Harren, Vincent A. Effects of leader disclosure on member disclosure in personal growth groups. *Small Group Behavior,* in press.

Neff, Richard. The group constellation. *Psychotherapy: Theory, Research and Practice*, 1974, *11*, 80-82.

O'Hare, Christopher. *Impact of intimacy and temporal orientation of helper self-disclosure on the helping process.* Unpublished doctoral dissertation, University of California, Los Angeles, 1975. *Dissertation Abstracts International*, 1976, *36* (7-B), 3618.

Pearson, Richard E. *Verbal behavior in the training group setting of individuals differing in conceptual style.* New York: Syracuse University, 1966. (ERIC Document Reproduction Service No. ED 050 420)

Wiener, Morton and Mehrabian, Albert. *Language within a language: Immediacy, a channel in verbal communication.* New York: Appleton-Century-Crofts, 1968.

B1.6 *Vocalic communication*

[for background on vocalic communication *see:* Hart, Roland J. and Brown, Bruce L. Interpersonal information conveyed by the content and vocal aspects of speech. *Speech Monographs*, 1974, *41*, 371-380; Pearce, W. Barnett and Brommel, Bernard J. Vocal communication and persuasion. *Quarterly Journal of Speech*, 1972, *58*, 298-306; and Pearce, W. Barnett and Conklin, Forrest. Nonverbal vocalic communication and perceptions of the speaker. *Speech Monographs*, 1971, *38*, 235-241.]

Fischer, Michael J. and Apostal, Robert A. Selected vocal cues and counselor's perceptions of genuineness, self-disclosure, and anxiety. *Journal of Counseling Psychology*, 1975, *22*, 92-96.

Moss, Carolyn J. *Effects of leader behavior in personal growth groups: Self-disclosure and experiencing.* Unpublished doctoral dissertation, Southern Illinois University, Carbondale, 1975. *Dissertation Abstracts International*, 1976, *36* (12-B), 6361.

Moss, Carolyn J. and Harren, Vincent A. Effects of leader disclosure on member disclosure in personal growth groups. *Small Group Behavior*, in press.

B1.7 *Duration, length, and frequency of the disclosure*

Hyink, Paul W. *The influence of client ego-stength, client sex and therapist sex on the frequency, depth, and focus of client self-*

disclosure. Unpublished doctoral dissertation, Michigan State University, 1974. *Dissertation Abstracts International, 1975, 35* (9-B), 4652.

Moss, Carolyn J. *Effects of leader behavior in personal growth groups: Self-disclosure and experiencing.* Unpublished doctoral dissertation, Southern Illinois University, Carbondale, 1975. *Dissertation Abstracts International, 1976, 36* (12-B), 6361.

Moss, Carolyn J. and Harren, Vincent A.   Effects of leader disclosure on member disclosure in personal growth groups. *Small Group Behavior*, in press.

Vondracek, Fred W.   Behavioral measurement of self-disclosure. *Psychological Reports, 1969, 25,* 914.

Wheeless, Lawrence R. and Grotz, Janis.   Conceptualization and measurement of reported self-disclosure. *Human Communication Research, 1976, 2,* 338-346.

B1.8 *Interpersonal dimensions of disclosure (see also E2. Interpersonal Process)*

B1.8.1 *Motivation for the disclosure (see also B1.8.2 Honesty and acuracy)*

Burke, Ronald J.; Weir, Tamara; and Harrison, Denise.   Disclosure of problems and tensions experienced by marital partners. *Psychological Reports, 1976, 38,* 531-542.

Carkhuff, Robert R.   Toward a comprehensive model of facilitative inter-personal processes. *Journal of Counseling Psychology, 1967, 14,* 67-72.

Carkhuff, Robert R.   *Helping and human relations: A primer for lay and professional helpers* (2 vols.).   New York: Holt, Rinehart and Winston, Inc., 1969.

Culbert, Samuel A.   The interpersonal process of self-disclosure: It takes two to see one.   *Explorations in Applied Behavioral Science, 1967, 3,* 2-31.

Granoff, Mendell.   *An analysis of meanings and consequences of self-disclosing behavior.*   Unpublished doctoral dissertation, Universtiy of Texas, 1970. *Dissertation Abstracts International, 1971, 31* (11-A), 5844.

Jourard, Sidney M. Healthy personality and self-disclosure. *Mental Hygiene*, 1959, *43*, 499-507. (a)

Jourard, Sidney M. I-thou relationship versus manipulation in counseling and psychotherapy. *Journal of Individual Psychology*, 1959, *15*, 174-179. (b)

Jourard, Sidney M. *Personal adjustment: An approach through the study of healthy personality.* New York: Macmillan, 1964. (a) [revised and expanded edition, *Healthy personality: An approach from the viewpoint of humanistic psychology.* New York: Macmillan, 1974.]

Jourard, Sidney M. *The transparent self.* Princeton: D. Van Nosstrand Company, 1964. (b)

Jourard, Sidney M. *Disclosing man to himself.* Princeton: D. Van Nostrand Company, 1968.

Komarovsky, Mirra. Patterns of self-disclosure of male undergraduates. *Journal of Marriage and the Family*, 1974, *36*, 677-686.

Levin, Fredrica M. and Gergen, Kenneth J. Revealingness, ingratiation, and the disclosure of self. *Proceedings of the 77th Annual Convention of the American Psychological Association*, 1969, *4*, 447-448.

Mowrer, O. Hobart. *The new group therapy.* Princeton: D. Van Nosstrand Company, 1964.

Rogers, Carl R. The necessary and sufficient conditions of therapeutic personality change. *Journal of Consulting Psychology*, 1957, *21*, 95-103.

Rogers, Carl R. *On becoming a person.* Boston: Houghton Mifflin Company, 1961.

Rogers, Carl R. The interpersonal relationship: The core of guidance. *Harvard Education Review*, 1962, *32*, 416-429.

Rogers, Carl R. The therapeutic relationship: Recent theory and research. *Australian Journal of Psychology*, 1965, *17*, 95-108.

Rogers, Carl R.; Gendlin, Eugene T.; Kiesler, Donald J.; and Truax, Charles B. (Eds.). *The therapeutic relationship and its impact: A study of psychotherapy with schizophrenics.* Madison: University of Wisconsin Press, 1967.

Rossiter, Charles M. Jr. and Pearce, W. Barnett. *Communicating personally: A theory of interpersonal communication and human relations.* Indianapolis: Bobbs-Merrill, 1975.

Truax, Charles B. Self-disclosure, genuineness, and the interpersonal relationship. *Counselor Education and Supervision,* 1971, *10,* 351-354.

Truax, Charles B.; Altmann, Hal; and Whittmer, Joe. Self-disclosure as a function of personal adjustment and the facilitative condition offered by the target person. *Journal of Community Psychology,* 1973, *1,* 319-322.

Truax, Charles B. and Carkhuff, Robert R. Client and therapist transparency in the therapeutic encounter. *Journal of Counseling Psychology,* 1965, *12,* 3-9.

Truax, Charles B. and Mitchell, Kevin M. The psychotherapeutic and the psychonoxious: Human encounters that change behavior. In Marvin J. Feldman (Ed.), *Studies in psychotherapy and behavioral change* (Vol. 1). Buffalo: State University of New York Press, 1968.

Truax, Charles B. and Mitchell, Kevin M. Research on certain therapist interpersonal skills in relation to process and outcome. In Allen E. Bergin and Sol L. Garfield (Eds.), *Handbook of psychotherapy and behavior change: An empirical analysis.* New York: John Wiley and Sons, 1971.

B1.8.2 *Honesty and accuracy (see also B1.1.2 Congruency, genuiness, authenticity)*

Ball, John C. The reliability and validity of interview data obtained from 59 narcotic addicts. *American Journal of Sociology,* 1967, *72,* 650-654.

Bayne, Rowan. Does the JSDQ measure authenticity? *Journal of Humanistic Psychology,* 1974, *14,* 79-86.

Gitter, A. George. *Studies in "hypocrisy."* Paper presented at the 18th International Congress of Psychology, Moscow, 1966.

Gitter, A. George; Antonellis, Richard; and Cohen, Steven. *Candor of communication about self* (CRC Report No. 69). Boston: Boston University, 1975.

B1.8.2 Methodology

Gitter, A. George and Blakely, L. *Veracity of self-disclosed information* (CRC Report No. 39). Boston: Boston University, 1968.

Gitter, A. George and Brown, Harvey. Is self-disclosure self-revealing? *Journal of Counseling Psychology,* 1976, *23,* 327-332.

Gitter, A. George and Frankfurt, Leslie P. *Expectations and gilding.* Paper presented at the Meeting of the Western Psychological Association, San Diego, March, 1968.

Hines, D. A. and Woodyard, H. D. *Accurate compared to inaccurate self-disclosure.* Unpublished manuscript, University of Florida, no date given. [*see* A1. Breed and Jourard, 1970, p. 14]

Levin, Fredrica and Gergen, Kenneth J. Revealingness, ingratiation, and the disclosure of self. *Proceedings of the 77th Annual Convention of the American Psychological Association,* 1969, *4,* 447-448.

Meares, Russell. The secret. *Psychiatry,* 1976, *39,* 258-265.

Moustakas, Clark. Honesty, idiocy, and manipulation. *Journal of Humanistic Psychology,* 1962, *2,* 1-15.

Polansky, Norman A. On duplicity in the interview. *American Journal of Orthopsychiatry,* 1967, *37,* 568-580.

Sobell, Linda C. and Sobell, Mark B. Outpatient alcoholics give valid self-reports. *Journal of Nervous and Mental Disease,* 1975, *161,* 32-42.

Sobell, Mark B.; Sobell, Linda C.; and Samuels, Fred H. Validity of self-reports of alcohol-related arrests by alcoholics. *Quarterly Journal of Studies on Alcohol,* 1974, *35,* 276-280.

Stephens, Richard. The truthfulness of addict respondents in research projects. *International Journal of the Addictions,* 1972, *7,* 549-558.

Summers, Trudy. Validity of alcoholics' self-reported drinking history. *Quarterly Journal of Studies on Alcohol,* 1970, *31,* 972-974.

Wheeless, Lawrence R. Self-disclosure and interpersonal solidarity: Measurement, validation, and relationships. *Human Communication Research,* 1976, *3,* 46-61.

Wheeless, Lawrence R. and Grotz, Janis. Conceptualization and measurement of reported self-disclosure. *Human Communication Research,* 1976, *2,* 338-346.

Woodyard, Howard D. and Hines, David A. Accurate compared to inaccurate self-disclosure. *Journal of Humanistic Psychology,* 1973, *13,* 61-67.

B1.8.3   *Appropriateness and flexibility*

Chaikin, Alan L. and Derlega, Valerian J. Variables affecting the appropriateness of self-disclosure. *Journal of Consulting and Clinical Psychology,* 1974, *42,* 588-593.

Chaikin, Alan L.; Derlega, Valerian J.; Bayma, Benjamin; and Shaw, Jacqueline. Neuroticism and disclosure reciprocity. *Journal of Consulting and Clinical Psychology,* 1975, *43,* 13-19.

Chelune, Gordon J. Self-disclosure: An elaboration of its basic dimensions. *Psychological Reports,* 1975, *36,* 79-85.

Chelune, Gordon J. A multidimensional look at sex and target differences in disclosure. *Psychological Reports,* 1976, *39,* 259-263. (a)

Chelune, Gordon J. Self-disclosure Situations Survey: A new approach to measuring self-disclosure. *Catalog of Selected Documents in Psychology,* 1976, *6,* 111-112. (b)

Chelune, Gordon J. *Studies in the behavioral and self-report assessment of self-disclosure.* Unpublished doctoral dissertation, University of Nevada, Reno, 1976. *Dissertation Abstracts International,* 1976, *37* (1-B), 453. (c)

Culbert, Samuel A. The interpersonal process of self-disclosure: It takes two to see one. *Explorations in Applied Behavioral Science,* 1967, *3,* 2-31.

Derlega, Valerian. Effects of therapist self-disclosure and its perceived appropriateness on client self-disclosure. *Journal of Consulting and Clinical Psychology,* in press.

Derlega, Valerian J. and Chaikin, Alan L. *Sharing intimacy: What we reveal to others and why.* Englewood Cliffs, New Jersey: Prentice-Hall, Inc., 1975.

Luft, Joseph. *Of human interaction.* Palo Alto: National Press Books, 1969.

Luft, Joseph. The Johari window and self-disclosure. In Gerald Egan (Ed.), *Encounter groups: Basic Readings.* Belmont, California: Brooks/Cole Publishing Company, 1971.

Stein, Waltraut J. The myth of the transparent self. *Journal of Humanistic Psychology,* 1975, *15,* 71-77.

B1.8.4 *Timing or ordering of the disclosure and stage of the relationship*

Altman, Irwin. Reciprocity of interpersonal exchange. *Journal for the Theory of Social Behavior,* 1973, *3,* 249-261.

Altman, Irwin and Haythorn, William W. Interpersonal exchange in isolation. *Sociometry,* 1965, *28,* 411-426.

Altman, Irwin and Taylor, Dalmas A. *Social penetration: The development of interpersonal relationships.* New York: Holt, Rinehart, and Winston, 1973.

Anchor, Kenneth N. and Sandler, Howard M. Psychotherapy sabotage and avoidance of self-disclosure. *Proceedings of the 81st Annual Convention of the American Psychological Association,* 1973, *8,* 485-486.

Anchor, Kenneth N. and Sandler, Howard M. Psychotherapy sabotage revisited: The better half of individual psychotherapy. *Journal of Clinical Psychology,* 1976, *32,* 146-148.

Bednar, Richard L.; Melnick, Joseph; and Kaul, Theodore J. Risk, responsibility, and structure: A conceptual framework for initiating group counseling and psychotherapy. *Journal of Counseling Psychology,* 1974, *21,* 31-37.

Culbert, Samuel A. The interpersonal process of self-disclosure: It takes two to see one. *Explorations in Applied Behavioral Science,* 1967, *3,* 2-31.

Dies, Robert R. Group therapist self-disclosure: An evaluation by clients. *Journal of Counseling Psychology,* 1973, *20,* 344-348.

Dies, Robert R.; Cohen, Lauren; and Pines, Sharon. Content considerations in group therapist self-disclosure. *Proceedings of the*

81st Annual Convention of the American Psychological Association, 1973, *8*, 481-482.

Gilbert, Shirley J. and Whiteneck, Gale G. Toward a multidimensional approach to the study of self-disclosure. *Human Communication Research*, 1976, *2*, 347-355.

Himelstein, Philip and Kimbrough, Wilson W. Jr. A study of self-disclosure in the classroom. *Journal of Psychology*, 1963, *55*, 437-440.

Jones, Edward E. and Gordon, Eric M. Timing of self-disclosure and its effects on personal attraction. *Journal of Personality and Social Psychology*, 1972, *24*, 358-365.

Mann, Brenda and Murphy, Kevin C. Timing of self-disclosure and reactions to an initial interview. *Journal of Counseling Psychology*, 1975, *22*, 304-308.

Nelson-Jones, Richard and Strong, Stanley R. Positive and negative self-disclosure, timing, and personal attraction. *The British Journal of Social and Clinical Psychology*, 1976, *15*, 323-325.

Olberz, Paul D. and Steiner, Ivan D. Order of disclosure and the attribution of dispositional characteristics. *Journal of Social Psychology*, 1969, *79*, 287-288.

Pearce, W. Barnett and Sharp, Stewart. Self-disclosing communication. *Journal of Communication*, 1973, *23*, 409-425.

Sousa-Poza, Joaquin F. and Rohrberg, Robert. Communicational and interactional aspects of self-disclosure in psychotherapy: Differences related to cognitive style. *Psychiatry*, 1976, *39*, 81-91.

Taylor, Dalmas A. *Some aspects of the development of interpersonal relationships: Social penetration processes.* ONR Technical Report, No. 1, Contract Number Nonr-2285(04), Center for Research on Social Behavior, University of Delaware, 1965.

Taylor, Dalmas A. The development of interpersonal relationships: Social penetration processes. *Journal of Social Psychology*, 1968, *75*, 79-90.

Taylor, Dalmas A. and Altman, Irwin. Self-disclosure as a function of reward-cost outcomes. *Sociometry*, 1975, *38*, 18-31.

B1.8.4 Methodology

Taylor, Dalmas A.; Altman, Irwin; and Sorrentino, Richard. Interpersonal exchange as a function of rewards and costs and situational factors: Expectancy confirmation-disconfirmation. *Journal of Experimental Social Psychology*, 1969, *5*, 324-339.

Taylor, Dalmas A.; Wheeler, Ladd; and Altman, Irwin. Self-disclosure in isolated groups. *Journal of Personality and Social Psychology*, 1973, *26*, 39-47.

Wortman, Camille B.; Adesman, Peter; Herman, Elliot; and Greenberg, Richard. Self-disclosure: An attributional perspective. *Journal of Personality and Social Psychology*, 1976, *33*, 184-191.

B1.8.5 *Reciprocity of disclosure, dyadic effect (see E2.1 Reciprocity, dyadic effect)*

B1.8.6 *Willingness to disclose (see C3.5.3 Willingness to disclose)*

B2. *Measures of Self-Disclosure*

B2.1 *Self-reports of disclosure*

B2.1.1 *Social accessibility scale*

Rickers-Ovsiankina, Maria A. Social accessibility in three age groups. *Psychological Reports*, 1956, *2*, 283-294. [25 item questionnaire]

Rickers-Ovsiankina, Maria A., and Kusmin, Arnold A. Individual differences in social accessibility. *Psychological Reports*, 1958, *4*, 391-406. [50 item questionnaire]

B2.1.2 *Verbal accessibility scale*

Plog, Stanley C. The disclosure of self in the United States and Germany. *Journal of Social Psychology*, 1965, *65*, 193-203. [questionnaire]

Polansky, Norman A. The concept of verbal accessibility. *Smith College Studies in Social Work*, 1965, *36*, 1-46.

Polansky, Norman A., and Brown, Sara Q. Verbal accessibility and fusion fantasy in a mountain country. *American Journal of Orthopsychiatry*, 1967, *37*, 651-660. [incomplete sentence method]

B2.1.3 *Jourard self-disclosure questionnaires*

Bayne, Rowan. Does the JSDQ measure authenticity? *Journal of Humanistic Psychology*, 1974, *14*, 79-86.

Drag, Lee R. *Experimenter-subject interation: A situational determinant of differential levels of self-disclosure.* Unpublished master's thesis, University of Florida, 1968. [40 item "Game of Invitations"]

Jourard, Sidney M. Self-disclosure and other-cathexis. *Journal of Abnormal Social Psychology*, 1959, *59*, 428-431. [15 item questionnaire]

Jourard, Sidney M. Self-disclosure scores and grades in nursing college. *Journal of Applied Psychology*, 1961, *45*, 244-247. [25 item questionnaire]

Jourard, Sidney M. The effects of experimenters' self-disclosure on subjects' behavior. In Charles D. Spielberger (Ed.), *Current topics in clinical and community psychology* (Vol. 1). New York: Academic Press, 1969. [40 item questionnaire scaled for intimacy level]

Jourard, Sidney M. *Self-disclosure: An experimental analysis of the transparent self.* New York: Wiley-Interscience, 1971. [all the questionnaires]

Jourard, Sidney M. and Lasakow, Paul. Some factors in self-disclosure. *Journal of Abnormal Social Psychology*, 1958, *56*, 91-98. [60 item questionnaire]

Kinder, Bill N. Evidence for a nonlinear relationship between self-disclosure and self-actualization. *Psychological Reports*, 1976, *38*, 631-634. [JSDQ-40 and Personal Orientation Inventory]

Lombardo, John P.; Franco, Raymond; Wolf, Thomas M.; and Fantasia, Saverio C. Interest in entering helping activities and self-disclosure to three targets on the Jourard Self-Disclosure Scale. *Perceptual and Motor Skills*, 1976, *42*, 299-302.

B2.1.3.1 *Modifications of the Jourard Self-Disclosure Questionnaire*

Low, A. B. *Sex and religious differences in self-disclosure as determined by a revised method of scoring the Jourard self-disclo-*

sure questionnaire. Unpublished master's thesis, University of Florida, 1964.

Lubin, Bernard J. A modified version of the self-disclosure inventory. *Psychological Reports,* 1965, *17,* 498.

Lubin, Bernard J. and Harrison, Roger L. Predicting small group behavior with the self-disclosure inventory. *Psychological Reports,* 1964, *15,* 77-78.

B2.1.3.2 *Reliability and validity studies of the Jourard questionnaires*

Abendroth, Walter R. *A validity study of the self-disclosure questionnaire.* Unpublished doctoral dissertation, Indiana University, 1974. *Dissertation Abstracts International,* 1975, *35* (8-A), 5005.

Burhenne, Dianne and Mirels, Herbert L. Self-disclosure in self-descriptive essays. *Journal of Consulting and Clinical Psychology,* 1970, *35,* 409-413.

DeLeon, Patrick H.; DeLeon, Jean L.; and Sheflin, Joseph A. A validation study of self-disclosure. *Proceedings of the 78th Annual Convention of the American Psychological Association,* 1970, *5,* 473-474.

Ehrlich, Howard J. and Graeven, David B. Reciprocal self-disclosure in a dyad. *Journal of Experimental Social Psychology,* 1971, *7,* 389-400.

Fiske, Donald W. Some hypotheses concerning the test adequacy. *Educational and Psychological Measurement,* 1966, *26,* 69-88.

Halverson, Charles F. and Shore, Roy E. Self-disclosure and interpersonal functioning. *Journal of Consulting and Clinical Psychology,* 1969, *33,* 213-217.

Himelstein, Philip and Kimbrough, Wilson W. Jr. A study of self-disclosure in the classroom. *Journal of Psychology,* 1963, *55,* 437-440.

Himelstein, Philip and Lubin, Bernard. Attempted validation of the self-disclosure inventory by the peer-nomination technique. *Journal of Psychology,* 1965, *61,* 13-16.

Hurley, John R. and Hurley, Shirley J. Toward authenticity in measuring self-disclosure. *Journal of Psychology,* 1969, *16,* 271-274.

Jourard, Sidney M. Self-disclosure and Rorschach productivity. *Perceptual and Motor Skills,* 1961, *13,* 232.

Jourard, Sidney M. Self-disclosure scores and grades in nursing college. *Journal of Applied Psychology,* 1961, *45,* 244-247.

Jourard, Sidney M. and Guertin, W. H. *Factor analysis of a measure of self-disclosure.* Unpublished manuscript. [*see* A1 Breed and Jourard, 1970]

Komaridis, George V. *A validation study of Jourard's self-disclosure scale.* Unpublished master's thesis, University of Nebraska, 1965.

Lind, Dennis R. *A study of the self-disclosure and self-presentation variables.* Unpublished doctoral dissertation, University of Colorado, 1970. *Dissertation Abstracts International,* 1971, *32* (2-B), 1217.

Lubin, Bernard J. and Harrison, Roger L. Predicting small group behavior with the self-disclosure inventory. *Psychological Reports,* 1964, *15,* 77-78.

O'Reilly, Edmund F. Jr. *An investigation of the contruct validity of self-disclosure questionnaire responses using a social judgment technique.* Unpublished doctoral dissertation, State University of New York, Albany, 1971. *Dissertation Abstracts International,* 1971, *32* (4-B), 2424.

Panyard, Christine M. A method to improve the reliability of the Jourard self-disclosure questionnare. *Journal of Counseling Psychology,* 1971, *18,* 606.

Panyard, Christine M. Self-disclosure between friends: A validity study. *Journal of Counseling Psychology,* 1973, *20,* 66-68.

Pearce, W. Barnett and Wiebe, Bernie. Item-analysis of Jourard's self-disclosure questionnaire-21. *Educational and Psychological Measurement,* 1975, *35,* 115-118.

Pedersen, Darhl M. and Breglio, Vincent J. The correlation of two self-disclosure inventories with actual self-disclosure: A validity study. *Journal of Psychology*, 1968, *68*, 291-298.

Pedersen, Darhl M. and Higbee, Kenneth L. An evaluation of the equivalence and construct validity of various measures of self-disclosure. *Educational and Psychological Measurement*, 1968, *28*, 511-523. [also includes Rickers-Ovsiankina and Kusmin (1958) Social Accessibility Scale]

Resnick, Jaquelyn L. *The effect of high revealing subjects on the self-disclosure of low revealing subjects.* Paper presented at Southeastern Psychological Association, Louisville, Kentucky, 1970.

Sullivan, Donald J. *Self-disclosure: Measurement, relationships with other personality dimensions, and modifiability.* Unpublished doctoral dissertation, University of Texas Southwestern Medical School, Dallas, 1972. *Dissertation Abstracts International*, 1972, *33* (1-B), 454.

Swensen, Clifford H. Jr.; Shapiro, Arnold; and Gilner, Frank. *The Validity of Jourard's self-disclosure scale.* Unpublished manuscript. [summary in A1. Breed and Jourard, 1970]

Taylor, Dalmas A. The development of interpersonal relationships: Social penetration processes. *Journal of Social Psychology*, 1968, *75*, 79-90.

Van Atta, Ralph E. *A correlational analysis of the construct of openness.* Unpublished manuscript, Southern Illinois University, Carbondale, 1971.

Vondracek, Fred W. The manipulation of self-disclosure in an experimental interview situation. Unpublished doctoral dissertation, Pennsylvania State University, 1968. *Dissertation Abstracts International*, 1969, *30* (3-B), 1350.

Vondracek, Fred W. Behavioral measurement of self-disclosure. *Psychological Reports*, 1969, *25*, 914. (a)

Vondracek, Fred W. The study of self-disclosure in experimental interviews. *Journal of Psychology*, 1969, *72*, 55-59. (b)

B2.1.4 *Other self-reports*

Allen, Jon G. When does exchanging personal information constitute self-disclosure? *Psychological Reports*, 1974, *35*, 195-198.

Barrell, James and Jourard, Sidney. Being honest with persons we like. *Journal of Individual Psychology*, 1976, *32*, 185-193. [a phenomenological measure]

Brodsky, Stanley L. An inventory for measuring prisoner disclosure of institutionally related events. *Correctional Psychologist*, 1969, *3*, 18-20.

Burke, Ronald J.; Weir, Tamara; and Harrison, Denise. Disclosure of problems and tensions experienced by marital partners. *Psychological Reports*, 1976, *38*, 531-542.

Callan, Joanne E. *A measure of self-disclosure in intensive small groups.* Unpublished doctoral dissertation, University of Texas at Austin, 1970. *Dissertation Abstracts International*, 1971, *31* (7-B), 4306. [Texas Inventory of Group Member Experience]

Chelune, Gordon J. Self-disclosure: An elaboration of its basic dimensions. *Psychological Reports*, 1975, *36*, 79-85.

Chelune, Gordon J. Self-Disclosure Situations Survey: A new approach to measuring self-disclosure. *Catalog of Selected Documents in Psychology*, 1976, *6*, 111-112. (a)

Chelune, Gordon J. *Studies in the behavioral and self-report assessment of self-disclosure.* Unpublished doctoral dissertation, University of Nevada, Reno, 1976. *Dissertation Abstracts International*, 1976, *37* (1-B), 453. (b)

Dies, Robert R. Group therapist self-disclosure: Development and validation of a scale. *Journal of Consulting and Clinical Psychology*, 1973, *41*, 97-103. [Therapist Orientation Scale]

Esposito, Ronald P.; McAdoo, Harriette; and Scher, Linda. The Johari Window as an evaluative instrument for group process. *Interpersonal Development*, 1975/76, *6*, 25-37.

Granoff, Mendell. *An analysis of meanings and consequences of self-disclosing behavior.* Unpublished doctoral dissertation, University of Texas at Austin, 1970. *Dissertation Abstracts International*, 1971, *31* (11-A), 5844. [Interpersonal Behaviors Scale]

Goodstein, Leonard D.; Goldstein, Joel J.; D'Orta, Carolyn V.; and Goodman, Margaret A. Measurement of self-disclosure in encounter groups: A methodological study. *Journal of Counseling Psychology*, 1976, *23*, 142-146. [self-ranking]

Hackett, Jay K. *An investigation of the correlation between teacher observed and self-reported affective behavior toward science.* Unpublished doctoral dissertation, University of Northern Colorado, 1972. *Dissertation Abstracts International,* 1972, *33* (3-A), 1078. [Affective Self-Report Instrument]

Hill, Clara E. *An investigation of the effects of therapist and client variables on the psychotherapy process.* Unpublished doctoral dissertation, Southern Illinois University, Carbondale, 1974. *Dissertation Abstracts International,* 1975, *35* (12-B), 6095.

Howard, Kenneth I.; Orlinsky, David E.; and Hill, James A. Content of dialogue in pshycotherapy. *Journal of Counseling Psychology,* 1969, *16,* 396-404.

Isaza, Judith L. *Cross-cultural self structure.* Unpublished doctoral dissertation, University of Florida, 1974. *Dissertation Abstracts International,* 1974, *35* (6-B), 2991.

Levinger, George and Senn, David J. Disclosure of feelings in marriage. *Merrill-Palmer Quarterly,* 1967, *13,* 237-249.

Luft, Joseph. *Of human interaction.* Palo Alto: National Press Books, 1969. [Johari Window]

Luft, Joseph. The Johari Window and self-disclosure. In Gerald Egan (Ed.), *Encounter groups: Basic readings.* Belmont, California: Brooks/Cole Publishing Company, 1971.

Mylet, M. *The Worthy-Mylet Self-Disclosure Scale.* Unpublished manuscript. [*see* A1. Breed and Jourard, 1970, p. 33]

Pearlman, Virginia H. *Development and validation of two companion instruments for measuring the quality of openness: The O. M. Semantic Differential and O. M. Graphic.* Unpublished doctoral dissertation, Purdue University, 1972. *Dissertation Abstracts International,* 1973, *34* (1-A), 139.

Pedersen, Darhl M. and Higbee, Kenneth L. Self-disclosure and relationship to the target person. *Merrill-Palmer Quarterly,* 1969, *15,* 213-220. [Target Person Rating Scale]

Potkay, Charles R.; Allen, Bem P.; and Haapoja, Nancy. Use of the adjective generation technique in a therapy context: Case application. *Psychotherapy: Theory, Research, and Practice,* 1973, *10,* 343-347. [Adjective Generation Technique]

Ricci, Joseph St. Elmo Jr. *Self-disclosure: Redefinition and remeasurement.* Unpublished doctoral dissertation, University of South Dakota, 1975. *Dissertation Abstracts International,* 1976, *37* (5-B), 2576 [Who Am I?]

Trafton, Richard. *Encounter group process: A descriptive analysis.* Unpublished master's thesis, Southern Illinois University, Carbondale, 1974. [Trafton Session Report]

West, Lloyd W. Mapping the communication patterns of adolescents. *Canadian Counselor,* 1974, *8,* 54-65. [Self-Disclosure Inventory for Adolescents]

West, Lloyd W. and Zingle, Harvey W. A self-disclosure inventory for adolescents. *Psychological Reports,* 1969, *24,* 439-445.

Wheeless, Lawrence R. Self-disclosure and interpersonal solidarity: measurement, validation, and relationships. *Human Communication Research,* 1976, *3,* 37-61.

Wheeless, Lawrence R. and Grotz, Janis. Conceptualization and measurement of reported self-disclosure. *Human Communication Research,* 1976, *2,* 338-346.

White, Roger L. *Adolescent and pubescent self-disclosure patterns: Phenomenal ratings of the privacy and importance of topics.* Unpublished doctoral dissertation, Claremont Graduate School, 1974. *Dissertation Abstracts International,* 1975, *35* (8-A), 5045.

Wile, Daniel B.; Bron, Gary D.; and Pollack, Herbert B. The Group Therapy Questionnaire: An instrument for study of leadership in small groups. *Psychological Reports,* 1970, *27,* 263-273.

B2.1.4.1 *Other validity studies*

DeShong, Hal G. Jr. *A factor analytic investigation of a measure of self-disclosure in intensive small groups.* Unpublished doctoral dissertation, University of Texas at Austin, 1971. *Dissertation Abstracts International,* 1972, *33* (2-A), 612.

West, Lloyd W. A study of the validity of the Self-Disclosure Inventory for Adolescents. *Perceptual and Motor Skills,* 1971, *33,* 91-100.

B2.2 Methodology

B2.2 Peer ratings and rankings: perceived self-disclosure

Allen, Jon G. When does exchanging personal information constitute self-disclosure? *Psychological Reports,* 1974, *35,* 195-198.

Banikiotes, Paul G. and McCabe, Sheridan P. Measurement of self-disclosure: Self-report, ratings of peers and supervisors. *Psychological Reports,* 1974, *34,* 754.

Goodstein, Leonard D.; Goldstein, Joel J.; D'Orta, Carolyn V.; and Goodman, Margaret A. Measurement of self-disclosure in encounter groups: A methodological study. *Journal of Counseling Psychology,* 1976, *23,* 142-146.

Himelstein, Philip and Lubin, Bernard. Attempted validation of the self-disclosure inventory by the peer-nomination technique. *Journal of Psychology,* 1965, *61,* 13-16.

Hurley, John R. and Hurley Shirley J. Toward authenticity in measuring self-disclosure. *Journal of Counseling Psychology,* 1969, *16,* 271-274.

Kahn, M. H. and Rudestam, K. E. The relationship between liking and perceived self-disclosure in small groups. *Journal of Psychology,* 1971, *78,* 81-85.

May, Orlan P. *Self-disclosure and mental health: A study of encounter-group members' perceptions of group leaders.* Unpublished doctoral dissertation, University of Tennessee, 1972. *Dissertation Abstracts International,* 1973, *33* (8-A), 4092.

Rogers, Richard and Wright, E. Wayne. Preliminary study of perceived self-disclosure. *Psychological Reports,* 1976, *38,* 1334.

Schrum, Jerry D. *The effects of empathy, self-disclosure, and the social desirability response set on the development of interpersonal relationships within growth-oriented psychotherapy groups.* Unpublished doctoral dissertation, Southern Illinois University, Carbondale, 1971. *Dissertation Abstracts International,* 1972, *33* (2-B), 922.

Steele, Dennis D. *Self-disclosure and peak experience in intensive small groups.* Unpublished doctoral dissertation, University of Utah, 1973. *Dissertation Abstracts International,* 1973, *34* (7-B), 3476.

Trafton, Richard. *Encounter group process: A descriptive analysis.*
Unpublished master's thesis. Southern Illinois University, Carbondale, 1974.

Weigel, Richard; Dinges, Norman; Dyer, Robert; and Straumfjord,
A. A. Perceived self-disclosure, mental health, and who is liked in
group treatment. *Journal of Counseling Psychology,* 1972, *19,* 47-
52.

Weigel, Richard and Warnath, Charles F. The effects of group therapy
on reported self-disclosure. *International Journal of Group Psychotherapy,* 1968, *18,* 31-41.

B2.3   *Judges' ratings of actual disclosure*

B2.3.1   *Written disclosure*

Burhenne, Dianne and Mirels, Herbert L. Self-disclosure in self-descriptive essays. *Journal of Consulting and Clinical Psychology,*
1970, *35,* 409-413.

Derlega, Valerian J.; Wilson, Midge; and Chaikin, Alan L. Friendship
and disclosure reciprocity. *Journal of Personality and Social Psychology,* 1976, *34,* 578-582.

Green, R. *A sentence completion procedure for measuring self-disclosure.* Unpublished master's thesis, Ohio State University,
1964. [*see* B2.1.3 Jourard, 1971]

Heifitz, M. L. *Experimenter effect upon openness of response to
the Rotter Incomplete Sentence Blank.* Unpublished honors
paper, University of Florida, 1967. [*see* B2.1.3 Jourard, 1969]

Levinger, G. and Senn, D. J. Disclosure of feelings in marriage.
Merrill-Palmer Quarterly, 1967, *13,* 237-249.

Lewis, David M. A TST based technique for the study of self-disclosure. *Sociological Quarterly,* 1970, *11,* 556-558. [Twenty Statements Test]

Mark, Elizabeth W. *Sex differences in intimacy motivation: A projective approach to the study of self-disclosure.* Unpublished
doctoral dissertation, Boston College, 1976. *Dissertation Abstracts International,* 1976, *37* (2-B), 1040.

Polansky, Norman A. and Brown, Sara Q. Verbal accessibility and fusion fantasy in a mountain country. *American Journal of Orthopsychiatry,* 1967, *37,* 651-660. [incomplete sentences]

Rubin, Zick. Disclosing oneself to a stranger: Reciprocity and its limits. *Journal of Experimental Social Psychology,* 1975, *11,* 233-260.

Sermat, Vello and Smyth, Michael. Content analysis of verbal communication in the development of a relationship: Conditions influencing self-disclosure. *Journal of Personality and Social Psychology,* 1973, *26,* 332-346. [teletypewritten messages]

Simon, William E. The AEPT: An adjunct in counseling. *Personnel and Guidance Journal,* 1973, *51,* 350-352. [Accuracy of Emotional Perception Technique]

Smyth, Michael. *Self-disclosure in homogeneous and heterogeneous dominant dyads.* Unpublished doctoral dissertation, York University, Canada, 1975. *Dissertation Abstracts International,* 1976, *37* (1-B), 530.

Sullivan, Donald J. *Self-disclosure: Measurement, relationships with other personality dimensions, and modifiability.* Unpublished doctoral dissertation. University of Texas, Southwestern Medical School, 1972. *Dissertation Abstracts International,* 1972, *33* (1-B), 454.

Worthy, Morgan; Gary, Albert L.; and Kahn, Gay M. Self-disclosure as an exchange process. *Journal of Personality and Social Psychology,* 1969, *13,* 59-63. [written notes exchanged in response to written questions]

B2.3.2 *Oral disclosure*

Abulsaad, Kamal G. Therapist's labeling statements and client's self-disclosure: A process psychotherapy study. Unpublished doctoral dissertation, University of Georgia, 1975. *Dissertation Abstracts International,* 1976, *36* (8-B), 4143.

Adler, Lois E. *The dimensions of self-disclosure from three vantage points.* Unpublished doctoral dissertation, Columbia University, 1973. *Dissertation Abstracts International,* 1973, *34* (5-B), 2294.

Allen, Jon G. When does exchanging personal information constitute self-disclosure? *Psychological Reports,* 1974, *35,* 195-198.

Althouse, Richard H. *Enhancing self-disclosure and cohesiveness in psychotherapy groups: An analogue study.* Unpublished doctoral dissertation, Pennsylvania University, 1975. *Dissertation Abstracts International,* 1976, *36* (7-B), 3668.

Anchor, Kenneth N. *Interaction patterns in experimental, marathon, and traditionally spaced groups.* Unpublished master's thesis, University of Connecticut, 1970. [Group Interaction Profile]

Anchor, Kenneth N. *High and low risk self-disclosure in group psychotherapy.* Paper presented at the Midwestern Psychological Association Meeting, Chicago, 1974. *Resources in Education* 1975, *10* (ERIC Document Reproduction Service No. ED 099746)

Axtell, Bryan and Cole, Charles W. Repression-sensitization response mode and verbal avoidance. *Journal of Personality and Social Psychology,* 1971, *18,* 133-137.

Berger, S. E. and Anchor, Kenneth N. The disclosure process in group interaction. *Proceedings of the 78th Annual Convention of the American Psychological Association,* 1970, *5,* 529-530.

Brooks, Linda. Interactive effects of sex and status on self-disclosure. *Journal of Counseling Psychology,* 1974, *21,* 469-474.

Carkhuff, Robert R. *Helping and human relations: A primer for lay and professional helpers* (2 vols.). New York: Holt, Rinehart, & Winston, Inc., 1969.

Carkhuff, Robert R. and Burstein, Julian W. Objective therapist and client ratings of therapist-offered facilitative conditions of moderate to low functioning therapists. *Journal of Clinical Psychology,* 1970, *26,* 394-395.

Cash, Thomas F. *Self-disclosure in the acquaintance process: Effects of sex, physical attractiveness, and approval motivation.* Unpublished doctoral dissertation, George Peabody College for Teachers, 1974. *Dissertation Abstracts International,* 1975, *35* (7-B), 3572. [The Confidential Information Questionnaire]

Cash, Thomas F. and Soloway, Deborah. Self-disclosure correlates of physical attractiveness: An exploratory study. *Psychological Reports,* 1975, *36,* 579-586.

Chaikin, Alan L.; Derlega, Valerian L.; Bayma, Benjamin; and Shaw, Jacqueline. Neuroticism and disclosure reciprocity. *Journal of Consulting and Clinical Psychology*, 1975, *43*, 13-19.

Chelune, Gordon J. A multidimensional look at sex and target differences in disclosure. *Psychological Reports*, 1976, *39*, 259-263. (a) [Self-Disclosure Coding System]

Chelune, Gordon J. *Studies in the behavioral and self-report assessment of self-disclosure.* Unpublished doctoral dissertation, University of Nevada, Reno, 1976. *Dissertation Abstracts International*, 1976, *37* (1-B), 453. (b)

Chinsky, Jack M. and Rappaport, Julian. Evaluation of a technique for the behavioral assessment of nonprofessional mental health workers. *Journal of Clinical Psychology*, 1971, *27*, 400-402. [Group Assessment of Interpersonal Traits]

Culbert, Samuel A. *Trainer self-disclosure and member growth in a T-group.* Unpublished doctoral dissertation, University of California, Los Angeles, 1966. *Dissertation Abstracts International*, 1966, *27* (6-B), 2131.

Culbert, Samuel A. Trainer self-disclosure and member growth in a T-group. *Journal of Applied Behavioral Science*, 1968, *4*, 47-73.

Daher, Douglas M. and Banikiotes, Paul G. Measurement of self-disclosure: Note on format and content of items. *Psychological Reports*, 1976, *38*, 1255-1256.

D'Augelli, Anthony R. and Chinsky, J. M. Interpersonal skills and pretraining: Implications for the use of group procedures for interpersonal learning and for the selection of nonprofessional mental health workers. *Journal of Consulting and Clinical Psychology*, 1974, *42*, 65-72.

Doster, Joseph A. and Strickland, B. R. Disclosing of verbal material as a function of information requested, information about the interviewer, and interviewee differences. *Journal of Consulting and Clinical Psychology*, 1971, *37*, 187-194.

Drag, Lee R. *Experimenter-subject interaction: A situational determinant of levels of self-disclosure.* Unpublished master's thesis, University of Florida, 1968.

Frankfurt, Leslie P. *The role of some individual and interpersonal factors in the acquaintance process.* Unpublished doctoral dissertation, The American University, 1965. *Dissertation Abstracts International,* 1965, *26* (3), 1809.

Gilbert, Carol J. *The relationship of locus of control, experimenter disclosure, and repeated encounters to "actual" disclosure, subject-perceived disclosure, anxiety, neuroticism, and social desirability.* Unpublished doctoral dissertation, University of Kansas, 1972. *Dissertation Abstracts International,* 1973, *33* (9-B), 4487.

Gilbert, Shirley J. *A study of the effects of self-disclosure on interpersonal attraction and trust as a function of situational appropriateness and the self-esteem of the recipient.* Unpublished doctoral dissertation, University of Kansas, 1972. *Dissertation Abstracts International,* 1973, *33* (8-A), 4566.

Gilbert, Shirley J. and Horenstein, David. The communication of self-disclosure: Level versus valence. *Human Communication Research,* 1975, *1,* 316-322.

Goodstein, Leonard D.; Goldstein, Joel J.; D'Orta, Carolyn V.; and Goodman, Margaret A. Measurement of self-disclosure in encounter groups: A methodological study. *Journal of Counseling Psychology,* 1976, *23,* 142-146. [Block's Q technique for rank-ordering self-disclosures]

Hancock, Brenda R. *An interaction analysis of self-disclosure.* Paper presented at the Annual Meeting of the Western Speech Communication Association, Honolulu, 1972. *Research in Education,* 1974, *9* (ERIC Document Reproduction Service No. ED 090 592).

Hayalian, Thomas. *The effect of trainer's level of self-disclosure and participants' inclusion orientation on participants' self-disclosures in an encounter group.* Unpublished doctoral dissertation, University of Kansas, 1975. *Dissertation Abstracts International,* 1976, *36* (7-B), 3674.

Haymes, M. Self-disclosure and the acquaintance process. In Sidney M. Jourard, *Self-disclosure: An experimental analysis of the transparent self.* New York: Wiley-Interscience, 1971.

Hayward, Richard H. *Process and outcome consequences of therapist self-disclosure.* Unpublished doctoral dissertation, University of Colorado, 1973. *Dissertation Abstracts International,* 1974, *34* (12-B), 6210.

Jourard, Sidney M. and Resnick, Jaquelyn L. Some effects of self-disclosure among college women. *Journal of Humanistic Psychology*, 1970, *10*, 84-93.

Kangas, Jon A. Group members' self-diclosure: A function of preceding self-disclosure by leader or other group member. *Comparative Group Studies*, 1971, *2*, 65-70.

Kirshner, Barry J. *The effects of experimental manipulation of self-disclosure on group cohesiveness.* Unpublished doctoral dissertation, University of Maryland, 1976. *Dissertation Abstracts International*, 1976, *37* (6-B), 3081. [Dies' Tape Rating]

Mayer, John E. Disclosing marital problems. *Social Casework*, 1967, *48*, 342-351.

Moss, Carolyn J. *Effects of leader behavior in personal growth groups: Self-disclosure and experiencing.* Unpublished doctoral dissertation, Southern Illinois University, Carbondale, 1975. *Dissertation Abstracts International*, 1976, *36* (12-B), 6361. [Moss Behavioral Rating of Disclosure]

Quimby, Scott L. *An experimental analysis of a proposed methology for investigating self-disclosure, feedback, leads, and impersonal communication in a T-group setting.* Unpublished doctoral dissertation, Purdue University, 1975. *Dissertation Abstracts International*, 1976, *36* (10-A), 6484.

Ribner, Neil G. *The effects of an explicit group contract on self-disclosure and group cohesiveness.* Unpublished doctoral dissertation, University of Cincinnati, 1971. *Dissertation Abstracts International*, 1972, *32* (7-B), 4226.

Ribner, Neil G. Effects of an explicit group contract on self-disclosure and group cohesiveness. *Journal of Counseling Psychology*, 1974, *21*, 116-120.

Ricci, Anthony M. *Content analysis of interviewee verbal communication: Type-token ratio as a function of repression-sensitization and self-disclosure.* Unpublished doctoral dissertation, Kent State University, 1973. *Dissertation Abstracts International*, 1974, *34* (9-A), 5642.

Rubin, Zick. Lovers and other strangers: The development of intimacy in encounters and relationships. *American Scientist*, 1974, *62*, 182-190.

Rubin, Zick. Naturalistic studies of self-disclosure. *Personality and Social Psychology Bulletin,* 1976, *2,* 260-263.

Sousa-Poza, Joaquin F. and Rohrberg, Robert. Communicational and interactional aspects of self-disclosure in psychotherapy: Differences related to cognitive style. *Psychiatry,* 1976, *39,* 81-91.

Sousa-Poza, Joaquin F. and Rohrberg, Robert. Communicational and interactional aspects of self-disclosure: A preliminary report on theory and method. *Semiotica,* in press.

Stein, Donald K. *Expectation and modeling in sensitivity groups.* Unpublished doctoral dissertation, University of Connecticut, 1971. *Dissertation Abstracts International,* 1971, *32* (1-B), 571-572.

Suchman, David I. *A scale for the measurement of revealingness in spoken behavior.* Unpublished master's thesis, Ohio State University, 1965. [summary in A1. Breed and Jourard, 1970, pp. 44-45]

Tittler, Bennett I.; Anchor, Kenneth N.; and Weitz, Lawrence J. Measuring change in openness: Behavioral assessment techniques and the problem of the examiner. *Journal of Counseling Psychology,* 1976, *23,* 473-478.

Vajner, P. R. *The effects of different types of interviewer self-disclosure on verbal behavior and relationship in the initial interview.* Unpublished doctoral dissertation, Ohio University, 1975. *Dissertation Abstracts International,* 1976, *36* (11-B), 5821.

Voight, Nancy L. *The effects of self-management strategies as initial training and as secondary training for affective self-disclosure of undergraduate males.* Unpublished doctoral dissertation, Michigan State University, 1975. *Dissertation Abstracts International,* 1976, *36* (9-A), 5842.

Vondracek, Fred W. *The manipulation of self-disclosure in an experimental interview situation.* Unpublished doctoral dissertation, Pennsylvania State University, 1968. *Dissertation Abstracts International,* 1969, *30* (3-B), 1350.

Vondracek, Fred W. Behavioral measurement of self-disclosure. *Psychological Reports,* 1969, *25,* 914. (a)

49

B2.3.2 Methodology

Vondracek, Fred W. The study of self-disclosure in experimental interviews. *Journal of Psychology*, 1969, 72, 55-59. (b)

Vondracek, Sarah I. *The measurement and correlates of self-disclosure in preadolescents.* Unpublished doctoral dissertation, Pennsylvania State University, 1969. *Dissertation Abstracts International*, 1970, 30 (11-B), 5230.

Vondracek, Sarah I. and Vondracek, Fred W. The manipulation and measurement of self-disclosure in preadolescents. *Merrill-Palmer Quarterly*, 1971, 17, 51-58.

Young, Taylor S. *The effects of cooperative and competitive interaction on self-disclosure.* Unpublished doctoral dissertation, Arizona State University, 1976. *Dissertation Abstracts International*, 1976, 37 (5-A), 2655.

B2.3.2.1 Taylor and Altman intimacy-scaled stimuli and some variations

Derlega, Valerian J.; Wilson, Midge; and Chaikin, Alan L. Friendship and disclosure reciprocity. *Journal of Personality and Social Psychology*, 1976, 34, 578-582.

Marshall, Marilyn J. *The effects of two interviewer variables on self-disclosure in an experimental interview situation.* Unpublished master's thesis, Pennsylvania State University, 1970.

Strassberg, Donald S. and Anchor, Kenneth N. Rating of self-disclosure. *Psychological Reports*, 1975, 37, 562.

Taylor, Dalmas A. and Altman, Irwin. *Intimacy-scaled stimuli for use in studies of interpersonal relationships.* Naval Medical Research Institute Report, No. 9, Contract Number MF 022.01.-03-1002, Bethesda, Maryland, 1966. (a)

Taylor, Dalmas A. and Altman, Irwin. Intimacy-scaled stimuli for use in studies of interpersonal relations. *Psychological Reports*, 1966, 19, 729-730. (b)

Tognoli, Jerome. Response matching in interpersonal information exchange. *British Journal of Social and Clinical Psychology*, 1969, 8, 116-123.

Vondracek, Fred W. and Marshall, Marilyn J. Self-disclosure and interpersonal trust: An exploratory study. *Psychological Reports*, 1971, 28, 235-240.

50

B3. *Methodological Issues*

Allen, Jon G. Implications of research in self-disclosure for group psychotherapy. *The International Journal of Group Psychotherapy,* 1973, *23,* 306-321.

Bridge, R. Gary. *Methodological issues in self-disclosure research: Would you like being a prostitute: Why or why not?* Paper presented at the Western Psychological Association Meeting, Anaheim, California, 1973. *Educational Research,* 1974, *9* (ERIC Document Reproduction Service No. ED 085 614).

Derlega, Valerian J. and Chaikin, Alan L. *Sharing intimacy: What we reveal to others and why.* Englewood Cliffs, N. J.: Prentice Hall, Inc., 1975.

Epting, Franz R.; Suchman, David I.; and Barker, E. N. *Some aspects of revealingness and disclosure: A review.* Unpublished manuscript, University of Florida, 1969. [see A1. Breed and Jourard, 1970, pp. 8-9](ERIC Document Reproduction Service No. ED 035 928)

Fantasia, Saverio C. *The effects of a moderate disclosing model on the subsequent disclosure level of high and low disclosers.* Unpublished master's thesis, SUNY College at Cortland, New York, 1974. [effect of instructions on response to questionnaire]

Fantasia, Saverio C. and Lombardo, John P. The effects of instructions on self-disclosure. *Journal of Psychology,* 1975, *91,* 183-186.

Fuchs, Kathleen F. *The effects of mode of presentation, training and sex of raters on self-disclosure, attraction, and confidence ratings.* Unpublished doctoral dissertation, St. Louis University, 1975. *Dissertation Abstracts International,* 1975, *36* (6-B), 3001.

Goodstein, Leonard D.; Goldstein, Joel J.; D'Orta, Carolyn V.; and Goodman, Margaret A. Measurement of self-disclosure in encounter groups: A methodological study. *Journal of Counseling Psychology,* 1976, *23,* 142-146.

Jourard, Sidney M. The beginnings of self-disclosure. *Voices: The Art and Science of Psychotherapy,* 1970, *6,* 42-51.

Jourard, Sidney M. *Self-disclosure: An experimental analysis of the transparent self.* New York: Wiley-Interscience, 1971.

Pearce, W. Barnett and Sharp, Stewart. Self-disclosing communication. *Journal of Communication,* 1973, *23,* 409-425.

B3. Methodology

Rubin, Zick. Lovers and other strangers: The development of intimacy in encounters and relationships. *American Scientist,* 1974, *62,* 182-190.

Rubin, Zick. Naturalistic studies of self-disclosure. *Personality and Social Psychology Bulletin,* 1976, *2,* 260-263.

C. DISCLOSER DIMENSIONS

C1. *Demographic Characteristics*

C1.1 *Age (see also* H1. *Children* and H2. *Adolescents)*

Jourard, Sidney M. Age trends in self-disclosure. *Merrill-Palmer Quarterly,* 1961, *7,* 191-198.

Jourard, Sidney M. *Self-disclosure: An experimental analysis of the transparent self.* New York: Wiley-Interscience, 1971.

Rickers-Ovsiankina, Maria A. Social accessibility in three age groups. *Psychological Reports,* 1956, *2,* 283-294.

Sinha, Virendra. Age differences in self-disclosure. *Developmental Psychology,* 1972, *7,* 257-258.

C1.2 *Sex*

Annicchiarico, Linda K. *Sex differences in self-disclosure as related to sex and status of the interviewer.* Unpublished doctoral dissertation, University of Texas, 1973. *Dissertation Abstracts International,* 1973, *34* (5-B), 2296.

Appelberg, Esther. Verbal accessibility of adolescents. *Child Welfare,* 1964, *43,* 86-90.

Bath, Kent E. and Daly, Daniel L. Self-disclosure: Relationships to self-described personality and sex differences. *Psychological Reports,* 1972, *31,* 623-628.

Brooks, Linda. Interactive effects of sex and status on self-disclosure. *Journal of Counseling Psychology*, 1974, *21*, 469-474.

Cash, Thomas F. *Self-disclosure in the acquaintance process: Effects of sex, physical attractiveness, and approval motivation.* Unpublished doctoral dissertation, George Peabody College for Teachers, 1974. *Dissertation Abstracts International*, 1975, *35* (7-B), 3572.

Chelune, Gordon J. A multidimensional look at sex and target differences in disclosure. *Psychological Reports*, 1976, *39*, 259-263.

Cozby, Paul C. Self-disclosure: A literature review. *Psychological Bulletin*, 1973, *79*, 73-91.

Derlega, Valerian J. and Chaikin, Alan L. Norms affecting self-disclosure in men and women. *Journal of Consulting and Clinical Psychology*, 1976, *44*, 376-380.

Dimond, Richard E. and Hellcamp, David T. Race, sex, ordinal position of birth and self-disclosure in high school students. *Psychological Reports*, 1969, *25*, 235-238.

Doster, Joseph A. Sex role learning and interview communication. *Journal of Counseling Psychology*, 1976, *23*, 482-485.

Eisman, Elena J. *The effect of leader sex and self-disclosure on member self-disclosure in marathon encounter-groups.* Unpublished doctoral dissertation, Boston University, 1975. *Dissertation Abstracts International*, 1975, *36* (3-B), 1429.

Exline, Ralph V.; Gray, David; and Schuette, Dorothy. Visual behavior in a dyad as affected by interview content and sex of respondent. *Journal of Personality and Social Psychology*, 1965, *1*, 201-09.

Feigenbaum, William M. *Self-disclosure in the psychological interview as a function of interviewer self-disclosure, sex of subjects, and seating arrangement.* Unpublished doctoral dissertation, University of South Carolina, 1974. *Dissertation Abstracts International*, 1975, *35* (10-B), 5108.

Gardner, Joseph A. *The effects of body motion, sex of counselor and sex of subject on counselor attractiveness and subject's self-disclosure.* Unpublished doctoral dissertation, University of Wyoming, 1973. *Dissertation Abstracts International*, 1973, *34* (5-B), 2337.

Gilbert, Shirley J. and Whiteneck, Gale G. Toward a multidimensional approach to the study of self-disclosure. *Human Communication Research*, 1976, *2*, 347-355.

Hall, Jon A. *The effect of interviewer expectation and level of self-disclosure on interviewee self-disclosure in a dyadic situation*. Unpublished doctoral dissertation, University of Arkansas, 1976. *Dissertation Abstracts International*, 1976, *37* (5-B), 2506.

Hill, Clara E. *An investigation of the effects of therapist and client variables on the psychotherapy process*. Unpublished doctoral dissertation, Southern Illinois University, Carbondale, 1974. *Dissertation Abstracts International*, 1975, *35* (12-B), 6095.

Hyink, Paul W. *The influence of client ego-strength, client sex and therapist sex on the frequency, depth, and focus of client self-disclosure*. Unpublished doctoral dissertation, Michigan State University, 1974. *Dissertation Abstracts International*, 1975, *35* (9-B), 4652.

Kassover, Carletta J. *Self-disclosure, sex and the use of personal distance*. Unpublished doctoral dissertation, University of Texas at Austin, 1971. *Dissertation Abstracts International*, 1972, *33* (1-B), 442.

Kraft, Lee W. and Vraa, Calvin W. Sex composition of groups and patterns of self-disclosure by high school females. *Psychological Reports*, 1975, *37*, 733-734.

Levinger, George and Senn, David J. Disclosure of feelings in marriage. *Merrill-Palmer Quarterly*, 1967, *13*, 237-249.

Lord, Charles G. and Velicer, Wayne F. Effects of sex, birth order, target's relationship and target's sex on self-disclosure by college students. *Psychological Reports*, 1975, *37*, 1167-1170.

Low, A. B. *Sex and religious differences in self-disclosure as determined by a revised method of scoring the Jourard Self-Disclosure Questionnaire*. Unpublished master's thesis, University of Florida, 1964. [*see* A1. Breed and Jourard, 1970, p. 29]

Mark, Elizabeth W. *Sex differences in intimacy motivation: A projective approach to the study of self-disclosure*. Unpublished doctoral dissertation, Boston College, 1976. *Dissertation Abstracts International*, 1976, *37* (2-B), 1040.

Melby, David J. *Self-disclosure as a function of self-actualization and sex of discloser and target person.* Unpublished master's thesis, Southern Illinois University, Carbondale, 1971.

Molinoff, Ada A. *Sex-related effects in the perception of self-disclosure.* Unpublished doctoral dissertation, University of California, Los Angeles, 1974, *Dissertation Abstracts International,* 1974, 35 (5-B), 2440.

Mulcahy, Gloria A. Sex differences in patterns of self-disclosure among adolescents: A developmental perspective. *Journal of Youth and Adolescence,* 1973, 2, 343-356.

Pedersen, Darhl M. and Higbee, Kenneth L. Self-disclosure and relationship to the target person. *Merrill-Palmer Quarterly,* 1969, 15, 213-220.

Rogers, Richard and Wright, E. Wayne. Preliminary study of perceived self-disclosure. *Psychological Reports,* 1976, 38, 1334.

Seffinger, Daniel J. *Deviance: A study in the perpetutation of stigmatization using persons with a hearing impairment.* Unpublished doctoral dissertation, California School of Professional Psychology, Los Angeles, 1973. *Dissertation Abstracts International,* 1974, 34 (10-B), 5209.

Smyth, Michael. *Self-disclosure in homogeneous and heterogeneous dominant dyads.* Unpublished doctoral dissertation, York University, Canada, 1975. *Dissertation Abstracts International,* 1976, 37 (1-B), 530.

Strassberg, Donald S. and Anchor, Kenneth N. Ratings of client self-disclosure and improvement as a function of sex of client and therapist. *Journal of Clinical Psychology,* in press.

Switkin, Linda R. *Self-disclosure as a function of sex roles, experimenter-subject distance, sex of experimenter and intimacy of topics.* Unpublished doctoral dissertation, St. Louis University, 1974. *Dissertation Abstracts International,* 1974, 35 (5-B), 2451.

Vondracek, Sarah I. *The measurement and correlates of self-disclosure in preadolescents.* Unpublished doctoral dissertation, Pennsylvania State University, 1969. *Dissertation Abstracts International,* 1970, 30 (11-B), 5230.

Weigel, Richard G.; Weigel, Virginia M.; and Chadwick, Patricia C. Reported and projected self-disclosure. *Psychological Reports,* 1969, 24, 283-287.

West, Lloyd W. Sex differences in the exercise of circumspection in self-disclosure among adolescents. *Psychological Reports,* 1970, *26,* 226.

White, Roger L. *Adolescent and pubescent self-disclosure patterns: Phenomenal ratings of the privacy and importance of topics.* Unpublished doctoral dissertation, Claremont Graduate School, 1974. *Dissertation Abstracts International,* 1975, *35* (8-A), 5045.

Williams, Bertha M. Trust and self-disclosure among black college students. *Journal of Counseling Psychology,* 1974, *21,* 522-525.

Wolff, Leanne O. *Self-disclosure in the marital dyad.* Unpublished doctoral dissertation, Bowling Green State University, 1976. *Dissertation Abstracts International,* 1976, *37* (5-B), 2581.

Young, Barbara A. *The effects of sex, assigned therapist or peer role, topic intimacy, and expectations of partner compatibility on dyadic communication patterns.* Unpublished doctoral dissertation, University of Southern California, 1969. *Dissertation Abstracts International,* 1969, *30* (2-B), 857.

C1.3 *Race*

Braithwaite, Ronald. A paired study of self-disclosure of black and white inmates. *Journal of Non-White Concerns in Personnel and Guidance,* 1973, *1,* 86-94.

Braithwaite, Ronald. *An analysis of proxemics and self-disclosing behavior of recidivist and non-recidivist adult social offenders from black, chicano, and white inmate populations.* Unpublished doctoral dissertation, Michigan State University, 1974. *Dissertation Abstracts International,* 1975, *35* (9-B), 4621.

Brown, Delindus R. *Self-disclosure and indentification: Dyadic communications of the new assistant black professor on a white campus.* Paper presented at the Annual Meeting of the Speech Communication Association, Chicago, 1974. (ERIC Document Reproduction Service No. ED 102 630)

Cozby, Paul C. Self-disclosure: A literature review. *Psychological Bulletin,* 1973, *79,* 73-91.

Dimond, Richard E. and Hellcamp, David T. Race, sex, ordinal position of birth, and self-disclosure. *Psychological Reports,* 1969, *25* 235-238.

Howard, Lydia R. *An exploratory analysis of differences in assertiveness and self-disclosure in blacks and whites.* Unpublished doctoral dissertation, West Virginia University, 1975. *Dissertation Abstracts International,* 1976, *36* (11-B), 5795.

Kurato, Yoshiya. *A feasibility study for measuring the intensity of self-disclosure between American and Japanese populations.* Unpublished doctoral dissertation, University of Massachusetts, 1975. *Dissertation Abstracts International,* 1975, *36* (6-A), 3407.

Littlefield, Robert P. *An analysis of the self-disclosure patterns of ninth grade public school students in three selected subcultural groups* [black, white, and Mexican-American]. Unpublished doctoral dissertation, Florida State University, 1968. *Dissertation Abstracts International,* 1969, *30* (2-A), 588.

Littlefield, Robert P. Self-disclosure among some negro, white, and Mexican-American adolescents. *Journal of Counseling Psychology,* 1974, *21,* 133-136.

Ramsey, Gene A. *Self-disclosure patterns among selected black and white high school students.* Unpublished doctoral dissertation, Auburn University, 1972. *Dissertation Abstracts International,* 1972, *33* (3-A), 9750.

Seffinger, Daniel J. *Deviance: A study in the perpetuation of stigmatization using persons with a hearing impairment.* Unpublished doctoral dissertation, California School of Professional Psychology, Los Angeles, 1973. *Dissertation Abstracts International,* 1974, *34* (10-B), 5209.

Williams, Bertha M. Trust and self-disclosure among black college students. *Journal of Counseling Psychology,* 1974, *21,* 522-525.

Wolkon, George H.; Moriwaki, Sharon; and Williams, Karen J. Race and social class as factors in the orientation towards psychotherapy. *Journal of Counseling Psychology,* 1973, *20,* 312-316.

C1.4 *Nationality, subculture, or ethnic group (see also C1.3 Race)*

Brown, Sara Q. *Subcultural background as a determinant of verbal accessibility and attitudes toward seeking help.* Unpublished master's thesis, University of Tennessee, 1966.

Isaza, Judith L. *Cross-cultural self structure.* Unpublished doctoral dissertation, University of Florida, 1974. *Dissertation Abstracts International,* 1974, *35* (6-B), 2991.

Jourard, Sidney M. Self-disclosure patterns in British and American college females. *Journal of Social Psychology*, 1961, *54*, 315-320.

Jourard, Sidney M. *Self-disclosure: An experimental analysis of the transparent self.* New York: Wiley-Interscience, 1971.

Jourard, Sidney M. and Devin, Linda. *Self-disclosure in Puerto Rico and the United States.* Unpublished manuscript, University of Florida, 1962. [*see* A1. Breed and Jourard, 1970]

Melikian, Levon H. Self-disclosure among university students in the Middle East. *Journal of Social Psychology*, 1962, *57*, 257-263.

Plog, Stanley C. The disclosure of self in the United States and Germany. *Journal of Social Psychology*, 1965, *65*, 193-203.

Polansky, Norman A. and Brown, Sara Q. Verbal accessibility and fusion fantasy in a mountain country. *American Journal of Orthopsychiatry*, 1967, *37*, 651-660.

Rickers-Ovsiankina, Maria A. Cross-cultural study of social accessibility. *Acta Psychologica*, 1961, *19*, 872-873.

Rickers-Ovsiankina, Maria A. and Kusmin, Arnold A. Individual differences in social accessibility. *Psychological Reports*, 1958, *4*, 391-406.

Rodriguez, Richard M. *The effect of a group leader's cultural identity upon self-disclosure.* Unpublished doctoral dissertation, Arizona State University, 1971. *Dissertation Abstracts International*, 1972, *32* (6-A), 3039.

Solberg, Oskar. *An analysis of Norwegian and American high school students' real and ideal self-disclosure in school as related to selected demographic and school variables.* Unpublished doctoral dissertation, Purdue University, 1973. *Dissertation Abstracts International*, 1974, *35* (1-A), 200.

Todd, Judy L. and Shapira, Ariella. U. S. and British self-disclosure, anxiety, empathy, and attitudes to psychotherapy. *Journal of Cross-Cultural Psychology*, 1974, *5*, 364-369.

Tiwari, J. G. and Singh, Sultan. Self-disclosure in urban and rural students. *Journal of Psychological Researches*, 1967, *11*, 7-12.

C1.4 Discloser Dimensions

Willerman, B. *The concealment of self: Method of study and some cross-cultural comparisons.* Paper read at the American Psychological Association Convention, St. Louis, 1962. [*see* A1. Breed and Jourard, 1970, p. 53]

C1.5 *Religion*

Cooke, Terence F. *Interpersonal correlates of religious behavior.* Unpublished doctoral dissertation, University of Florida, 1962. *Dissertation Abstracts International*, 1962, *23* (3), 1103.

Jennings, Floyd L. Religious beliefs and self-disclosure. *Psychological Reports,* 1971, *28,* 193-194.

Jourard, Sidney M. Religious denomination and self-disclosure. *Psychological Reports,* 1961, *8,* 446. [*see* summary in C1.4 Jourard, 1971]

Low, A. B. *Sex and religious differences in self-disclosure as determined by a revised method of scoring the Jourard Self-Disclosure Questionnaire.* Unpublished master's thesis, University of Florida, 1964. [*see* A1. Breed and Jourard, 1979, p. 29]

Wiebe, Bernhard. *Self-disclosure and perceived relationships of Mennonite adolescents in senior high school.* Unpublished doctoral dissertation, University of North Dakota, 1974. *Dissertation Abstracts International*, 1975, *35* (10-A), 6472.

Wiebe, Bernie and Scott, Thomas B. Self-disclosure patterns of Mennonite adolescents to parents and their perceived relationships. *Psychological Reports,* 1976, *39,* 355-358.

Wiebe, Bernhard and Williams, John D. Self-disclosure to parents by high school seniors. *Psychological Reports,* 1972, *31,* 690.

C1.6 *Socio-economic class*

Cozby, Paul C. Self-disclosure: A literature review. *Psychological Bulletin,* 1973, *79,* 73-91.

Jones, Lawrence K. *Relationship between self-disclosure and positive mental health, modeled self-disclosure, and socio-economic status.* Unpublished doctoral dissertation, University of Missouri, Columbia, 1971. *Dissertation Abstracts International*, 1972, *32* (9-A), 4953.

Mayer, John E. Disclosing marital problems. *Social Casework,* 1967, *48,* 342-351.

Peterson, Ronald E. *The effects of self-disclosure on self-concept in a group of low-income clients.* Unpublished doctoral dissertation, United States International University, 1975. *Dissertation Abstracts International,* 1975, *36* (6-B), 3127.

C1.7 *Educational level (see H1., H2., and H3. elementary, high school, and college students)*

C1.8 *Occupational or professional status*

Jourard, Sidney M. and Shain, E. K. *The status of nurses and self-disclosure.* Unpublished manuscript, 1968. [*see* A1. Breed and Jourard, 1970, p. 25]

Myers, Raymond A. *The role of self-disclosure as related to selected professional and predictive variables in a graduate humanistic teacher education program.* Unpublished doctoral dissertation, George Washington University, 1975. *Dissertation Abstracts International,* 1976, *36* (11-A), 7358.

Silver, Robert J. Effects of subject status and interviewer response program on subject self-disclosure in standardized interviews. *Proceedings of the Annual Convention of the American Psychological Association,* 1970, *5,* 539-540.

Slobin, Dan I.; Miller, Stephen H.; Porter, Lyman W. Forms of address and social relations in a business organization. *Journal of Personality and Social Psychology,* 1968, *8,* 289-293.

C2. *Family Characteristics*

C2.1 *Birth order*

Dimond, Richard E. and Hellcamp, David T. Race, sex, and ordinal position of birth and self-disclosure in high school students. *Psychological Reports,* 1969, *25,* 235-238.

Dimond, Richard E. and Munz, David C. Ordinal position of birth and self-disclosure in high school students. *Psychological Reports,* 1967, *21,* 829-833.

C2.1 Discloser Dimensions

Lord, Charles G. and Velicer, Wayne F. Effects of sex, birth order, target's relationship and target's sex on self-disclosure by college students. *Psychological Reports,* 1975, *37,* 1167-1170.

Ohlson, Edward L. *The effects of the female-based family and birth order on the ability to self-disclose.* Unpublished doctoral dissertation, University of Oklahoma, 1970, *Dissertation Abstracts International,* 1970, *31* (6-A), 2742.

Ohlson, Edward L. The effects of the female-based family and birth order on the ability to self-disclose. *Journal of Psychology,* 1974, *87,* 59-69.

C2.2 *Family structure: both parents or one parent present*

Ohlson, Edward L. *The effects of the female-based family and birth order on the ability to self-disclose.* Unpublished doctoral dissertation, University of Oklahoma, 1970. *Dissertation Abstracts International,* 1970, *31* (6-A), 2742.

Ohlson, Edward L. The effects of the female-based family and birth order on the ability to self-disclose. *Journal of Psychology,* 1974, *87,* 59-69.

White, Roger L. *Adolescent and pubescent self-disclosure patterns: Phenomenal ratings of the privacy and importance of topics.* Unpublished doctoral dissertation, Claremont Graduate School, 1974. *Dissertation Abstracts International,* 1975, *35* (8-A), 5045.

C2.3 *Family interaction patterns*

Ableman, Adrienne K. *The relationship between family self-disclosure, adolescent adjustment, family satisfaction, and family congruence.* Unpublished doctoral dissertation, Northwestern University, 1975. *Dissertation Abstracts International,* 1976, *36* (7-A), 4248.

Beckert, Charles B. *The effect of self-disclosure within a family on the perceived family environment and on individual personality traits.* Unpublished doctoral dissertation, Brigham Young, 1975. *Dissertation Abstracts International,* 1975, *35* (7-A), 4714.

Carpenter, James C. *Patterns of self-disclosure and confirmation in mother-daughter communication.* Unpublished doctoral dissertation, Ohio State University, 1970. *Dissertation Abstracts International*, 1970, *31* (7-B), 4331.

Cooke, Terence F. *Interpersonal correlates of religious behavior.* Unpublished doctoral dissertation, University of Florida, 1962. *Dissertation Abstracts International*, 1962, *23* (3), 1103.

Cozby, Paul C. Self-disclosure: A literature review. *Psychological Bulletin*, 1973, *79*, 73-91.

Daluiso, Victor E. *Self-disclosure and perception of that self-disclosure between parents and their teen-age children.* Unpublished doctoral dissertation, United States International University, 1972. *Dissertation Abstracts International*, 1972, *33* (1-B), 420.

Davis, Wesley A. *Academic achievement and self-disclosure of high school students and their parents.* Unpublished doctoral dissertation, University of Florida, 1969. *Dissertation Abstracts International*, 1970, *31* (1-A), 144.

Derlega, Valerian J. and Chaikin, Alan L. *Sharing intimacy: What we reveal to others and why.* Englewood Cliffs, New Jersey: Prentice-Hall, Inc., 1975.

Doster, Joseph A. and Strickland, Bonnie R. Perceived child-rearing practices and self-disclosure patterns. *Journal of Consulting and Clinical Psychology*, 1969, *33*, 382.

Feldman, Ronald L. *Self-disclosure patterns in the parents of stuttering children.* Unpublished doctoral dissertation, New York University, 1970. *Dissertation Abstracts International*, 1971, *32* (6-B), 3688.

Iversen, Craig A. *Style of adaptation to aversive maternal control and self-disclosure.* Unpublished doctoral dissertation, Emory University, 1974. *Dissertation Abstracts International*, 1974, *35* (5-B), 2433.

Martin, William T. *Parental and situational determinants of trust.* Unpublished doctoral dissertation, Emory University, 1972. *Dissertation Abstracts International*, 1972, *33* (6-B), 2816.

Mellers, A. E. *Self-disclosure and the perception of parents.* Unpublished master's thesis, Ohio State University, 1965.

Mullaney, Anthony J. *Relationships among self-disclosive behavior, personality, and family interaction.* Unpublished doctoral dissertation, Fordham University, 1963. *Dissertation Abstracts International*, 1964, *24* (10), 4290.

Ohlson, Edward L. The meaningfulness of play for children and parents: An effective counseling strategy. *Journal of Family Counseling*, 1974, *2*, 53-54. [disclosure of problems in play]

Wiebe, Bernhard and Williams, John D. Self-disclosure to parents by high school seniors. *Psychological Reports*, 1972, *31*, 690.

C3. *Self*

C3.1 *Self-concept, self-esteem, and self-acceptance*

Archibald, W. Peter and Cohen, Ronald I. Self-presentation, embarrassment, and facework as a function of self-evaluation, conditions of self-presentation, and feedback from others. *Journal of Personality and Social psychology*, 1971, *20*, 287-297.

Dietlein, John R. *Self-disclosure in an interview situation as a function of self-esteem and immediacy.* Unpublished master's thesis, California State University, Long Beach, 1975.

Doyne, Stephen E. *The relationship between self-disclosure and self-esteem in encounter groups.* Unpublished doctoral dissertation, George Peabody College for Teachers, 1972. *Dissertation Abstracts International*, 1972, *33* (4-B), 1786.

Ellison, Craig W. *The development of interpersonal trust as a function of self-esteem, status, and style.* Unpublished doctoral dissertation, Wayne State University, 1972. *Dissertation Abstracts International*, 1972, *33* (5-B), 2319-2320.

Ellison, Craig W. and Firestone, Ira J. Development of interpersonal trust as a function of self-esteem, target status, and target style. *Journal of Personality and Social Psychology*, 1974, *29*, 655-663.

Fitzgerald, Maureen P. *Relationship between expressed self-esteem, assumed similarity and self-disclosure.* Unpublished doctoral dissertation, Fordham University, 1961. *Dissertation Abstracts International*, 1962, *22*, 4402.

Fitzgerald, Maureen P. Self-disclosure and expressed self-esteem, social distance and areas of the self revealed. *Journal of Social Psychology*, 1963, *56*, 405-412.

Fullerton, Wayne S. *Self-disclosure, self-esteem, and risk-taking: A study of their convergent and discriminate validity in elementary school children.* Unpublished doctoral dissertation, University of California, Berkeley, 1972. *Dissertation Abstracts International,* 1973, *33* (10-B), 5014.

Granoff, Mendell. *An analysis of meanings and consequences of self-disclosing behavior.* Unpublished doctoral dissertation, University of Texas, Austin, 1970. *Dissertation Abstracts International,* 1971, *31* (11-A), 5844.

Green, Richard B. *Self-disclosure, self-esteem, and perceived similarity.* Unpublished doctoral dissertation, City University of New York, 1976. *Dissertation Abstracts International,* 1976, *37* (3-B), 1434.

Green, Robert A. and Murray, Edward J. Instigation to aggression as a function of self-disclosure and threat to self-esteem. *Journal of Consulting and Clinical Psychology,* 1973, *40,* 440-443.

Hyink, Paul W. *The influence of client ego-strength, client sex and therapist sex on the frequency, depth, and focus of client self-disclosure.* Unpublished doctoral dissertation, Michigan State University, 1974. *Dissertation Abstracts International,* 1975, *35* (9-B), 4652.

James, Charles R. *The socialization process of psychotherapy training: Self-disclosure, self-concept, and conformity of value orientation as mediated by trainer influence.* Unpublished doctoral dissertation, George Peabody College for Teachers, 1973. *Dissertation Abstracts International,* 1973, *34* (7-B), 3498.

Jourard, Sidney M. *Self-disclosure and self-acceptance.* Unpublished manuscript. [*see* A1. Breed and Jourard, 1970, p. 19]

Lind, Dennis R. *A study of the self-disclosure and self-presentation variables.* Unpublished doctoral dissertation, University of Colorado, 1970. *Dissertation Abstracts International,* 1971, *32* (2-B), 1217.

Petersen, Dwight J. *The relationship between self-concept and self-disclosure of underachieving college students in group counseling.* Unpublished doctoral dissertation, Brigham Young University, 1972. *Dissertation Abstracts International,* 1972, *33* (5-B), 2354.

Peterson, Ronald, E. *The effects of self-disclosure on self-concept in a group of low-income clients.* Unpublished doctoral dissertation, United States International University, 1975. *Dissertation Abstracts International,* 1975, *36* (6-B), 3127.

Russell, John K. *A study of the relationships between self-actualization, self-concept, and self-disclosure.* Unpublished doctoral dissertation, United Staes International University, 1974. *Dissertation Abstracts International,* 1974, *35* (3-B), 1395.

Scherz, Malcolm E. *Changes in self-esteem following experimental manipulation of self-disclosure and feedback conditions in a sensitivity laboratory.* Unpublished doctoral dissertation, George Peabody College for Teachers, 1972. *Dissertation Abstracts International,* 1972, *33* (4-B), 1805.

Shapiro, Arnold. *The relationship between self-concept and self-disclosure.* Unpublished doctoral dissertation, Purdue University, 1968. *Dissertation Abstracts International,* 1968, *29* (3-B), 1180.

Sparks, Dennis C. *Self-disclosure and its relationship to self-concept among students in a selected high school.* Unpublished doctoral dissertation, University of Michigan, 1976. *Dissertation Abstracts International,* 1976, *37* (3-A), 1412.

Sussman, Gilbert. *The effects of writing about self on the self-esteem of fifth and sixth grade children.* Unpublished doctoral dissertation, Fordham University, 1973. *Dissertation Abstracts International,* 1973, *34* (1-A), 179.

Thomas, Ivor J. *An investigation of the relationships among self-disclosure, self-concept, and counseling effectiveness.* Unpublished doctoral dissertation, University of Southern California, 1968. *Dissertation Abstracts International,* 1968, *29* (1-A), 130.

Tolor, Alexander; Cramer, Marie; D'Amico, Denis; and O'Marra, Margaret. The effects of self-concept, trust, and imagined positive or negative self-disclosures on psychological space. *Journal of Psychology,* 1975, *89,* 9-24.

Vosen, Leonard M. *The relationship between self-disclosure and self-esteem.* Unpublished doctoral dissertation, University of California, Los Angeles, 1966. *Dissertation Abstracts International,* 1967, *27* (8-B), 2882.

Webb, Donald G. *Relationship of self-acceptance and self-disclosure to empathy and marital need satisfaction.* Unpublished doctoral dissertation, United States International University, 1972. *Dissertation Abstracts International*, 1972, *33* (1-B), 432-433.

Wildman, Laura L. *The effect of dyadic exercises in self-disclosure on the self-concept and social acceptability of preadolescents.* Unpublished doctoral dissertation, University of Maryland, 1972. *Dissertation Abstracts International*, 1973, *33* (8-B), 3968.

Willingham, Mary E. *The relationship between self-concept, self-disclosure, and peer selection.* Unpublished doctoral dissertation, George Washington University, 1971. *Dissertation Abstracts International*, 1972, *32* (8-A), 4365.

Woolfolk, Anita E. and Woolfolk, Robert L. Student self-disclosure in response to teacher verbal and nonverbal behavior. *Journal of Experimental Education*, 1975, *44*, 36-40.

C3.2 *Adjustment, mental health, and self-actualization (see also C3.3.21 Neuroticism; C3.4.3 Maudsley Personality Inventory; and H6 Psychiatric Patients)*

Beaven, Mary H. Beyond language arts and reading: Self-disclosure. *Elementary English*, 1974, *51*, 437-439.

Bennett, Chester C. What price privacy? *American Psychologist*, 1967, *22*, 371-376.

Booth, Robert E. *Self-disclosure and personality adjustment.* Unpublished doctoral dissertation, University of Colorado, 1974. *Dissertation Abstracts International*, 1975, *35* (11-B), 5633.

Burke, Ronald J.; Weir, Tamara; and Harrison, Denise. Disclosure of problems and tensions experienced by marital partners. *Psychological Reports*, 1976, *38*, 531-542.

Chaikin, Alan L. and Derlega, Valerian J. *Self-disclosure.* Morristown, New Jersey: General Learning Press, 1974.

Clark, James V. Authentic interaction and personal growth in sensitivity training groups. *Journal of Humanistic Psychology*, 1963, Spring, 1-13.

Clark, William H. *A study of the relationships between the client personality traits of dogmatism, empathy, self-disclosure, and the behavioral changes resulting from a therapeutic group experience.* Unpublished doctoral dissertation, The American University, 1972. *Dissertation Abstracts International,* 1973, *33* (10-A), 5488.

Cozby, Paul C. Self-disclosure: A literature review. *Psychological Bulletin,* 1973, *79,* 73-91.

Culbert, Samuel A. The interpersonal process of self-disclosure: It takes two to see one. *Explorations in Applied Behavioral Science,* 1967, *3,* 2-31.

Davis, Terry S. *Relationship of personality and task demands to self-disclosing behavior and psychological health.* Unpublished doctoral dissertation, University of Southern California, 1973. *Dissertation Abstracts International,* 1973, *33* (12-B), 6073.

Derlega, Valerian J. and Chaikin, Alan L. *Sharing intimacy: What we reveal to others and why.* Englewood Cliffs, New Jersey: Prentice-Hall, Inc., 1975.

Derlega, Valerian J. and Chaikin, Alan L. Norms affecting self-disclosure in men and women. *Journal of Consulting and Clinical Psychology,* 1976, *44,* 376-380.

Gorman, John R. *Adjustment and self-disclosing behavior of Roman Catholic priests.* Unpublished doctoral dissertation, Loyola University of Chicago, 1973. *Dissertation Abstracts International,* 1973, *34* (1-B), 413.

Greene, Ronald. *Self-disclosure, dogmatism, and sensory acuity as they relate to humanistic concepts of mental health.* Unpublished doctoral dissertation, Ohio State University, 1971. *Dissertation Abstracts International,* 1972, *32* (11-B), 6647.

Jones, Lawrence K. *Relationship between self-disclosure and positive mental health, modeled self-disclosure and socio-economic status.* Unpublished doctoral dissertation, University of Missouri, Columbia, 1971. *Dissertation Abstracts International,* 1972, *32* (9-A), 4953.

Jourard, Sidney M. Healthy personality and self-disclosure. *Mental Hygiene,* 1959, *43,* 499-507.

Jourard, Sidney M. *Personal adjustment: An approach through the study of healthy personality.* New York: Macmillan, 1964. (a) [revised and expanded edition, *Healthy personality: An approach from the viewpoint of humanistic psychology.* New York: Macmillan, 1974]

Jourard, Sidney M. *The transparent self.* Princeton, New Jersey:
D. Van Nostrand Co., 1964. (b) [Revised ed., 1971]

Jourard, Sidney M. *Disclosing man to himself.* Princeton, New Jersey:
D. Van Nostrand, 1968.

Jourard, Sidney M. The beginnings of self-disclosure. *Voices: The Art
and Science of Psychotherapy,* 1970, *6,* 42-51.

Kim, Jee-Il. *The effect of self-disclosure on emotion perception and
social adjustment.* Unpublished doctoral dissertation, University of
Toronto, 1973. *Dissertation Abstracts International,* 1975, *35*
(7-B), 3647.

Kinder, Bill N. Evidence for a nonlinear relationship between self-disclosure and self-actualization. *Psychological Reports,* 1976, *38*
631-634. [JSDQ-40 and Personal Orientation Inventory]

Kuppersmith, Joel H. *The relative effects of here-and-now versus
there-and-then self-disclosure upon personality and cohesiveness in
marathon encounter groups.* Unpublished doctoral dissertation,
University of Mississippi, 1975. *Dissertation Abstracts International,* 1975, *36* (4-A), 2028.

Lind, Dennis R. *A study of the self-disclosure and self-presentation
variables.* Unpublished doctoral dissertation, University of Colorado,1970. *Dissertation Abstracts International,* 1971, *32* (2-B),
1217.

Luft, Joseph. *Of human interaction.* Palo Alto: National Press Books,
1969.

May, Orlan P. *Self-disclosure and mental health: A study of encounter-group members' perceptions of group leaders.* Unpublished dissertation, University of Tennessee, 1972. *Dissertation Abstracts
International,* 1973, *33* (8-A), 4092.

May, Orlan P. and Thompson, Charles L. Perceived level of self-disclosure, mental health, and helpfulness of group leaders. *Journal
of Counseling Psychology,* 1973, *20,* 349-352.

Melby, David J. *Self-disclosure as a function of self-actualization and
sex of discloser and target person.* Unpublished master's thesis,
Southern Illinois University, Carbondale, 1971.

Moriwaki, Sharon M. *Correlates of mental health in an aged population: An analysis of supported self-disclosure.* Unpublished doc-

toral dissertation, University of Southern California, 1971. *Dissertation Abstracts International*, 1972, *32* (10-A), 5917.

Moriwaki, Sharon M. Self-disclosure, significant others, and psychological well-being in old age. *Journal of Health and Social Behavior*, 1973, *14*, 226-232.

Moustakas, Clark. Honesty, idiocy, and manipulation. *Journal of Humanistic Psychology*, 1962, *2*, 1-15.

Mowrer, O. Hobart. *The new group therapy*. Princeton: D. Van Nostrand Company, 1964.

Noel, Joseph R. and De'Chenne, Timothy K. Three dimensions of psychotherapy: I-We-Thou. In David A. Wexler and Laura N. Rice, (Eds.), *Innovations in client-centered therapy*. New York: John Wiley and Sons, 1974.

Paulson, Marguerite J. *Differences in self-disclosure patterns between a group of madadjusted and a group of adjusted male adolescents*. Unpublished master's thesis, University of Calgary, Canada, 1976.

Powell, John. *Why am I afraid to tell you who I am?* Chicago: Peacock, 1969.

Powell, W. J. and Jourard, Sidney M. Some objective evidence of immaturity in under-achieving college students. *Journal of Counseling Psychology*, 1963, *10*, 276-282.

Prophit, Sister Penny. *The relationship of the psychological construct of self-disclosure to post-coronary adjustment*. Unpublished doctoral dissertation, The Catholic University of America, 1974. *Dissertation Abstracts International*, 1975, *36* (1-B), 163.

Rogers, Carl R. *On becoming a person*. Boston: Houghton Mifflin, 1961.

Rothenberg, Eugenia. *The effect of self-disclosure and pseudo-self-disclosure on social adjustment of institutionalized delinquent girls*. Unpublished doctoral dissertation, University of New Mexico, 1969. *Dissertation Abstracts International*, 1970, *30* (12-A), 5246.

Rudisill, John R. *Self-disclosure and adjustment*. Unpublished doctoral dissertation, Indiana University, 1974. *Dissertation Abstracts International*, 1975, *35* (10-B), 5134.

Russell, John K. *A study of the relationships between self-actualiza-tion, self-concept, and self-disclosure.* Unpublished doctoral disser-tation, United States International University, 1974. *Dissertation Abstracts International*, 1974, *35* (3-B), 1395.

Shere, Stephen H. *The relationship between self-disclosure and psy-chological defense.* Unpublished doctoral dissertation, George Washington University, 1972. *Dissertation Abstracts International*, 1973, *33* (11-B), 5525.

Sinha, Virendra. Self-disclosure: Its clinical importance. *Indian Jour-nal of Clinical Psychology*, 1974, *1*, 81-83.

Starr, Paul D. Self-disclosure and stress among Middle-Eastern univer-sity students. *Journal of Social Psychology*, 1975, *97*, 141-142.

Truax, Charles B.; Altmann, Hal; and Whittmer, Joe. Self-disclosure as a function of personal adjustment and the facilitative condition offered by the target person. *Journal of Community Psychology*, 1973, *1*, 319-322.

Truax, Charles B. and Whittmer, Joe. Self-disclosure and personality adjustment. *Journal of Clinical Psychology*, 1971, *27*, 535-537.

Tubbs, Stewart L. and Baird, John W. *The open person . . . Self-dis-closure and personal growth.* Columbus, Ohio: Charles E. Merrill Publishing Company, 1976.

Weigel, Richard; Dinges, Norman; Dyer, Robert; and Straumfjord, A. A. Perceived self-disclosure, mental health, and who is liked in group treatment. *Journal of Counseling Psychology*, 1972, *19*, 47-52.

Wharton, Mary C. *Some personality characteristics of frequent and infrequent visitors to a university infirmary.* Unpublished doctoral dissertation, University of Florida, 1962. *Dissertation Abstracts International*, 1962, *23* (9), 3483.

C3.3 *Personality: needs and traits*

C3.3.1 *Achievement*

Altman, Irwin and Haythorn, William W. Interpersonal exchange in isolation. *Sociometry*, 1965, *28*, 411-426.

C3.3.2 Discloser Dimensions

C3.3.2 *Affiliation*

Altman, Irwin and Haythorn, William W. Interpersonal exchange in isolation. *Sociometry,* 1965, *28,* 411-426.

Dietch, James and House, James. Affiliative conflict and individual differences in self-disclosure. *Representative Research in Social Psychology,* 1975, *6,* 69-75.

Ksionzky, Sheldon M. *Some determinants of breadth and depth of self-disclosure.* Unpublished doctoral dissertation, University of California, Los Angeles, 1974. *Dissertation Abstracts International,* 1975, *35* (10-B), 5117.

Pelletier, Cheryl S. *The relationship between reported affiliative needs of women and their self-disclosure tendencies and affiliative behaviors.* Unpublished doctoral dissertation, Ohio University, 1974. *Dissertation Abstracts International,* 1975, *35* (8-B), 4192.

C3.3.3 *Anxiety*

Anchor, Kenneth N.; Vojtisek, John E.; and Patterson, Roger L. Trait anxiety, initial structuring, and self-disclosure in groups of schizophrenic patients. *Psychotherapy: Theory, Research, and Practice,* 1973, *10,* 155-158.

Carlson, Christopher R. *The relationship of anxiety, openness, and group psychotherapy experience with perceptions of therapist self-disclosure among psychiatric patients.* Unpublished doctoral dissertation, University of Texas, Austin, 1975. *Dissertation Abstracts International,* 1976, *37* (1-B), 453.

Fritchey, Kathleen H. *The effects of anxiety and threat on self-disclosure.* Unpublished doctoral dissertation, University of Southern California, 1970. *Dissertation Abstracts International,* 1971, *31* (7-B), 4336.

Garrigan, James J. *Effects of modeling on self-disclosure of emotionally disturbed preadolescent boys.* Unpublished doctoral dissertation, Lehigh University, 1975. *Dissertation Abstracts International,* 1975, *36* (5-B), 2467.

Lind, Dennis R. *A study of the self-disclosure and self-presentation variables.* Unpublished doctoral dissertation, University of Colorado, 1970. *Dissertation Abstracts International,* 1971, *32* (2-B), 1217.

Martin, Paul L. Jr. and Barry, John R. Autonomic concomitants of self-disclosure. JSAS *Catalog of Selected Documents in Psychology,* 1971, *1,* 14. [galvanic skin response and heart-rate indicators of anxiety]

Nieto-Cardoso, Ezequiel. *Relationship of level of self-disclosure and levels of facilitative functioning and manifest anxiety.* Unpublished doctoral dissertation, Loyola University of Chicago, 1975. *Dissertation Abstracts International,* 1975, *36* (1-A), 134.

Sullivan, Donald J. *Self-disclosure: Measurement, relationships with other personality dimensions, and modifiability.* Unpublished doctoral dissertation, University of Texas Southwestern Medical School, 1972. *Dissertation Abstracts International,* 1972, *33* (1-B), 454.

Ure, Douglas W. *An assessment of the effect of introversion-extroversion as a moderator variable in the relationship between anxiety and self-disclosure for a sample of university students.* Unpublished master's thesis, University of Calgary, Canada, 1972.

West, Lloyd W. *Patterns of self-disclosure for a sample of adolescents and the relationship of disclosure style to anxiety and psychological differentiation.* Unpublished doctoral dissertation, University of Alberta, Canada, 1968. [not abstracted by *Dissertation Abstracts*]

C3.3.4 *Approval: social desirability (see* C3.4.2 *Marlowe-Crowne Social Desirability Scale)*

C3.3.5 *Ascendancy-submissions (see* C3.3.11 *Dominance)*

C3.3.6 *Authoritarianism*

Halverson, Charles F. and Shore, Roy E. Self-disclosure and interpersonal functioning. *Journal of Consulting and Clinical Psychology,* 1969, *33,* 213-217.

C3.3.7 *Compliance-conformity and conventionality*

Lacey, Marylyn and Levinger, George. Is conventionality a determinant of stereotype and self-disclosure in close and casual relationships? *Catalog of Selected Documents in Psychology,* 1975, *5, 330.*

C3.3.7 Discloser Dimensions

Mouton, Jane S.; Blake, Robert R.; and Olmstead, Joseph A. The relationship between frequency of yielding and the disclosure of personal identity. *Journal of Personality*, 1956, *24*, 339-347.

Mulligan, William L. *The effects of induced self-disclosure and interviewer feedback on compliance and liking.* Unpublished doctoral dissertation, Yale University, 1973. *Dissertation Abstracts International*, 1973, *34* (2-B), 878.

C3.3.8 *Conceptual complexity (see also C3.3.1.5 Field dependence)*

Delia, Jesse G. Attitude toward the disclosure of self-attributions and the complexity of interpersonal constructs. *Speech Monographs*, 1974, *41*, 119-126.

Halverson, Charles F. and Shore, Roy E. Self-disclosure and interpersonal functioning. *Journal of Consulting and Clinical Psychology*, 1969, *33*, 213-217.

Pearson, Richard E. *Verbal behavior in the training group setting of individuals differing in conceptual style.* New York: Syracuse University, 1966. (ERIC Document Reproduction Service No. ED 050 420)

Roth, Marvin and Kuiken, Don. Communication immediacy, cognitive compatibility, and immediacy of self-disclosure. *Journal of Counseling Psychology*, 1975, *22*, 102-107.

Tuckman, Bruce W. Interpersonal probing and revealing and systems of integrative complexity. *Journal of Personality and Social Psychology*, 1966, *3*, 655-664.

C3.3.9 *Defensiveness*

Sarason, Irwin G.; Ganzer, Victor; and Singer, Michael. Effects of modeled self-disclosure on the verbal behavior of persons differing in defensiveness. *Journal of Consulting and Clinical Psychology*, 1972, *39*, 483-490.

C3.3.10 *Dogmatism*

Clark, William H. *A study of the relationships between the client personality traits of dogmatism, empathy, self-disclosure, and the behavioral changes resulting from a therapeutic group experience.* Unpublished doctoral dissertation, The American University, 1972. *Dissertation Abstracts International,* 1973, *33* (10-A), 5488.

Crapo, Steven E. *The influence of belief systems upon self-disclosure.* Unpublished doctoral dissertation, Arizona State University, 1970. *Dissertation Abstracts International,* 1970, *31* (1-A), 144.

Davis, Terry B.; Frye, Roland L.; and Joure, Sylvia. Perceptions and behaviors of dogmatic subjects in a T-group setting. *Perceptual and Motor Skills,* 1975, *41,* 375-381.

Field, Timothy F. Relationship of dogmatism to self-disclosure. *Psychological Reports,* 1975, *36,* 594.

Gitter, A. George; Antonellis, Richard; and Cohen, Steven. *Candor of communication about self* (CRC Report No. 69), Boston: Boston University, 1975.

Gitter, A. George and Brown, Harvey. Is self-disclosure self-revealing? *Journal of Counseling Psychology,* 1976, *23,* 327-332.

Kidd, Virginia. *A study of the effects of philosophic mindedness and dogmatism upon self-disclosing communication.* Unpublished master's thesis, Sacramento State College, 1970.

Taylor, Dalmas A.; Altman, Irwin; and Frankfurt, Leslie P. *Personality correlates of self-disclosure.* Unpublished manuscript, Naval Medical Research Institute, 1965.

Worthy, Morgan; Gary, Albert L.; and Kahn, Gay M. Self-disclosure as an exchange process. *Journal of Personality and Social Psychology,* 1969, *13,* 59-63.

Wright, Wilbert. Counselor dogmatism, willingness to disclose, and client's empathy ratings. *Journal of Counseling Psychology,* 1975, *22,* 390-394.

C3.3.11 *Dominance or ascendancy-submission*

Chittick, Eldon V. and Himelstein, Philip. The manipulation of self-disclosure. *Journal of Psychology,* 1967, *65,* 117-121.

Jones, Mary G. *Self-disclosure among deaf adolescents and its relationship to social sensitivity and personality.* Unpublished doctoral dissertation, The Catholic University of America, 1975. *Dissertation Abstracts International,* 1975, *36* (3-B), 1437.

Kurth, Suzanne B. *Determinants of verbal self-disclosure.* Unpublished doctoral dissertation, University of Illinois at Chicago Circle, 1971. *Dissertation Abstracts International,* 1972, *32* (7-A), 4106.

Smyth, Michael. *Self-disclosure in homogeneous and heterogeneous dominant dyads.* Unpublished doctoral dissertation, York University, Canada, 1975. *Dissertation Abstracts International,* 1976, *37* (1-B), 530.

C3.3.12 *Empathy*

Clark, William H. *A study of the relationships between the client personality traits of dogmatism, empathy, self-disclosure, and the behavioral changes resulting from a therapeutic group experience.* Unpublished doctoral dissertation, The American University, 1972. *Dissertation Abstracts International,* 1973, *33* (10-A), 5488.

C3.3.13 *Extroversion-introversion (see also C3.4.5 Pedersen Personality Inventory)*

Becker, Jane F. and Munz, David C. Extroversion and reciprocation of interviewer disclosures. *Journal of Consulting and Clinical Psychology,* 1975, *43,* 593.

Shapiro, Arnold. *The relationship between self-concept and self-disclosure.* Unpublished doctoral dissertation, Purdue University, 1968. *Dissertation Abstracts International,* 1968, *29* (3-B), 1180.

Ure, Douglas W. *An assessment of the effect of introversion-extroversion as a moderator variable in the relationship between anxiety and self-disclosure for a sample of university students.* Unpublished master's thesis, University of Calgary, Canada, 1972.

C3.3.14 *Femininity-masculinity (see C3.4.5 Pedersen Personality Inventory)*

C3.3.15   *Field dependence (see also* C3.3.8 *Conceptual complexity)*

Rohrberg, Robert. *The effects of alcohol and cognitive style on dyadic self-disclosure.* Unpublished master's thesis. Brooklyn College, 1973.

Sousa-Poza, Joaquin F. and Rohrberg, Robert. Communicational and interactional aspects of self-disclosure in psychotherapy: Differences related to cognitive style. *Psychiatry,* 1976, *39,* 81-91.

Sousa-Poza, Joaquin F.; Shulman, Ernest; and Rohrberg, Robert. Field dependence and self-disclosure. *Perceptual and Motor Skills,* 1973, *36,* 735-738.

C3.3.16   *Identity*

Kinsler, Philip J. *Ego identity status and intimacy.* Unpublished doctoral dissertation, State University of New York at Buffalo, 1972. *Dissertation Abstracts International,* 1973, *33* (8-B), 3946.

Simmons, Dale D. Further psychometric correlates of the Identity Achievement Scale. *Psychological Reports,* 1973, *32,* 1042.

C3.3.17   *Impulsiveness*

Stunkel, Erwin H. *Interviewee self-disclosure among impulsive and nonimpulsive college students as a function of instructions and interviewer disclosure.* Unpublished doctoral dissertation, Emory University, 1972. *Dissertation Abstracts International,* 1973, *33* (11-B), 5526.

C3.3.18   *Inclusion*

Hayalian, Thomas. *The effect of trainer's level of self-disclosure and participants' inclusion orientation on participants' self-disclosures in an encounter group.* Unpublished doctoral dissertation, University of Kansas, 1975. *Dissertation Abstracts International,* 1976, *36* (7-B), 3674.

C3.3.19   *Internal-external locus of control (see* C3.4.6 *Rotter's Internal-External Locus of Control)*

C3.3.20   Discloser Dimensions

C3.3.20   *Interpersonal distance: body space, personal space, proxemics, and social distance (see E2.7 Interpersonal distance)*

C3.3.21   *Neuroticism (see also C3.4.3 Maudsley Personality Inventory)*

> Chaikin, Alan L; Derlega, Valerian L.; Bayma, Benjamin; and Shaw, Jacqueline. Neuroticism and disclosure reciprocity. *Journal of Consulting and Clinical Psychology, 1975, 43,* 13-19.

> Mayo, P. R. Self-disclosure and neurosis. *British Journal of Social and Clinical Psychology,* 1968, *7,* 140-148.

> Pedersen, Darhl M. and Breglio, Vincent J. Personality correlates of actual self-disclosure. *Psychological Reports, 1968, 22,* 495-501.

C3.3.22   *Repression-sensitization (see C3.4.1 Byrne's Repression-Sensitization Scale)*

C3.3.23   *Sensitivity to rejection*

> Ksionzky, Sheldon M. *Some determinants of breadth and depth of self-disclosure.* Unpublished doctoral dissertation, University of California, Los Angeles, 1974. *Dissertation Abstracts International, 1975, 35* (10-B), 5117.

C3.4   *Personality: inventory correlates*

C3.4.1   *Byrne's Repression-Sensitization Scale*

> Axtell, Bryan and Cole, Charles W. Repression-sensitization response mode and verbal avoidance. *Journal of Personality and Social Psychology, 1971, 18,* 133-137.

> Baldwin, Bruce A. Self-disclosure and expectations for psychotherapy in repressors and sensitizers. *Journal of Counseling Psychology, 1974, 21,* 455-456.

> Chelune, Gordon J. *Studies in the behavioral and self-report assessment of self-disclosure.* Unpublished doctoral dissertation, University of Nevada, Reno, 1976. *Dissertation Abstracts International, 1976, 37* (1-B), 453.

> Dudgeon, Thomas B. *The effect of status and task manipulations on the interview responsivity of sensitizing and repressing juvenile*

delinquents. Unpublished doctoral dissertation, Indiana University, 1972. *Dissertation Abstracts International,* 1973, *33* (8-B), 3933-3934.

Fabricatore, Joseph M. *The effects of high and low self-disclosure on repressors and sensitizers.* Unpublished doctoral dissertation, University of California, Los Angeles, 1973. *Dissertation Abstracts International,* 1974, *34* (7-B), 3494.

Ricci, Anthony M. *Content analysis of interviewee verbal communication: Type-token ratio as a function of repression-sensitization and self-disclosure.* Unpublished doctoral dissertation, Kent State University, 1973. *Dissertation Abstracts International,* 1974, *34* (9-A), 5642.

C3.4.2   *Marlowe-Crowne Social Desirability Scale*

Anchor, Kenneth N.; Vojtisek, John E.; and Berger, Stephen E. Social desirability as a predictor of self-disclosure in groups. *Psychotherapy: Theory, Research, and Practice,* 1972, *9,* 262-264.

Burhenne, Dianne and Mirels, Herbert L. Self-disclosure in self-descriptive essays. *Journal of Consulting and Clinical Psychology,* 1970, *35,* 409-413.

Cash, Thomas F. *Self-disclosure in the acquaintance process: Effects of sex, physical attractiveness, and approval motivation.* Unpublished doctoral dissertation, George Peabody College for Teachers, 1974. *Dissertation Abstracts International,* 1975, *35* (7-B), 3572.

Cravens, Richard W. The need for approval and the private versus public disclosure of self. *Journal of Personality,* 1975, *43,* 503-514.

Davis, Terry S. *Relationship of personality and task demands to self-disclosing behavior and psychological health.* Unpublished doctoral dissertation, University of Southern California, 1973. *Dissertation Abstracts International,* 1973, *33* (12-B), 6073.

Doster, Joseph A. and Slaymaker, Judith. Need for social approval, uncertainty anxiety, and expectancies of interview behavior. *Journal of Counseling Psychology,* 1972, *19,* 522-528.

Doster, Joseph A. and Strickland, Bonnie R. Disclosing of verbal material as a function of information requested, information about the interviewer, and interviewee differences. *Journal of Consulting and Clinical Psychology,* 1971, *37,* 187-194.

Reck, Jon J. *Psychological tests as invasions of privacy in personnel settings, students reactions' approval motivation and self-disclosure patterns.* Unpublished doctoral dissertation, University of Houston, 1967. *Dissertation Abstracts International,* 1967, *28* (6-B), 2630.

Ricci, Joseph St. Elmo Jr. *Self-disclosure: Redefinition and remeasurement.* Unpublished doctoral dissertation, University of South Dakota, 1975. *Dissertation Abstracts International,* 1976, *37* (5-B), 2576.

Schrum, Jerry D. *The effects of empathy, self-disclosure, and the social desirability response set on the development of interpersonal relationships within growth-oriented psychotherapy groups.* Unpublished doctoral dissertation, Southern Illinois University, Carbondale, 1971. *Dissertation Abstracts International,* 1972, *33* (2-B), 922.

C3.4.3 *Maudsley Personality Inventory*

Chaikin, Alan L.; Derlega, Valerian L.; Bayma, Benjamin; and Shaw, Jacqueline. Neuroticism and disclosure reciprocity. *Journal of Consulting and Clinical Psychology,* 1975, *43,* 13-19.

Hamilton, Larry K. *The relationship between self-disclosure and neuroticism.* Unpublished doctoral dissertation, Northwestern University, 1971. *Dissertation Abstracts International,* 1971, *32* (6-B), 3635.

Stanley, Gordon and Bownes, A. F. Self-disclosure and neuroticism. *Psychological Reports,* 1966, *18,* 350.

Swensen, Clifford H. Jr. *Self-disclosure as a function of personality variables.* Paper presented at the meeting of the American Psychological Association, san Francisco, 1968. [*see* A2. Cozby, 1973, p. 79]

C3.4.4 *Minnesota Multiphasic Personality Inventory*

Forrest, Gary G. *Transparency as a prognostic variable in psychotherapy.* Unpublished doctoral dissertation, University of North Dakota, 1970. *Dissertation Abstracts International,* 1971, *31* (9-A), 4457.

Himelstein, Philip and Lubin, Bernard. Relationship of MMPI K scale and a measure of self-disclosure in a normal population. *Psychological Reports*, 1966, *19*, 166.

Persons, Roy W. and Marks, Philip A. Self-disclosure with recidivists: Optimum interviewer-interviewee matching. *Journal of Abnormal Psychology*, 1970, 76, 387-391.

Smith, S. A. *Self-disclosure behavior associated with two MMPI code types.* Unpublished master's thesis, University of Alabama, 1958. [*see* summary in B2.1.3 Jourard, 1971]

Stump, Walter L. *Early and late dimensions of client perceived therapist self-disclosure as they relate to constructive client change and to outcome in psychotherapy.* Unpublished doctoral dissertation, Michigan State University, 1968. *Dissertation Abstracts International*, 1969, *29* (10-B), 3923.

Taylor, Dalmas; Altman, Irwin; and Frankfurt, L. P. *Personality correlates of self-disclosure.* Unpublished manuscript, 1965. [*see* A2. Cozby, 1973, pp. 77, 79]

Truax, Charles B. and Wittmer, Joe. Self-disclosure and personality adjustment. *Journal of Clinical Psychology*, 1971, *27*, 535-537.

C3.4.5 *Pedersen Personality Inventory*

Pedersen, Darhl M. and Breglio, Vincent J. Personality correlates of actual self-disclosure. *Psychological Reports*, 1968, *22*, 495-501.

Pedersen, Darhl M. and Higbee, Kenneth L. Personality correlates of self-disclosure. *Journal of Social Psychology*, 1969, *78*, 81-89.

C3.4.6 *Rotter's Internal-External Locus of Control (see also* E2.4 *Trust)*

Cash, Thomas F.; Stack, James J.; and Luna, Gloria C. Convergent and discriminant behavioral aspects of interpersonal trust. *Psychological Reports*, 1975, *37*, 983-986.

Ellison, Craig W. *The development of interpersonal trust as a function of self-esteem, status, and style.* Unpublished doctoral dissertation, Wayne State University, 1972. *Dissertation Abstracts International*, 1972, *33* (5-B), 2319-2320.

C3.4.6 Discloser Dimensions

Ellison, Craig W. and Firestone, Ira J. Development of interpersonal trust as a function of self-esteem, target status, and target style. *Journal of Personality and Social Psychology*, 1974, *29*, 655-663.

Fuller, James B. *An investigation of self-disclosing behavior and the affective response within a T-group.* Unpublished doctoral dissertation, West Virginia University, 1971. *Dissertation Abstracts International*, 1971, *32* (4-A), 1852.

Gilbert, Carol J. *The relationship of locus of control, experimenter disclosure and repeated encounters to "actual" disclosure, subject-perceived disclosure, anxiety, neuroticism, and social desirability.* Unpublished doctoral dissertation, University of Kansas, 1972. *Dissertation Abstracts International*, 1973, *33* (9-B), 4487.

Kinder, Billy N. *The relationship of pretherapy self-disclosure, the structure of group therapy and locus-of-control on therapeutic outcome.* Unpublished doctoral dissertation, University of South Carolina, 1975. *Dissertation Abstracts International*, 1976, *37* (1-B), 465.

Lieberman, Lewis R. and Begley, Carl E. Studies of the patient version of the A. I. D.: Internal-external control, interactive style, self-disclosure. *Psychological Reports*, 1972, *30*, 493-494.

Ryckman, Richard M.; Sherman, Martin F.; and Burgess, Gary D. Locus of control and self-disclosure of public and private information by college men and women: A brief note. *Journal of Psychology*, 1973, *84*, 317-318.

Sherman, Richard M. *The effects of peer modeling and instructions on self-disclosure of internally and externally controlled male college undergraduate students: An interview-analogue situation.* Unpublished doctoral dissertation, University of Georgia, 1975. *Dissertation Abstracts International*, 1976, *36* (9-B), 4708.

Stone, Gerald L. and Jackson, Ted. Internal-external control as a determinant of the effectiveness of modeling and instructions. *Journal of Counseling Psychology*, 1975, *22*, 294-298.

C3.4.7 *Other personality inventories*

Jones, Mary G. *Self-disclosure among deaf adolescents and its relationship to social sensitivity and personality.* Unpublished doctoral dissertation, The Catholic University of America, 1975. *Dissertation Abstracts International,* 1976, *36* (3-B), 1437. [O'Sullivan-Guilford Test of Social Intelligence]

Jourard, Sidney M. Self-disclosure and Rorschach productivity. *Perceptual and Motor Skills,* 1961, *13,* 232.

Kim, Jee-Il. *The effect of self-disclosure on emotion perception and social adjustment.* Unpublished doctoral dissertation, University of Toronto, 1973. *Dissertation Abstracts International,* 1975, *35* (7-B), 3647. [Bell's Adjustment Inventory and Izard's Emotion Recognition Test]

Kormann, Leo A. *Getting to know the experimenter and its effect on EPPS test performance.* Unpublished master's thesis, University of Florida, 1967. [Edwards Personal Preference Schedule: *see* B2.1.3 Jourard, 1969 for summary]

Pedersen, Darhl M. and Breglio, Vincent J. Personality correlates of actual self-disclosure. *Psychological Reports,* 1968, *22,* 495-501. [Gough Femininity Scale]

Pedersen, Darhl M. and Higbee, Kenneth L. Personality correlates of self-disclosure. *Journal of Social Psychology,* 1969, *78,* 81-89. [Gough Femininity Scale]

Simmons, Dale D. Further psychometric correlates of the Identity Achievement Scale. *Psychological Reports,* 1973, *32,* 1042.

C3.5   *Verbal accessibility, social accessibility, and willingness to disclose*

C3.5.1   *Verbal accessibility*

Appelberg, Esther. *Verbal accessibility of adolescents.* Unpublished doctoral dissertation, Western Reserve University, 1961. [not abstracted by *Dissertation Abstracts*]

Appelberg, Esther. Verbal accessibility of adolescents. *Child Welfare,* 1964, *43,* 86-90.

Blum, Arthur. Peer-group structure and a child's verbal accessibility in a treatment institution. *Social Service Review,* 1962, *36,* 385-395.

Brown, Sara Q. *Subcultural background as a determinant of verbal accessibility and attitudes toward seeking help.* Unpublished master's thesis, University of Tennessee, 1966.

C3.5.1 Discloser Dimensions

Ganter, Grace and Polansky, Norman A. Predicting a child's accessibility to individual treatment from diagnostic groups. *Social Work*, 1964, *9*, 56-63.

Ganter, Grace; Yeakel, Margaret; and Polansky, Norman A. Intermediary group treatment of inaccessible children. *American Journal of Orthopsychiatry*, 1965, *35*, 739-746.

Jaffee, Lester D. and Polansky, Norman A. Verbal inaccessibility in young adolescents showing delinquent trends. *Journal of Health and Human Behavior*, 1962, *3*, 105-111.

Nooney, James B. *Verbal accessibility as determined by perceived similarity and personality.* Unpublished doctoral dissertation, Western Reserve University, 1960. [not abstracted in Dissertation Abstracts]

Nooney, James B. The influence of perceived similarity and personality on verbal accessibility. *Merrill-Palmer Quarterly*, 1962, *8*, 33-40.

Polansky, Norman A. The concept of verbal accessibility. *Smith College Studies in Social Work*, 1965, *36*, 1-46.

Polansky, Norman A. On duplicity in the interview. *American Journal of Orhtopsychiatry*, 1967, *37*, 568-580.

Polansky, Norman A. and Brown, Sara Q. Verbal accessibility and fusion fantasy in a mountain country. *American Journal of Orthopsychiatry*, 1967, *37*, 651-660.

Polansky, Norman A. and Weiss, Erwin S. Determinants of accessibility to treatment in a children's institution. *Journal of Jewish Communal Service*, 1959, *36*, 130-137.

Polansky, Norman A.; Weiss, Ervin S.; and Blum, Arthur. Children's verbal accessibility as a function of content and personality. *American Journal of Orthopsychiatry*, 1961, *31*, 153-169.

Tessler, R. C. and Polansky, Norman A. Perceived similarity: A paradox in interviewing. *Social Work*, 1975, *20*, 359-363.

Tucker, Gregory E. *A study of verbal accessibility in hospitalized paranoid schizophrenics in response to two styles of interviewing.* Unpublished doctoral dissertation, Western Reserve University, 1961. [not abstracted in *Dissertation Abstracts*]

Weber, Ruth. *Children's verbal accessibility as a predictor of treatment outcome.* Unpublished doctoral dissertation, Western Reserve University, 1963. [not abstracted in *Dissertation Abstracts*]

C3.5.2 *Social accessibility*

Pedersen, Darhl M. and Higbee, Kenneth L. Self-disclosure and relationship to the target person. *Merrill-Palmer Quarterly,* 1969, *15,* 213-220.

Rickers-Ovsiankina, Maria A. Social accessibility in three age groups. *Psychological Reports,* 1956, *2,* 283-294.

Rickers-Ovsiankina, Maria A. Cross-cultural study of social accessibility. *Acta Psychologica,* 1961, *19,* 872-873.

Rickers-Ovsiankina, Maria A. and Kusmin, Arnold. Individual differences in social accessibility. *Psychological Reports,* 1958, *4,* 391-406.

Young, Taylor S. *The effects of cooperative and competitive interaction on self-disclosure.* Unpublished doctoral dissertation, Arizona State University, 1976. *Dissertation Abstracts International,* 1976, *37* (5-A), 2655.

C3.5.3 *Willingness to disclose (see also B2.1 Self-reports of disclosure)*

Barrell, James and Jourard, Sidney. Being honest with persons we like. *Journal of Individual Psychology,* 1976, *32,* 185-193.

Bundza, Kenneth A. and Simonson, Norman R. Therapist self-disclosure: Its effect on impressions of therapist and willingness to disclose. *Psychotherapy: Theory, Research, and Practice,* 1973, *10,* 215-217.

Jourard, Sidney M. The effects of experimenters' self-disclosure on subjects' behavior. In Charles D. Spielberger (Ed.), *Current topics in clinical and community psychology* (Vol. 1). New York: Academic Press, 1969.

Jourard, Sidney M. *Self-disclosure: An experimental analysis of the transparent self.* New York: Wiley-Interscience, 1971.

Meares, Russell. The secret. *Psychiatry,* 1976, *39,* 258-265.

C3.5.3 Discloser Dimensions

Plog, Stanley C. The disclosure of self in the United States and Germany. *Journal of Social Psychology,* 1965, *65,* 193-203.

Schrum, Jerry D. *The effects of empathy, self-disclosure and the social desirability response set on the development of interpersonal relationships within growth-oriented psychotherapy groups.* Unpublished doctoral dissertation, Southern Illinois University, Carbondale, 1971. *Dissertation Abstracts International,* 1972, *33* (2-B), 922.

Stehura, Eugene F. The relationship between the experiencing scale and the focusing method regarding the counselor in the clinical interview. Unpublished doctoral dissertation, Illinois Institute of Technology, 1973. *Dissertation Abstracts International,* 1974, *35* (2-B), 1065.

Wheeless, Lawrence R. and Grotz, Janis. Conceptualization and measurement of reported self-disclosure. *Human Communication Research,* 1976, *2,* 338-346.

C3.6 *Attitudes, beliefs, and values*

Delia, Jesse G. Attitude toward the disclosure of self-attributions and the complexity of interpersonal constructs. *Speech Monographs,* 1974, *41,* 119-126.

Graham, Sharon J. *Level of self-disclosure as a variable of death attitudes.* Unpublished master's thesis, University of Florida, 1970. [*see* C3.5.3 Jourard, 1971, pp. 158-165]

Koerper, Leslie. *The effects of self-disclosure in attitude change and ethos.* Unpublished master's thesis, Bowling Green University, 1971.

Leuchtmann, Hanna. *Self-disclosure, attitudes, and sociometric choice.* Unpublished doctoral dissertation, Yeshiva University, 1968. *Dissertation Abstracts International,* 1969, *30* (1-B), 371.

Liske, Carol. *Self-disclosure and similarity of values among adolescents.* Unpublished master's thesis, University of Calgary, Canada, 1975.

Nathanson, Barry F. *The relationship of personality self-disclosure to occupational choice of college freshmen.* Unpublished doctoral dissertation, University of Kentucky, 1967. *Dissertation Abstracts International,* 1969, *30* (5-A), 1874.

Phalen, Paul W. *Self-disclosure and attitudes about interpersonal encounters.* Unpublished master's thesis, San Francisco State, 1970.

Small, L. S. *Personal values and self-disclosure.* Unpublished doctoral dissertation, University of Florida, 1970. [not in *Dissertation Abstracts International*; [*see* A1. Breed and Jourard, 1970, p. 42]

Wilson, Thurlow R. and Rosen, Theodore H. *Self-disclosure on army surveys: Survey procedures and respondent beliefs related to candidness.* (HumRRO Tech. Rep. 75-2). Alexandria, Virginia: Human Resources Research Organization, April, 1975.

Zeif, R. M. *Values and self-disclosure.* Unpublished honors thesis, Harvard University, 1962.

C3.7 *Perception and sensory awareness*

Beckert, Charles B. *The effect of self-disclosure within a family on the perceived family environment and on individual personality traits.* Unpublished doctoral dissertation, Brigham Young, 1975. *Dissertation Abstracts International,* 1975, *35* (7-A), 4714.

Campbell, William. Role perception and self-disclosure. *Human Mosaic,* 1971, *5,* 1-28.

Daluiso, Victor E. *Self-disclosure and perception of that self-disclosure between parents and their teen-age children.* Unpublished doctoral dissertation, United States International University, 1972. *Dissertation Abstracts International,* 1972, *33* (1-B), 420.

Higbee, Kenneth L. Group influence on self-disclosure. *Psychological Reports,* 1973, *32,* 903-909.

Kim, Jee-Il. *The effect of self-disclosure on emotion perception and social adjustment.* Unpublished doctoral dissertation, University of Toronto, Canada, 1973. *Dissertation Abstracts International,* 1975, *35* (7-B), 3647.

Knops, G. M. *The influence of an experimentally transient increase in sensory awareness (tactile) upon self-disclosure, momentary anxiety, and ratings of social desirability.* Unpublished doctoral dissertation, University of Kansas, 1970. *Dissertation Abstracts International,* 1971, *31* (11-B), 6906.

Lefkowitz, Mark B. *The role of self-disclosure and physical attractiveness in person-perception.* Paper presented at the Meeting of the

Southeastern Psychological Association, Louisville, 1970. (a) [*see* A1. Breed and Jourard, 1970, p. 27]

Lefkowitz, Mark B. *The role of self-disclosure and physical attractiveness in person-perception: A hypothetical first date situation.* Unpublished master's thesis, University of Florida, 1970. (b) [*see* C3.5.3 Jourard, 1971, pp. 89-93; 235-238]

Mellers, A. E. *Self-disclosure and the perception of parents.* Unpublished master's thesis, Ohio State University, 1965.

Moldowski, Edward W. *Some judgmental effects of self-disclosure.* Unpublished doctoral dissertation, University of New York at Buffalo, 1962. *Dissertation Abstracts International,* 1966, *27* (5-B), 1626.

Plym, Donald L. *Employee self-disclosure as related to illness, absenteeism, self-perceived wellness and job satisfaction.* Unpublished doctoral dissertation, University of Arizona, 1966. *Dissertation Abstracts International,* 1967, *27* (8-A), 2617.

Shapiro, Jeffrey G.; McCarroll, J. E. and Fine, H. Perceived therapeutic conditions and disclosure to significant others. *Discussion Papers,* Arkansas Rehabilitation Research and Training Center, 1967, *1.* [*see* A1. Breed and Jourard, 1970, pp. 40-41.]

Sousa-Poza, Joaquin F.; Shulman, Ernest; and Rohrberg, Robert. Field-dependence and self-disclosure. *Perceptual and Motor Skills,* 1973, *36,* 735-738.

Taylor, Dalmas A. The development of interpersonal relationships: Social penetration processes. *Journal of Social Psychology,* 1968, *75,* 79-90. [see person perception]

Taylor, Dalmas A. and Oberlander, Leonard. Person-perception and self-disclosure: Motivational mechanisms in interpersonal processes. *Journal of Experimental Research in Personality,* 1969, *4,* 14-28.

Wiebe, Bernhard. *Self-disclosure and perceived relationships of Mennonite adolescents in senior high school.* Unpublished doctoral dissertation, University of South Dakota, 1974. *Dissertation Abstracts International,* 1975, *35* (10-A), 6472.

C3.8 *Experiencing*

Moss, Carolyn J. *Effects of leader behavior in personal growth groups: Self-disclosure and experiencing.* Unpublished doctoral dissertation, Southern Illinois University, 1975. *Dissertation Abstracts International,* 1976, *36* (12-B), 6361.

Rogers, Carl R.; Gendlin, Eugene T.; Kiesler, Donald J.; Truax, Charles B. (Eds.). *The therapeutic relationship and its impact: A study of psychotherapy with schizophrenics.* Madison: University of Wisconsin Press, 1967. [theoretical background on experiencing]

Schoeninger, Douglas W. *Client experiencing as a function of therapist self-disclosure and pre-therapy training in experiencing.* Unpublished doctoral dissertation, University of Wisconsin, 1965. *Dissertation Abstracts International,* 1966, *26* (9), 5551.

Stehura, Eugene F. *The relationship between the experiencing scale and the focusing method regarding the counselor in the clinical interview.* Unpublished doctoral dissertation, Illinois Institute of Technology, 1973. *Dissertation Abstracts International,* 1974, *35* (2-B), 1065.

Vargas, R. *A study of certain personality characteristics of male college students who report frequent positive experiencing and behaving.* Paper presented at the Meeting of the Southeastern Psychological Association, New Orleans, 1969. [*see* A1. Breed and Jourard, 1970, p. 49]

C3.9 *Performance and achievement*

Davis, Wesley A. *Academic achievement and self-disclosure of high school students and their parents.* Unpublished doctoral dissertation, University of Florida, 1969. *Dissertation Abstracts International,* 1970, *31* (1-A), 144.

Dunn, Joseph R. *The effect of cognitive and aggressive humor stimuli and grade point average on self-disclosure and creativity.* Unpublished doctoral dissertation, Mississippi State University, 1975. *Dissertation Abstracts International,* 1976, *36* (11-A), 7287.

Dutton, E. *Some relationships between self-reports of emotional and social behavior and measures of academic achievement, interest, and talent.* Paper presented at the Annual Meeting of the National Council on Measurement in Education. [*see* A1. Breed and Jourard, 1970, p. 8]

Frey, Marshall. *The effects of self-disclosure and social reinforcement on performance in paired-associate learning.* Unpublished honors paper, University of Florida, 1967. Summary in Charles D. Spielberger (Ed.), *Current topics in clinical and community psychology* (Vol. 1). New York: Academic Press, 1969.

Hoyt, Michael F. and Janis, Irving L. Increasing adherence to a stressful decision via a motivational balance sheet procedure: A field experiment. *Journal of Personality and Social Psychology,* 1975, *31,* 833-839.

Jourard, Sidney M. Self-disclosure scores and grades in nursing college. *Journal of Applied Psychology,* 1961, *45,* 244-247.

Nieto-Cardoso, Ezequiel. *Relationships of level of self-disclosure and levels of facilitative functioning and manifest anxiety.* Unpublished doctoral dissertation, Loyola University of Chicago, 1975. *Dissertation Abstracts International,* 1975, *36* (1-A), 134.

Petersen, Dwight J. *The relationship between self-concept and self-disclosure of underachieving college students in group counseling.* Unpublished doctoral dissertation, Brigham Young University, 1972. *Dissertation Abstracts International,* 1972, *33* (5-B), 2354.

Powell, W. J. and Jourard, Sidney M. Some objective evidence of immaturity in underachieving college students. *Journal of Counseling Psychology,* 1963, *10,* 276-282.

Schofield, Janet W. Effect of norms, public disclosure, and need for approval on volunteering behavior consistent with attitudes. *Journal of Personality and Social Psychology,* 1975, *31,* 1126-1133.

Solberg, Oskar. *An analysis of Norwegian and American high school students' real and ideal self-disclosure in school as related to selected demographic and school variables.* Unpublished doctoral dissertation, Purdue University, 1973. *Dissertation Abstracts International,* 1974, *35* (1-A), 200. [language and mathematics grades]

Tapp, Jack T. and Spanier, Deborah. Personal characteristics of volunteer phone counselors. *Journal of Consulting and Clinical Psychology,* 1973, *41,* 245-250.

C3.10 *Physical appearance*

Cash, Thomas F. *Self-disclosure in the acquaintance process: Effects of sex, physical attractiveness, and approval motivation.* Unpublished doctoral dissertation, George Peabody College for Teachers, 1974. *Dissertation Abstracts International,* 1975, *35* (7-B), 3572.

Cash, Thomas F. and Soloway, Deborah. Self-disclosure correlates of physical attractiveness: An exploratory study. *Psychological Reports,* 1975, *36,* 579-586.

Derlega, Valerian J.; Walmer, James; and Furman, Gail. Mutual disclosure in social interaction. *Journal of Social Psychology,* 1973, *90,* 159-160. ["hippie" vs. conventional dress]

Lefkowitz, Mark B. *The role of self-disclosure and physical attractiveness in person-perception.* Paper presented at the Meeting of the Southeastern Psychological Association, Louisville, 1970. (a) [Summary in Sidney M. Jourard, *Self-disclosure: An experimental analysis of the transparent self.* Wiley-Interscience, 1971]

Lefkowitz, Mark B. *The role of self-disclosure and physical attractiveness in person-perception: A hypothetical first date situation.* Unpublished master's thesis, University of Florida, 1970. (b) [*see* Lefkowitz above in Jourard, 1971, pp. 89-93; 235-238]

Marcus, Bette B. *Self-disclosure as a function of attitude similarity and physical attractiveness.* Unpublished doctoral dissertation, University of Maryland, 1976. *Dissertation Abstracts International,* 1976, *37* (6-B), 3155.

Robison, Joan T. *The role of self-disclosure, interpersonal attraction, and physical attractiveness in the initial stages of relationship development within single-sex female dyads.* Unpublished doctoral dissertation, University of Georgia, 1975. *Dissertation Abstracts International,* 1976, *36* (9-B), 4760.

D. DISCLOSEE (RECIPIENT OR TARGET OF DISCLOSURE) DIMENSIONS

(See also E1.2.1.1 *Therapist, counselor, interviewer* and E1.2.2 *Laboratory relationships)*

D1. *Choice of Disclosee and Relationship to Discloser*

Braithwaite, Ronald. A paired study of self-disclosure of black and white inmates. *Journal of Non-White Concerns in Personnel and Guidance,* 1973, *1,* 86-94.

Braithwaite, Ronald L. *An analysis of proxemics and self-disclosing behavior of recidivist and non-recidivist adult social offenders from black, chicano, and white inmate populations.* Unpublished doctoral dissertation, Michigan State University, 1974. *Dissertation Abstracts International,* 1975, *35* (9-B), 4621.

Brodsky, Stanley L. and Komaridis, George V. Self-disclosure in prisoners. *Psychological Reports,* 1968, *23,* 403-407.

Culbert, Samuel A. The interpersonal process of self-disclosure: It takes two to see one. *Explorations in Applied Behavioral Science,* 1967, *3,* 2-31.

Derlega, Valerian J.; Wilson, Midge; and Chaikin, Alan L. Friendship and disclosure reciprocity. *Journal of Personality and Social Psychology,* 1976, *34,* 578-582.

Gaebelein, Jacquelyn W. Self-disclosure among friends, acquaintances, and strangers. *Psychological Reports,* 1976, *38,* 967-970.

D1. Disclosee Dimensions

Gilbert, Shirley J. and Whiteneck, Gale G. Toward a multidimensional approach to the study of self-disclosure. *Human Communication Research*, 1976, *2*, 347-355.

Gitter, A. George; Antonellis, Richard; and Cohen, Steven. *Candor of communication about self.* (Report No. 69). Boston: Boston University, Communication Research Center, 1975.

Gitter, A. George and Brown, Harvey. Is self-disclosure self-revealing? *Journal of Counseling Psychology*, 1976, *23*, 327-332.

Jones, Edward E. and Archer, Richard L. Are there special effects of personalistic self-disclosure? *Journal of Experimental Social Psychology*, 1976, *12*, 180-193.

Jourard, Sidney M. Age trends in self-disclosure. *Merrill-Palmer Quarterly*, 1961, *7*, 191-197.

Jourard, Sidney M. *Self-disclosure: An experimental analysis of the transparent self.* New York: Wiley-Interscience, 1971.

Jourard, Sidney M. and Lasakow, Paul. Some factors in self-disclosure. *Journal of Abnormal Social Psychology*, 1958, *56*, 91-98.

Jourard, Sidney M. and Richman, Patricia. Disclosure output and input in college students. *Merrill-Palmer Quarterly*, 1963, *9*, 141-148.

Komarovsky, Mirra. Patterns of self-disclosure of male undergraduates. *Journal of Marriage and the Family*, 1974, *36*, 677-686.

Lord, Charles G. and Velicer, Wayne F. Effects of sex, birth order, target's relationship and target's sex on self-disclosure by college students. *Psychological Reports*, 1975, *37*, 1167-1170.

McRae, Stuart D. *A study of the relationship between self-disclosure and predictive accuracy for a sample of adolescent subjects.* Unpublished master's thesis, University of Calgary, Canada, 1974.

Rivenbark, Wilburn H. III. *Self-disclosure target choice preferences in female college students.* Paper presented at Meeting of the Southeastern Psychological Association, New Orleans, 1969. [*see* A1. Breed and Jourard, 1970, p. 38]

Rivenbark, Wilburn H. III. Self-disclosure patterns among adolescents. *Psychological Reports*, 1971, *28*, 35-42.

Solberg, Oskar. *An analysis of Norwegian and American high school students' real and ideal self-disclosure in school as related to selected demographic and school variables.* Unpublished doctoral dissertation, Purdue University, 1973. *Dissertation Abstracts International,* 1974, *35* (1-A), 200.

West, Lloyd W. Sex differences in the exercise of circumspection in self-disclosure among adolescents. *Psychological Reports,* 1970, *26,* 226.

West, Lloyd W. Mapping the communication patterns of adolescents. *Canadian Counselor,* 1974, *8,* 54-65.

D2. *Characteristics of the Disclosee*

Barrowcliffe, W. T. *Target authoritarianism as a correlate of self-disclosure of adolescents.* Unpublished master's thesis, University of Calgary, Canada, 1971.

Campbell, William. Role perception and self-disclosure. *Human Mosaic,* 1971, *5,* 1-28.

Cash, Thomas F. *Self-disclosure in the acquaintance process: Effects of sex, physical attractiveness, and approval motivation.* Unpublished doctoral dissertation, George Peabody College for Teachers, 1974. *Dissertation Abstracts International,* 1975, *35* (7-B), 3572.

Cash, Thomas F. and Soloway, Deborah. Self-disclosure correlates of physical attractiveness: An exploratory study. *Psychological Reports,* 1975, *36,* 579-586.

Chaikin, Alan L. and Derlega, Valerian J. Variables affecting the appropriateness of self-disclosure. *Journal of Consulting and Clinical Psychology,* 1974, *42,* 588-593.

Chelune, Gordon J. A multidimensional look at sex and target differences in disclosure. *Psychological Reports,* 1976, *39,* 259-263.

Copeland, Edna D. *Leadership status, leadership style and self-disclosure.* Unpublished doctoral dissertation, Georgia State University, 1970. *Dissertation Abstracts International,* 1971, *32* (1-B), 553.

Fitzgerald, Maureen P. *Relationship between expressed self-esteem, assumed similarity, and self-disclosure.* Unpublished doctoral dissertation, Fordham University, 1961. *Dissertation Abstracts International,* 1962, *22* (12), 4402.

D2. Disclosee Dimensions

Frankel, Gail. *Reported self-disclosure and perceived characteristics of the disclosee.* Unpublished doctoral dissertation, University of Rochester, 1970. *Dissertation Abstracts International,* 1970, *31* (4-B), 2279.

Gilbert, Shirley J. *A study of the effects of self-disclosure on interpersonal attraction and trust as a function of situational appropriateness and the self-esteem of the recipient.* Unpublished doctoral dissertation, University of Kansas, 1972. *Dissertation Abstracts International,* 1973, *33* (8-A), 4566.

Jourard, Sidney M. and Resnick, Jaquelyn L. Some effects of self-disclosure among college women. *Journal of Humanistic Psychology,* 1970, *10,* 84-93.

Knecht, Laura; Lippman, Daniel; and Swap, Walter. Similarity, attraction, and self-disclosure. *Proceedings of the 81st Annual Convention of the American Psychological Association,* 1973, *8,* 205-206.

Lefkowitz, Mark B. *The role of self-disclosure and physical attractiveness in person-perception.* Paper presented at the meeting of the Southeastern Psychological Association, Louisville, 1970. (a)

Lefkowitz, Mark B. *The role of self-disclosure and physical attractiveness in person-perception: A hypothetical first date situation.* Unpublished master's thesis, University of Florida, 1970. (b) [*see* summary in Sidney M. Jourard, *Self-disclosure: An experimental analysis of the transparent self.* New York: Wiley-Interscience, 1971]

Long, Lynette N. and Long, Thomas J. Influence of religious status and religious attire on interviewees. *Psychological Reports,* 1976, *39,* 25-26.

Lord, Charles G. and Velicer, Wayne F. Effects of sex, birth order, target's relationship, and target's sex on self-disclosure by college students. *Psychological Reports,* 1975, *37,* 1167-1170.

Moldowski, Edward W. *Some judgmental effects of self-disclosure.* Unpublished doctoral dissertation, State University of New York at Buffalo, 1962. *Dissertation Abstracts International,* 1966, *27* (5-B), 1626.

Nooney, James B. *Verbal accessibility as determined by perceived similarity and personality.* Unpublished doctoral dissertation, Western Reserve University, 1960. [not abstracted in *Dissertation Abstracts*]

Nooney, James B. and Polansky, Norman A. The influence of perceived similarity and personality on verbal accessibility. *Merrile-Palmer Quarterly*, 1962, *8*, 33-40.

Pedersen, Darhl M. and Higbee, Kenneth L. Self-disclosure and relationship to the target person. *Merrill-Palmer Quarterly*, 1969, *15*, 213-220.

D3. *Response Style of the Disclosee to the Disclosure (see also E1.2.1.1.4 Response style of therapist)*

Archibald, W. Peter and Cohen, Ronald I. Self-presentation, embarrassment, and facework as a function of self-evaluation, conditions of self-presentation, and feedback from others. *Journal of Personality and Social Psychology*, 1971, *20*, 287-297.

Brasfield, Charles R. *Intimacy of self-disclosure, availability of reaction to disclosure, and formation of interpersonal relationships.* Unpublished doctoral dissertation, University of British Columbia, Canada, 1971. *Dissertation Abstracts International*, 1972, *32* (10-B), 6043.

Carpenter, James C. *Patterns of self-disclosure and confirmation in mother-daughter communication.* Unpublished doctoral dissertation, Ohio State University, 1970. *Dissertation Abstracts International*, 1970, *31* (7-B), 4331.

Colson, W. N. *Self-disclosure as a function of social approval.* Unpublished master's thesis, Howard University, Washington, D. C., 1968.

Gergen, Kenneth J. and Wishnov, Barbara. Others' self-evaluations and interaction anticipation as determinants of self-presentation. *Journal of Personality and Social Psychology*, 1965, *2*, 348-358.

Green, Robert A. and Murray, Edward J. Instigation to aggression as a function of self-disclosure and threat to self-esteem. *Journal of Consulting and Clinical Psychology*, 1973, *40*, 440-443.

Heilbrun, Alfred B. Jr. Interviewer style, client satisfaction, and premature termination following the initial counseling contact. *Journal of Counseling Psychology*, 1974, *21*, 346-350.

Johannesen, Richard L. The emerging concept of communication as dialogue. *Quarterly Journal of Speech*, 1971, *57*, 373-382.

D3. Disclosee Dimensions

Lum, Kenneth. Towards multicentered marital therapy. *Psychotherapy: Theory, Research, and Practice,* 1973, *10,* 208-211.

Moriwaki, Sharon M. *Correlates of mental health in an aged population: An analysis of supported self-disclosure.* Unpublished doctoral dissertation, University of Southern California, 1971. *Dissertation Abstracts International,* 1972, *32,* (10-A), 5917.

Moriwaki, Sharon M. Self-disclosure, significant others and psychological well-being in old age. *Journal of Health and Social Behavior,* 1973, *14,* 226-232.

Resnick, Jaquelyn L. *The effectiveness of a brief communications skills program involving facilitative responding and self-disclosure training for student volunteers in college residence halls.* Unpublished doctoral dissertation, University of Florida, 1972. *Dissertation Abstracts International,* 1973, *34* (6-A), 3069.

Sermat, Vello and Smyth, Michael. Content analysis of verbal communication in the development of a relationship: Conditions influencing self-disclosure. *Journal of Personality and Social Psychology,* 1973, *26,* 332-346.

Smith, Samuel C. *The effects of feedback on self-disclosure in a dyadic interaction.* Unpublished doctoral dissertation, University of Wisconsin, Madison, 1974. *Dissertation Abstracts International,* 1974, *35* (3-B), 1418.

Sundstrom, Eric D. *A study of crowding: Effects of intrusion, goal-blocking, and density on self-reported stress, self-disclosure, and nonverbal behavior.* Unpublished doctoral dissertation, University of Utah, 1973. *Dissertation Abstracts International,* 1974, *34* (7-A), 4412.

Sundstrom, Eric D. Experimental study of crowding: Effects of room size, intrusion and goal-blocking on nonverbal behavior, self-disclosure and self-reported stress. *Journal of Personality and Social Psychology,* 1975, *32,* 645-654.

Taylor, Dalmas A. *Self-disclosure as an exchange process: Reinforcement effects.* Paper presented at the Meeting of the American Psychological Association, Montreal, Canada, 1973. (ERIC Document Reproduction Service No. ED 083 521)

Taylor, Dalmas A.; Altman, Irwin; and Sorrentino, Richard. Interpersonal exchange as a function of rewards and costs and situational

factors: Expectancy confirmation-disconfirmation. *Journal of
Social Psychology,* 1969, *5,* 324-339.

Truax, Charles B.; Altmann, Hal; and Whittmer, Joe. Self-disclosure as
a function of personal adjustment and the facilitative condition
offered by the target person. *Journal of Community Psychology,*
1973, *1,* 319-322.

Wagner, Mary P. *Intimacy of self-disclosure and response processes as
factors affecting the development of interpersonal relationships.*
Unpublished doctoral dissertation, University of Minnesota, 1975.
Dissertation Abstracts International, 1976, *36* (7-B), 3684.

Zoberi, Seemie. *Rapport by operant conditioning.* Unpublished doctoral dissertation, University of South Dakota, 1973. *Dissertation
Abstracts International,* 1974, *34* (5-B), 2324.

D4. *Effect of the Disclosure on the Disclosee (see also* E2.1 *Reciprocity,
dyadic effect;* E2.2 *Attraction, liking, and sociometric choice)*

Ashworth, Clark; Furman, Gail; Chaikin, Alan; and Derlega, Valerian.
Physiological responses to self-disclosure. *Journal of Humanistic
Psychology,* 1976, *16,* 71-80.

Horenstein, David and Gilbert, Shirley. Anxiety, likeability, and avoidance as responses to self-disclosing communication. *Small Group
Behavior,* 1976, 7, 423-432.

Kamerschen, Karen S. *Multiple therapy: Variables relating to co-therapist satisfaction.* Unpublished doctoral dissertation, Michigan State
University, 1969. *Dissertation Abstracts International,* 1970, *31*
(2-B), 915.

Randolph, Christie C. *Multiple therapy co-therapist satisfaction as related to the variables of affection and self-disclosure.* Unpublished
doctoral dissertation, Michigan State University, 1970. *Dissertation
Abstracts International,* 1971, *31* (7-B), 4344.

Sawyer, Jesse C. *The level of self-disclosure and its effect on counselor
anxiety.* Unpublished doctoral dissertation, Mississippi State University, 1975. *Dissertation Abstracts International,* 1976, *36* (7-A),
4271.

E. INTERPERSONAL DIMENSIONS

E1. *Context of the Disclosure*

E1.1 *Personal relationships*

E1.1.1 *Marriage and the family (see also C2.3 Family interaction patterns)*

Blaker, Karen L. *Self-disclosure and depression during the ante-partum and postpartum periods among primiparous spouses.* Unpublished doctoral dissertation, New York University, 1973. *Dissertation Abstracts International,* 1974, *34* (12-B), 6190.

Burke, Ronald J.; Weir, Tamara; and Harrison, Denise. Disclosure of problems and tensions experienced by marital partners. *Psychological Reports,* 1976, *38* 531-542.

Campbell, Edson E. *The effects of couple communication training on married couples in the child rearing years: A field experiment.* Unpublished doctoral dissertation, Arizona State University, 1974. *Dissertation Abstracts International,* 1974, *35* (4-A), 1942-1943.

Cutler, Beverly and Dyer, William G. Initial adjustment processes in young married couples. *Social Forces,* 1965, *44,* 195-201.

Derlega, Valerian J. and Chaikin, Alan L. *Sharing intimacy: What we reveal to others and why.* Englewood Cliffs, New Jersey: Prentice-Hall, 1975.

Diethelm, Daniel R. *Changes in levels of self-disclosure and perceived self-disclosure between partners following participation in a weekend encounter group for couples.* Unpublished doctoral dissertation, University of Connecticut, 1974. *Dissertation Abstracts International,* 1974, *34* (9-A), 5622.

Freed, Frank H. *Self-disclosure as a facilitator of satisfaction in marriage.* Unpublished doctoral dissertation, Fuller Theological Seminary, 1974. *Dissertation Abstracts International,* 1975, *36* (1-B), 440.

Jourard, Sidney M. *The transparent self.* New Jersey: Van Nostrand Company, 1964 (Rev. ed. 1971).

Katz, Irwin. *Some aspects of self-disclosure in marriage.* Unpublished manuscript. [*see* A1. Breed and Jourard, 1970, p. 26]

Katz, Irwin; Goldstein, Judith; Cohen, Melvin; and Stucker, Solomon. Need satisfaction, perception, and cooperative interaction in married couples. *Marriage and Family Living,* 1963, *25*, 209-214.

Komarovsky, Mirra. *Blue-collar marriage.* New York: Random House, 1964.

Levinger, George. *Letter to research participants concerning husband-wife communication,* June, 1964. Unpublished manuscript. [*see* A1. Breed and Jourard, 1970, p. 27]

Levinger, George. *Self-disclosure in marriage.* Unpublished manuscript, no date given. [*see* A1. Breed and Jourard, 1970, p. 28]

Levinger, George and Senn, David J. Disclosure of feelings in marriage. *Merrill-Palmer Quarterly,* 1967, *13*, 237-249.

Lum, Kenneth. Towards multicentered marital therapy. *Psychotherapy: Theory, Research, and Practice,* 1973, *10*, 208-211.

Mayer, John E. Disclosing marital problems. *Social Casework,* 1967, *48*, 342-351.

Pasternack, Thomas L. and Van Landingham, Martha. A comparison of the self-disclosure behavior of female undergraduates and married women. *Journal of Psychology,* 1972, *82*, 233-240.

Shapiro, Arnold and Swensen, Clifford. Patterns of self-disclosure among married couples. *Journal of Counseling Psychology,* 1969, *16*, 179-180.

Strassberg, Donald S.; Gabel, Harris; and Anchor, Kenneth. Patterns of self-disclosure in parent discussion groups. *Small Group Behavior*, 1976, *7*, 369-378.

Swensen, Clifford H. Jr.; Gilner, Frank; and Gelburd, S. *Love: A self-report analysis with married and single college students.* Unpublished manuscript [*see* A1. Breed and Jourard, 1970, p. 46]

Tubbs, Stewart L. and Baird, John W. *The open person...Self-disclosure and personal growth.* Columbus, Ohio: Charles E. Merrill Publishing Company, 1976.

Voss, F. *The relationship of disclosure to marital satisfaction: An exploratory study.* Unpublished master's thesis, University of Wisconsin, Milwaukee, 1969.

Webb, Donald G. *Relationship of self-acceptance and self-disclosure to empathy and marital need satisfaction.* Unpublished doctoral dissertation, United States International University, 1972. *Dissertation Abstracts International*, 1972, *33* (1-B), 432-433.

Wolf, Leanne O. *Self-disclosure in the marital dyad.* Unpublished doctoral dissertation, Bowling Green State University, 1976. *Dissertation Abstracts International*, 1976, *37* (5-B), 2581.

E1.1.2 *Acquaintanceship, friendship, love: the social penetration process (see also E1.1.1 Marriage and E2.2 Attraction, liking, and sociometric choice)*

Altman, Irwin. Reciprocity of interpersonal exchange. *Journal for the Theory of Social Behavior*, 1973, *3*, 249-261.

Altman, Irwin and Haythorn, William W. Interpersonal exchange in isolation. *Sociometry*, 1965, *28*, 411-426.

Altman, Irwin and Taylor, Dalmas A. *Disclosure as a measure of social penetration.* Paper presented at a symposium on "Self-Disclosure and the Interpersonal Relationship," of the American Psychological Association, San Francisco, 1968.

Altman, Irwin and Taylor, Dalmas A. *Social penetration: The development of interpersonal relationships.* New York: Holt, Rinehart, and Winston, 1973.

Argyle, Michael. *The psychology of interpersonal behavior.* Baltimore: Penguin, 1967.

E1.1.2 Interpersonal Dimensions

Ayres, Joe and Ivie, Robert L. *Verbal patterns in dyadic interaction.* Paper presented at the Annual Meeting of the Western Speech Communication Association, Newport Beach, California, 1974. (ERIC Document Reproduction Service No. ED 099 919)

Bochner, Arthur P. and Kelly, Clifford W. Interpersonal communication instruction—Theory and practice: A symposium. *The Speech Teacher*, 1974, *23*, 279-301.

Brasfield, Charles R. *Intimacy of self-disclosure, availability of reaction to disclosure, and formation of interpersonal relationships.* Unpublished doctoral dissertation, University of British Columbia, Canada, 1971. *Dissertation Abstracts International*, 1972, *32* (10-B).

Brockner, Joel B. and Swap, Walter C. Effects of repeated exposure and attitudinal similarity on self-disclosure and interpersonal attraction. *Journal of Personality and Social Psychology*, 1976, *33*, 531-540.

Brooks, William D. *Speech Communication.* Dubuque, Iowa: William C. Brown Company, 1971.

Cash, Thomas F. *Self-disclosure in the acquaintance process: Effects of sex, physical attractiveness, and approval motivation.* Unpublished doctoral dissertation, George Peabody College for Teachers, 1974. *Dissertation Abstracts International*, 1975, *35* (7-B), 3572.

Certner, Barry C. *The exchange of self-disclosures in same-sexed and heterosexual groups of strangers.* Unpublished doctoral dissertation, University of Cincinnati, 1970. *Dissertation Abstracts International*, 1971, *31* (9-A), 4885.

Certner, Barry C. Exchange of self-disclosures in same-sexed groups of strangers. *Journal of Consulting and Clinical Psychology*, 1973, *40*, 292-297.

Chaikin, Alan L. and Derlega, Valerian J. Liking for the normbreaker in self-disclosure. *Journal of Personality*, 1974, *42*, 117-129. (a)

Chaikin, Alan L. and Derlega, Valerian J. *Self-disclosure.* Morristown, New Jersey: General Learning Press, 1974. (b)

Chaikin, Alan L. and Derlega, Valerian J. Variables affecting the appropriateness of self-disclosure. *Journal of Consulting and Clinical Psychology*, 1974, *42*, 588-593. (c)

104

Conley, Susan J. *Strategies of maneuvers during the acquaintance process.* Unpublished doctoral dissertation, Michigan State University, 1968. *Dissertation Abstracts International,* 1969, *30* (1-B), 378.

Culbert, Samuel A. The interpersonal process of self-disclosure: It takes two to see one. *Explorations in Applied Behavioral Science,* 1967, *3,* 2-31.

D'Augelli, Anthony R.; Deyss, Christine; Guerney, Bernard G., Jr.; Hershenberg, Bernard; and Sborofsky, Sandra. Interpersonal skill training for dating couples: An evaluation of an educational mental health service. *Journal of Counseling Psychology,* 1974, *21,* 385-389.

Davis, John D. Self-disclosure in an acquaintance exercise: Responsibility for level of intimacy. *Journal of Personality and Social Psychology,* 1976, *33,* 787-792.

Derlega, Valerian J.; and Chaikin, Alan L. *Sharing intimacy: What we reveal to others and why.* Englewood Cliffs, New Jersey: Prentice-Hall, Inc., 1975.

Derlega, Valerian J.; Walmer, James; and Furman, Gail. Mutual disclosure in social interactions. *Journal of Social Psychology,* 1973, *90,* 159-160.

Derlega, Valerian J.; Wilson, Midge; and Chaikin, Alan L. Friendship and disclosure reciprocity. *Journal of Personality and Social Psychology,* 1976, *34,* 578-582.

Drag, Lee R. *The bus rider phenomenon and its generalizability: A study of self-disclosure in student stranger versus college room-mate dyads.* Unpublished doctoral dissertation, University of Florida, 1971. *Dissertation Abstracts International,* 1972, *32* (11-B), 6616.

Ehrlich, Howard J. and Graeven, David B. Reciprocal self-disclosure in a dyad. *Journal of Experimental Social Psychology,* 1971, *7,* 389-400.

Gaebelein, Jacquelyn W. Self-disclosure among friends, acquaintances, and strangers. *Psychological Reports,* 1976, *38,* 967-970.

Granoff, Mendell. *An analysis of meanings and consequences of self-disclosing behavior.* Unpublished doctoral dissertation, University of Texas at Austin, 1970. *Dissertation Abstracts International,* 1971, *31* (11-A), 5844.

E1.1.2 Interpersonal Dimensions

Green, Robert A. and Murray, Edward J. Instigation to aggression as a function of self-disclosure and threat to self-esteem. *Journal of Consulting and Clinical Psychology,* 1973, *40,* 440-443.

Halverson, Charles F. and Shore, Roy E. Self-disclosure and interpersonal functioning. *Journal of Consulting and Clinical Psychology,* 1969, *33,* 213-217.

Haythorn, William W. and Altman, Irwin. Together in isolation. In Dalmas A. Taylor (Ed.), *Small groups.* Chicago: Markham, 1971.

Hope, G. M. *Some relationships between first impressions and self-disclosure.* Unpublished master's thesis, University of Florida, 1967. [*see* A1. Breed and Jourard, 1970, p. 14]

Huesmann, L. R. and Levinger, George. Incremental exchange theory: A formal model for progression in dyadic interaction. *Proceedings of the 80th Annual Meeting of the American Psychological Association,* 1972, *7,* 903-904.

Johnson, David W. *Reaching out: Interpersonal effectiveness and self-actualization.* Englewood Cliffs, New Jersey: Prentice-Hall, Inc., 1972.

Jourard, Sidney M. *Personal adjustment: An approach through the study of healthy personality.* New York: Macmillan, 1964. (a) [revised and expanded edition, *Healthy personality: An approach from the viewpoint of humanistic psychology.* New York: Macmillan, 1974.]

Jourard, Sidney M. *The transparent self.* New Jersey: D. Van Nostrand Company, 1964. (b) [Rev. ed., 1971.]

Jourard, Sidney M. *Self-disclosure: An experimental analysis of the transparent self.* New York: Wiley-Interscience, 1971.

Keiser, George J. and Altman, Irwin. The relationship of nonverbal behavior to the social penetration process. *Catalog of Selected Documents in Psychology,* 1974, *4,* 10-11.

Keiser, George J. and Altman, Irwin. Relationship of nonverbal behavior to the social penetration process. *Human Communication Research,* 1976, *2,* 147-161.

Kimble, Charles E. *The effects of acquaintanceship, disclosure level, and attributional variables on attraction and self-disclosure.*

Unpublished doctoral dissertation, University of Texas at Austin, 1972. *Dissertation Abstracts International,* 1973, *34* (2-A), 862.

Kohen, Janet A. Self-disclosing behavior in cross-sex dyads. Unpublished doctoral dissertation, University of Iowa, 1972. *Dissertation Abstracts International,* 1972, *33* (4-A), 1851.

Kohen, Janet. Liking and self-disclosure in opposite sex dyads. *Psychological Reports,* 1975, *36,* 695-698.

Krause, Fred. *An investigation of verbal exchanges between strangers.* Unpublished doctoral dissertation, Yeshiva University, 1969. *Dissertation Abstracts International,* 1969, *30* (3-A), 1235.

Lichtig, Leo K. *A study of close interpersonal relationships.* Paper presented at the Annual Meeting of the International Communication Association, Chicago, 1975. (ERIC Document Reproduction Service No. ED 106 889)

Luft, Joseph. *Of human interaction.* Palo Alto: National Press Books, 1969.

MacDoniels, J.; Yarbrough, E.; Kaszmaul, C.; and Giffin, K. *Openness: Personalized expression in interpersonal communication.* Paper presented at the Meeting of the International Communication Association, Phoenix, 1971.

Mark, Elizabeth W. *Sex differences in intimacy motivation: A projective approach to the study of self-disclosure.* Unpublished doctoral dissertation, Boston College, 1976. *Dissertation Abstracts International,* 1976, *37* (2-B), 1040.

McLaughlin, H. G. *Interpersonal effects of self-disclosure.* Unpublished master's thesis, Ohio State University, 1965. [*see* A1. Breed and Jourard, 1970, p. 31]

Miller, Sherod L. *The effects of communication training in small groups upon self-disclosure and openness in engaged couples' systems of interaction: A field experiment.* Unpublished doctoral dissertation, University of Minnesota, 1971. *Dissertation Abstracts International,* 1971, *32* (5-A), 2819.

Newcomb, Theodore M. *The acquaintance process.* New York: Holt, Rinehart and Winston, 1961.

Olberz, Paul D. and Steiner, Ivan D. Order of disclosure and the attribution of dispositional characteristics. *Journal of Social Psychology*, 1969, *79*, 287-288.

Page, Janice M. *Social penetration processes: The effects of interpersonal reward and cost factors on the stability of dyadic relationships.* Unpublished doctoral dissertation, The American University, 1969. *Dissertation Abstracts International*, 1969, *30* (4-A), 1638.

Panyard, Christine Marie. Self-disclosure between friends: A validity study. *Journal of Counseling Psychology*, 1973, *20*, 66-68.

Pearce, W. Barnett and Wiebe, Bernie. Relationship with and self-disclosure to friends. *Perceptual and Motor Skills*, 1973, *37*, 610.

Pearce, W. Barnett; Wright, Paul H.; Sharp, Stewart M. and Slama, Katherine M. Affection and reciprocity in self-disclosing communication between same-sexed friends. *Human Communication Research*, 1974, *1*, 5-14.

Pedersen, Darhl M. and Higbee, Kenneth L. Self-disclosure and relationship to the target person. *Merrill-Palmer Quarterly*, 1969, *15*, 213-220.

Powell, John. *Why am I afraid to tell you who I am?* Chicago: Peacock, 1969.

Quinn, P. T. *Self-disclosure as a function of degree of acquaintance and potential power.* Unpublished master's thesis, Ohio State University, 1965. [see A1. Breed and Jourard, 1970, p. 36]

Rickers-Ovsiankina, Maria A. Social accessibility in three age groups. *Psychological Reports*, 1956, *2*, 283-294.

Rickers-Ovsiankina, Maria A. Cross-cultural study of social accessibility. *Acta Psychologica*, 1961, *19*, 872-873.

Rickers-Ovsiankina, Maria A. and Kusmin, Arnold. Individual differences in social accessibility. *Psychological Reports*, 1958, *4*, 391-406.

Robison, Joan T. *The role of self-disclosure, interpersonal attraction, and physical attractiveness in the initial stages of relationship development within single-sex female dyads.* Unpublished doctoral dissertation, University of Georgia, 1975. *Dissertation Abstracts International*, 1976, *36* (9-B), 4760.

Rossiter, Charles M. Jr. and Pearce, W. Barnett. *Communicating personally: A theory of interpersonal communication and human relations.* Indianapolis: Bobbs-Merrill, 1975.

Rubin, Jane E. *Impression change as a function of level of self-disclosure.* Unpublished master's thesis, University of Florida. Summary in Charles D. Spielberger (Ed.), *Current topics in clinical and community psychology* (Vol. 1). New York: Academic Press, 1969.

Rubin, Zick. Lovers and other strangers: The development of intimacy in encounters and relationships. *American Scientist,* 1974, *62,* 182-190.

Rubin, Zick. Disclosing oneself to a stranger: Reciprocity and its limits. *Journal of Experimental Social Psychology,* 1975, *11,* 233-260.

Rubin, Zick. Naturalistic studies of self-disclosure. *Personality and Social Psychology Bulletin,* 1976, *2,* 260-263.

Rytting, Marvin B. *Self-disclosure in the development of a heterosexual relationship.* Unpublished doctoral dissertation, Purdue University, 1975. *Dissertation Abstracts International,* 1976, *36* (7-B), 3582.

Savicki, Victor E. *Self-disclosure strategy and personal space proximity in intimacy development.* Unpublished doctoral dissertation, University of Massachusetts, 1971. *Dissertation Abstracts International,* 1971, *31* (8-B), 5008.

Schlein, Stephen P. *Training dating couples in empathic and open communication: An experimental evaluation of a potential preventive mental health program.* Unpublished doctoral dissertation, Pennsylvania State University, 1971. *Dissertation Abstracts International,* 1972, *32* (11-B), 6487.

Sermat, Vello and Smyth, Michael. Content analysis of verbal communication in the development of a relationship: Conditions influencing self-disclosure. *Journal of Personality and Social Psychology,* 1973, *26,* 332-346.

Shapiro, Jeffrey G.; Krauss, Herbert H.; and Truax, Charles B. Therapeutic conditions and disclosure beyond the therapeutic encounter. *Journal of Counseling Psychology,* 1969, *16,* 290-294.

Smith, Samuel C. *The effects of feedback on self-disclosure in a dyadic interaction.* Unpublished doctoral dissertation, University of Wisconsin, 1974. *Dissertation Abstracts International,* 1974, *35* (3-B), 1418.

Smyth, Michael. *Self-disclosure in homogeneous and heterogeneous dominant dyads.* Unpublished doctoral dissertation, York University, Canada, 1975. *Dissertation Abstracts International,* 1976, *37* (1-B), 530.

Stewart, John (Ed.). *Bridges not walls: A book about interpersonal communication.* Reading, Massachusetts: Addison-Wesley, 1973.

Swensen, Clifford H. Jr. Love: A self-report analysis with college students. *Journal of Individual Psychology,* 1961, *17,* 167-171.

Swensen, Clifford H. Jr. and Gilner, Frank. Factor analysis of self-report statements of love relationships. *Journal of Individual Psychology,* 1964, *20,* 186-188.

Swensen, Clifford H. Jr.; Gilner, Frank; and Gelburd, S. *Love: A self-report analysis with married and single college students.* Unpublished manuscript, no date given. [*see* A1. Breed and Jourard, 1970, p. 46.]

Taylor, Dalmas A. *Some aspects of the development of interpersonal relationships: Social penetration processes.* ONR Technical Report, No. 1, Contract Number Nonr-2285(04), Center for Research on Social Behavior, University of Delaware, 1965.

Taylor, Dalmas A. *Some aspects of the development of interpersonal relationships: Social penetration processes.* Unpublished doctoral dissertation, University of Delaware, 1966. *Dissertation Abstracts International,* 1967, *28* (4-A), 1530.

Taylor, Dalmas A. The development of interpersonal relationships: Social penetration processes. *Journal of Social Psychology,* 1968, *75,* 79-90.

Taylor, Dalmas A. *Reinforcement of self-disclosing behaviors: Contrast effects.* Paper presented at a symposium on "Theory and Research on the Devlopment of Dyadic Relationships," American Psychological Association, Honolulu, 1972.

Taylor, Dalmas A. and Altman, Irwin. Self-disclosure as a function of reward-cost outcomes. *Sociometry,* 1975, *38,* 18-31.

Taylor, Dalmas A.; Altman, Irwin; and Sorrentino, Richard. Interpersonal exchange as a function of rewards and costs and situational factors: Expectancy confirmation-disconfirmation. *Journal of Experimental Social Psychology*, 1969, *5*, 324-339.

Taylor, Dalmas A. and Kleinhans, Bruce. *Beyond words: Other aspects of self-disclosure.* Paper presented at the Meeting of the American Psychological Association, New Orleans, 1974. (ERIC Document Reproduction Service No. ED 099 757)

Taylor, Dalmas A. and Oberlander, Leonard. Person-perception and self-disclosure: Motivational mechanisms in interpersonal processes. *Journal of Experimental Research in Personality*, 1969, *4*, 14-28.

Taylor, Dalmas A.; Wheeler, Ladd; and Altman, Irwin. Self-disclosure in isolated groups. *Journal of Personality and Social Psychology*, 1973, *26*, 39-47.

Tubbs, Stewart L. and Baird, John W. *The open person . . . Self-disclosure and personal growth.* Columbus, Ohio: Charles E. Merrill Publishing Company, 1976.

Truax, Charles B. Self-disclosure, genuineness, and the interpersonal relationship. *Counselor Education and Supervision*, 1971, *10*, 351-354.

Wagner, Mary P. *Intimacy of self-disclosure and response processes as factors affecting the development of interpersonal relationships.* Unpublished doctoral dissertation, University of Minnesota, 1975. *Dissertation Abstracts International*, 1976, *36* (7-B), 3684.

Walker, Lilly J. *Friendship patterning as affected by intimate and nonintimate self-disclosure.* Unpublished doctoral dissertation, University of North Dakota, 1972. *Dissertation Abstracts International*, 1973, *33* (7-B), 3326.

Walker, Lilly J. and Wright, Paul H. Self-disclosure in friendship. *Perceptual and Motor Skills*, 1976, *42*, 735-742.

Wenburg, John R. and Wilmot, William W. *The personal communication process.* New York: John Wiley and Sons, 1973.

Wheeless, Lawrence R. Self-disclosure and interpersonal solidarity: Measurement, validation, and relationships. *Human Communication Research*, 1976, *3*, 47-61.

E1.1.2 Interpersonal Dimensions

Willingham, Mary E. *The relationship between self-concept, self-disclosure, and peer selection.* Unpublished doctoral dissertation, George Washington University, 1971. *Dissertation Abstracts International*, 1972, *32* (8-A), 4365.

Woodyard, Howard D. and Hines, David A. Accurate compared to inaccurate self-disclosure. *Journal of Humanistic Psychology*, 1973, *13*, 61-67.

Worthy, Morgan; Gary, Albert L.; and Kahn, Gay M. Self-disclosure as an exchange process. *Journal of Personality and Social Psychology*, 1969, *13*, 59-63.

Wortman, Camille B.; Adesman, Peter; Herman, Elliot; and Greenberg, Richard. Self-disclosure: An attributional perspective. *Journal of Personality and Social Psychology*, 1976, *33*, 184-191.

E1.2 *Professional relationships: dyadic*

E1.2.1 *Clinical relationships*

E1.2.1.1 *Therapist, counselor and interviewer dimensions*

E1.2.1.1.1 *General dimensions*

Dublin, James E. A further motive for psychotherapists: Communicative intimacy. *Psychiatry*, 1971, *34*, 401-409.

Gibb, Jack R. The counselor as a role free person. In Clyde A. Parker (Ed.). *Counseling Theories and Counselor Education.* Boston: Houghton Mifflin, 1968.

Hall, Jon A. *The effect of interviewer expectation and level of self-disclosure on interviewee self-disclosure in a dyadic situation.* Unpublished doctoral dissertation, University of Arkansas, 1976. *Dissertation Abstracts International*, 1976, *37* (5-B), 2506.

Kamerschen, Karen S. *Multiple therapy: Variables relating to co-therapist satisfaction.* Unpublished doctoral dissertation, Michigan State University, 1969. *Dissertation Abstracts International*, 1970, *31* (2-B), 915.

Kempler, Walter. The therapist's merchandise. *Voices: The Art and Science of Psychotherapy,* 1969-1970, *5*, 57-60.

Noel, Joseph R. and De Chenne, Timothy K. Three dimensions of psychotherapy: I-we-thou. In David A. Wexler and Laura N. Rice (Eds.). *Innovations in client-centered therapy.* New York: John Wiley & Sons, 1974.

Randolph, Christie C. *Multiple therapy co-therapist satisfaction as related to the variables of affection and self-disclosure.* Unpublished doctoral dissertation, Michigan State University, 1970. *Dissertation Abstracts International,* 1971, *31* (7-B), 4344.

Sawyer, Jesse C. *The level of self-disclosure and its effect on counselor anxiety.* Unpublished doctoral dissertation, Mississippi State University, 1975. *Dissertation Abstracts International,* 1976, *36* (7-A), 4271.

E1.2.1.1.2 *Characteristics of the therapist, counselor, and interviewer*

Annicchiarico, Linda K. *Sex differences in self-disclosure as related to sex and status of the interviewer.* Unpublished doctoral dissertation, University of Texas, Austin, 1973. *Dissertation Abstracts International,* 1973, *34* (5-B), 2296.

Brooks, Linda. Interactive effects of sex and status on self-disclosure. *Journal of Counseling Psychology,* 1974, *21,* 469-474.

Donahue, Gerald E. *The relative effects of positive statements regarding counselor ability and experience on self-disclosure and relationship satisfaction with respect to selected personality variables.* Unpublished doctoral dissertation, University of Mississippi, 1974. *Dissertation Abstracts International,* 1975, *35* (7-A), 4155.

Doster, Joseph A. and Strickland, Bonnie R. Disclosing of verbal material as a function of information requested, information about the interviewer, and interviewee differences. *Journal of Consulting and Clinical Psychology,* 1971, *37,* 187-194.

Graff, Mary A. *Sex pairing and self-disclosure in counseling.* Unpublished doctoral dissertation, University of Minnesota, 1975. *Dissertation Abstracts International,* 1976, *37* (1-B), 460.

Hill, Clara E. *An investigation of the effects of therapist and client variables on the psychotherapy process.* Unpublished

113

doctoral dissertation, Southern Illinois University, Carbondale, 1974. *Dissertation Abstracts International*, 1975, *35* (12-B), 6095.

Hyink, Paul W. The *influence of client ego-strength, client sex, and therapist sex on the frequency, depth, and focus of client self-disclosure.* Unpublished doctoral dissertation, Michigan State University, 1974. *Dissertation Abstracts International*, 1975, *35* (9-B), 4652.

Jackson, Russel H. and Pepinsky, Harold B. Interviewer activity and status effects upon revealingness in the initial interview. *Journal of Clinical Psychology*, 1972, *28*, 400-404.

Lombardo, John P.; Franco, Raymond; Wolf, Thomas M.; and Fantasia, Saverio C. Interest in entering helping activities and self-disclosure to three targets on the Jourard Self-Disclosure Scale. *Perceptual and Motor Skills*, 1976, *42*, 299-302.

Persons, Roy W. and Marks, Philip A. Self-disclosure with recidivists: Optimum interviewer-interviewee matching. *Journal of Abnormal Psychology*, 1970, *76*, 387-391.

Rogers, Carl R.; Gendlin, Eugene T.; Kiesler, Donald J.; and Truax, Charles B. (Eds.). *The therapeutic relationship and its impact: A study of psychotherapy with schizophrenics.* Madison: University of Wisconsin Press, 1967.

Shaffer, Warren S. *The effects of counselor self-disclosure, status, and length of time of intimacy on subject evaluation and selection of counselor.* Unpublished doctoral dissertation, University of Arkansas, 1976. *Dissertation Abstracts International*, 1976, *37* (5-A), 2650.

Stehura, Eugene F. *The relationship between the experiencing scale and the focusing method regarding the counselor in the clinical interview.* Unpublished doctoral dissertation, Illinois Institute of Technology, 1973. *Dissertation Abstracts International*, 1974, *35* (2-B), 1065.

Tapp, Jack T. and Spanier, Deborah. *Personal characteristics of* volunteer phone counselors. *Journal of Consulting and Clinical Psychology*, 1973, *41*, 245-250.

Williams, Bertha M. *The effects of two models of counseling— peer and professional—on the levels of self-disclosure and trust of black college students.* Unpublished doctoral dissertation, Arizona State University, 1973. *Dissertation Abstracts International,* 1973, *34* (6-A), 3076.

Williams, Bertha M. Trust and self-disclosure among black college students. *Journal of Counseling Psychology,* 1974, *21,* 522-525.

Wright, Wilbert. Counselor dogmatism, willingness to disclose, and clients' empathy ratings. *Journal of Counseling Psychology,* 1975, *22,* 390-394.

Young, Barbara A. *The effects of sex, assigned therapist or peer role, topic intimacy, and expectations of partner compatibility on dyadic communication patterns.* Unpublished doctoral dissertation, University of Southern California, 1969. *Dissertation Abstracts International,* 1969, *30* (2-B), 857.

E1.2.1.1.3 *Training of the therapist, counselor, and interviewer (see also* G. MODIFICATION OF SELF-DISCLOSING BEHAVIOR)

Briggs, Sherry A. *The effects of microcounseling on counselor-trainee anxiety and client self-disclosure.* Unpublished doctoral dissertation, Mississippi State University, 1975. *Dissertation Abstracts International,* 1975, *36* (4-A), 2016.

Coughlin, David D. *Differential rehabilitation training models, self-disclosure, and the acquisition of basic helping skills by resident advisors.* Unpublished doctoral dissertation, Syracuse University, 1975. *Dissertation Abstracts International,* 1976, *36* (10-A), 6544.

Lovett, Jerry A. *Self-disclosure: An inservice training process for volunteers in helping roles.* Unpublished doctoral dissertation, Memphis State University, 1975. *Dissertation Abstracts International,* 1976, *36* (11-A), 7212.

Milliren, Alan P. *The training of counselor self-disclosure utilizing micro-counseling techniques.* Unpublished doctoral dissertation, University of Illinois at Urbana-Champaign, 1971. *Dissertation Abstracts International,* 1972, *32* (8-A), 4355.

E1.2.1.1.4 *Response style*

E1.2.1.1.4.1 Interpersonal Dimensions

E1.2.1.1.4.1 *Facilitative conditions: empathy, genuineness, and positive regard*

Barrett-Lennard, G. T. Dimensions of therapist response as causal factors in therapeutic change. *Psychological Monographs,* 1962, *76* (43, Whole No. 562).

Carkhuff, Robert R. Toward a comprehensive model of facilitative inter-personal processes. *Journal of Counseling Psychology,* 1967, *14,* 67-72.

Carkhuff, Robert R. *Helping and human relations: A primer for lay and professional helpers* (2 vols.). New York: Holt, Rinehart and Winston, 1969.

Carkhuff, Robert R. and Burstein, Julian W. Objective therapist and client ratings of therapist-offered facilitative conditions of moderate to low functioning therapists. *Journal of Clinical Psychology,* 1970, *26,* 394-395.

Melby, David J. *Self-disclosure as a function of self-actualization and sex of discloser and target person.* Unpublished master's thesis, Southern Illinois University, Carbondale, 1971.

Muehlberg, Nancy; Pierce, Richard; and Drasgow, James. A factor analysis of therapeutically facilitative conditions. *Journal of Clinical Psychology,* 1969, *25,* 93-95.

Rogers, Carl R. The necessary and sufficient conditions of therapeutic personality change. *Journal of Consulting Psychology,* 1957, *21,* 95-103.

Rogers, Carl R. The interpersonal relationship: The core of guidance. *Harvard Education Review,* 1962, *32,* 416-429.

Rogers, Carl R. The therapeutic relationship: Recent theory and research. *Australian Journal of Psychology,* 1965, *17,* 95-108.

Sasso, Lawrence A. *An investigation of the relationship between self-disclosure and facilitative counselor communication.* Unpublished doctoral dissertation, Fairleigh Dickinson University, 1975. *Dissertation Abstracts International,* 1976, *36* (10-A), 6487.

Shapiro, Jeffrey G.; McCarroll, J. E. and Fine, H. Perceived therapeutic conditions and disclosure to significant others.

Facilitative conditions: empathy, genuineness, and positive regard E1.2.1.1.4.1

Discussion Papers, Arkansas Rehabilitation Research and Training Center, 1967, *1.*

Shapiro, Jeffrey G. and Truax, Charles B. *Therapeutic conditions and disclosure in a normal population.* Unpublished manuscript. [*see* A1. Breed and Jourard, 1970, p. 41]

Simonson, Norman R. The impact of therapist disclosure on patient disclosure. *Journal of Counseling Psychology,* 1976, *23,* 3-6.

Truax, Charles B. Self-disclosure, genuineness, and the interpersonal relationship. *Counselor Education and Supervision,* 1971, *10,* 351-354.

Truax, Charles B. and Mitchell, Kevin M. The psychotherapeutic and the psychonoxious: Human encounters that change behavior. In Marvin J. Feldman (Ed.), *Studies in psychotherapy and behavioral change* (Vol. 1). *Research in individual psychotherapy.* Buffalo: State University of New York, 1968.

Truax, Charles B. and Mitchell, Kevin M. Research on certain therapist interpersonal skills in relation to process and outcome. In Allen E. Bergin and Sol L. Garfield (Eds.), *Handbook of psychotherapy and behavior change: An empirical analysis.* New York: John Wiley and Sons, 1971.

E1.2.1.1.4.2 *Response style: evaluative, intrusive, reflective, and reinforcing (see also* D3. *Response Style of the Disclosee)*

Abulsaad, Kamal G. *Therapist's labeling statements and client's self-disclosure: A process psychotherapy study.* Unpublished doctoral dissertation, University of Georgia, 1975. *Dissertation Abstracts International,* 1976, *36* (8-B), 4143.

Auerswald, Mary C. Differential reinforcing power of restatement and interpretation on client production of affect. *Journal of Counseling Psychology,* 1974, *21,* 9-14.

Beharry, Edward A. *The effect of interviewing style upon self-disclosure in a dyadic interaction.* Unpublished doctoral dissertation, University of Windsor, Canada, 1975. *Dissertation Abstracts International,* 1976, *36* (9-B), 4677.

Cline, Rebecca J. *An experimental study of the effects of interviewee locus of evaluation and interviewer style on depth and amount of interviewee self-disclosure and other-disclosure.* Unpublished doctoral dissertation, Pennsylvania State University, 1975. *Dissertation Abstracts International,* 1976, *37* (2-A), 690. [open and closed question and reflecting listening]

Crowley, Thomas J. The *conditionability of positive and negative self-reference emotional affect statements in a counseling type interview.* Unpublished doctoral dissertation, University of Massachusetts, 1970. *Dissertation Abstracts International,* 1970, *31* (5-A), 2100.

Ellison, Craig W. *The development of interpersonal trust as a function of self-esteem, status, and style.* Unpublished doctoral dissertation, Wayne State University, 1972. *Dissertation Abstracts International,* 1972, *33* (5-B), 2319-2320.

Ellison, Craig W. and Firestone, Ira J. Development of interpersonal trust as a function of self-esteem, target status, and target style. *Journal of Personality and Social Psychology,* 1974, *29,* 655-663.

Heilbrun, Alfred B. Jr. Interviewer style, client satisfaction, and premature termination following the initial counseling contact. *Journal of Counseling Psychology,* 1974, *21,* 346-350.

Kertes, Joseph. *The relationship between counselor initiated confrontation and client self-disclosure and self-exploration.* Unpublished doctoral dissertation, University of Southern California, 1975. *Dissertation Abstracts International,* 1975, *36* (6-A), 3407.

Klepper, Irwin L. *The effects of pre-interview exposure to vicarious reinforcement on disclosure and attraction in alcoholics: A psychotherapy analogue.* Unpublished doctoral dissertation, Syracuse University, 1971. *Dissertation Abstracts International,* 1971, *32* (1-B), 563-564.

Lieberman, Lewis R. and Begley, Carl E. Studies of the A. I. D.: Internal-external control, interactive style, self-disclosure. *Psychological Reports,* 1972, *30,* 493-494.

Mann, Joe W. *The effects of reflection and race on verbal conditioning of affective self-disclosure in black and white males.* Unpublished doctoral dissertation, Auburn University, 1972. *Dissertation Abstracts International,* 1972, *33* (6-A), 2717.

Marlatt, G. Alan; Jacobson, Edward A.; Johnson, Donald L.; and Morrice, D. James. Effects of exposure to a model receiving evaluative feedback upon subsequent behavior in an interview. *Journal of Consulting and Clinical Psychology,* 1970, *34,* 104-112.

Mulligan, William L. *The effects of induced self-disclosure and interviewer feedback on compliance and liking.* Unpublished doctoral dissertation, Yale University, 1973. *Dissertation Abstracts International,* 1973, *34* (2-B), 878.

Olson, Gordon K. *The effects of interviewer self-disclosing and reinforcing behavior upon subject self-disclosure.* Unpublished doctoral dissertation, University of Arizona, 1972. *Dissertation Abstracts International,* 1973, *33* (11-A), 6096.

Powell, W. J. Jr. Differential effectiveness of interviewer interventions in an experimental interview. *Journal of Consulting and Clinical Psychology,* 1968, *32,* 210-215.

Silver, Robert J. Effects of subject status and interviewer response program on subject self-disclosure in standardized interviews. *Proceedings of the 78th Annual Convention of the American Psychological Association,* 1970, *5,* 539-540.

Silver, Robert J. *Effects of relative interviewer status and interviewer program upon subject self-disclosure in standardized interviews.* Unpublished doctoral dissertation, Indiana University, 1973. *Dissertation Abstracts International,* 1973, *33* (8-B), 3962.

Turoczi, John C. *The effects of interviewer evaluative statements and self-disclosure on the self-disclosing behavior of interviewees.* Unpublished doctoral dissertation, Lehigh University, 1972. *Dissertation Abstracts International,* 1973, *33* (11-A), 5990.

E1.2.1.1.4.3 *Self-disclosure of therapist, counselor, or interviewer (see also E1.2.2 Experimenter-subject and E1.3.1.1 Group leader)*

Blackburn, James R. *The efficacy of modeled self-disclosure on subjects response in an interview situation.* Unpublished doctoral dissertation, University of Arkansas, 1970. *Dissertation Abstracts International,* 1970, *31* (3-B), 1529.

Bloch, Ellin L.; Goodstein, Leonard D.; Jourard, Sidney M.; and Jaffe, Peggy E. Comment on "Influence of an interviewer's disclosure on the self-disclosing behavior of interviewees." *Journal of Counseling Psychology,* 1971, *18,* 595-600.

Bradford, Eregina G. *Therapist self-disclosure and client expectations.* Unpublished doctoral dissertation, Kent State University, 1975. *Dissertation Abstracts International,* 1975, *36* (6-B), 3024.

Branan, John M. Client reaction to counselor's use of self-experience. *Personnel and Guidance Journal,* 1967, *45,* 568-572.

Bundza, Kenneth A. and Simonson, Norman R. Therapist self-disclosure: Its effect on impressions of therapist and willingness to disclose. *Psychotherapy: Theory, Research, and Practice,* 1973, *10,* 215-217.

Chafey, Richard L. *The effects of counselor self-disclosure on the self-disclosure of clients with high and low pre-counseled levels of self-disclosure in a counseling analogue.* Unpublished doctoral dissertation, University of Virginia, 1973. *Dissertation Abstracts International,* 1974, *34* (8-A), 4731.

Davis, John D. and Skinner, Adrian E. Reciprocity of self-disclosure in interviews: Modeling or social exchange? *Journal of Personality and Social Psychology,* 1974, *29,* 779-784.

Derlega, Valerian J. and Chaikin, Alan L. *Sharing intimacy: What we reveal to others and why.* Englewood Cliffs, New Jersey: Prentice-Hall, Inc., 1975.

Dickenson, Walter A. *Therapist self-disclosure as a variable in psychotherapeutic process and outcome.* Unpublished doctoral dissertation, University of Kentucky, 1965. *Dissertation Abstracts International,* 1969, *30* (5-B), 2434.

Doster, Joseph A. and Brooks, Samuel J. Interviewer disclosure modeling, information revealed, and interviewee verbal behavior. *Journal of Consulting and Clinical Psychology,* 1974, *42,* 420-426.

Feigenbaum, William M. *Self-disclosure in the psychological interview as a function of interviewer self-disclosure, sex of subjects, and seating arrangement.* Unpublished doctoral dissertation, University of South Carolina, 1974. *Dissertation Abstracts International*, 1975, *35* (10-B), 5108.

Gabbert, Larry C. *Interviewee self-disclosure as a function of two forms of interviewer disclosure.* Unpublished doctoral dissertation, State University of New York, Albany, 1975. *Dissertation Abstracts International*, 1976, *36* (11-A), 7205.

Gay, Evan G. *Interviewer role and self-disclosure level as determinants of interviewee self-disclosure level and reactions to an interview.* Unpublished doctoral dissertation, University of Minnesota, 1975. *Dissertation Abstracts International*, 1975, *36* (6-B), 3039.

Giannandrea, Vincenzo and Murphy, Kevin C. Similarity self-disclosure and return for a second interview. *Journal of Counseling Psychology*, 1973, *20*, 545-548.

Hall, Jon A. *The effect of interviewer expectation and level of self-disclosure on interviewee self-disclosure in a dyadic situation.* Unpublished doctoral dissertation, University of Arkansas, 1976. *Dissertation Abstracts International*, 1976, *37* (5-B), 2506.

Halpern, Tamar P. *A study of self-disclosure in a client-counselor relationship: The interrelationship of client perception of client self-disclosure in counseling with client perception of counselor self-disclosure, counselor characteristics and some general characteristics.* Unpublished doctoral dissertation, State University of New York, Buffalo, 1975. *Dissertation Abstracts International*, 1976, *36* (7-A), 4260.

Hays, Charles F. *The effects of initial disclosure level and interviewer disclosure level upon interviewees' subsequent disclosure level.* Unpublished doctoral dissertation, Emory University, 1971. *Dissertation Abstracts International*, 1972, *32* (7-B), 4215.

Hayward, Richard H. *Process and outcome consequences of therapist self-disclosure.* Unpublished doctoral dissertation, University of Colorado, 1973. *Dissertation Abstracts International*, 1974, *34* (12-B), 6210.

E1.2.1.1.4.3 Interpersonal Dimensions

Heller, Kenneth. Laboratory interview research as analogue to treatment. In Allen E. Bergin and Sol L. Garfield (Eds.), *Handbook of psychotherapy and behavior change: An empirical analysis.* New York: John Wiley and Sons, 1971.

Horner, Beverly M. *The effect of counselor similarity self-disclosure on clients with differing role expectations.* Unpublished doctoral dissertation, University of Iowa, 1974. *Dissertation Abstracts International,* 1975, *35* (7-A), 4158.

Hutchins, Trova K. *Therapist self-disclosure behavior within the psychotherapeutic context.* Unpublished doctoral dissertation, Washington University, 1974. *Dissertation Abstracts International,* 1975, *35* (9-A), 6238.

James, Charles R. *The socialization process of psychotherapy training: Self-disclosure, self-concept and conformity of value orientation as mediated by trainer influence.* Unpublished doctoral dissertation, George Peabody College for Teachers, 1973. *Dissertation Abstracts International,* 1973, *34* (7-B), 3498.

Jourard, Sidney M. The phenomenon of resistance in the psychotherapist. *Counseling Center Discussion Papers,* University of Chicago, 1961, 7 (13). (a)

Jourard, Sidney M. Some implications of self-disclosure research for counseling and psychotherapy. *Counseling Center Discussion Papers,* University of Chicago, 1961, 7 (14). (b)

Jourard, Sidney M. and Jaffe, Peggy E. Influence of an interviewer's disclosure on the self-disclosing behavior of interviewees. *Journal of Counseling Psychology,* 1970, *17,* 252-257.

Jourard, Sidney M. and Resnick, Jaquelyn. Some effects of self-disclosure among college women. *Journal of Humanistic Psychology,* 1970, *10,* 84-93.

McLeod, Michael A. *Orienting ninth-grade students to counseling services: A study of counselor self-disclosure.* Unpublished doctoral dissertation, St. Louis University, 1973. *Dissertation Abstracts International,* 1974, *34* (8-A), 234.

Murphy, Kevin C. and Strong, Stanley R. Some effect of similarity self-disclosure. *Journal of Counseling Psychology*, 1972, *19*, 121-124.

Nieto-Cardoso, Ezequiel. *Relationships of level of self-disclosure and levels of facilitative functioning and manifest anxiety.* Unpublished doctoral dissertation, Loyola University of Chicago, 1975. *Dissertation Abstracts International*, 1975, *36* (1-A), 134.

Olson, Gordon K. *The effects of interviewer self-disclosing and reinforcing behavior upon subject self-disclosure.* Unpublished doctoral dissertation, University of Arizona, 1972. *Dissertation Abstracts International*, 1973, *33* (11-A), 6096.

Powell, W. J. Jr. Differential effectiveness of interviewer interventions in an experimental interview. *Journal of Consulting and Clinical Psychology*, 1968, *32*, 210-215.

Rabin, Marilyn S. *The effectiveness of helper self-disclosure as a function of role-expectations and levels of self-disclosure.* Unpublished doctoral dissertation, University of Cincinnati, 1975. *Dissertation Abstracts International*, 1975, *36* (4-B), 1929.

Robison, Philip D. *The effects of level of therapist self-disclosure on high and low disclosing subject's perception of the therapist.* Unpublished doctoral dissertation, Ohio State University, 1973. *Dissertation Abstracts International*, 1974, *34* (12-B), 6223.

Schoeninger, Douglas W. *Client experiencing as a function of therapist self-disclosure and pre-therapy training in experiencing.* Unpublished doctoral dissertation, University of Wisconsin, 1965. *Dissertation Abstracts International*, 1966, *26* (9), 5551.

Shaffer, Warren S. *The effects of counselor self-disclosure, status, and length of time of intimacy on subject evaluation and selection of counselor.* Unpublished doctoral dissertation, University of Arkansas, 1976. *Dissertation Abstracts International*, 1976, *37* (5-A), 2650.

Simonson, Norman R. The impact of therapist disclosure on patient disclosure. *Journal of Counseling Psychology*, 1976, *23*, 3-6.

E1.2.1.1.4.3 Interpersonal Dimensions

Simonson, Norman R. and Bahr, Susan. Self-disclosure by the professional and paraprofessional therapist. *Journal of Consulting and Clinical Psychology,* 1974, *42,* 359-363.

Sodikoff, Charles L.; Firestone, Ira J.; and Kaplan, Kalman J. Distance matching and distance equilibrium in the interview dyad. *Personality and Social Psychology Bulletin,* 1974, *1,* 243-245.

Stunkel, Erwin H. *Interviewee self-disclosure among impulsive and nonimpulsive college students as a function of instructions and interviewer disclosure.* Unpublished doctoral dissertation, Emory University, 1972. *Dissertation Abstracts International,* 1973, *33* (11-B), 5526.

Sykes, John David Jr. *A study of self-disclosure prediction and two types of interviewer modeling in the counseling interview.* Unpublished doctoral dissertation, The College of William and Mary in Virginia, 1976. *Dissertation Abstracts International,* 1976, *37* (6-A), 3431.

Thompson, Claude W. *A study of the effects of therapist self-disclosure on the therapist-client relationship.* Unpublished doctoral dissertation, Vanderbilt University, 1973. *Dissertation Abstracts International,* 1973, *34* (4-B), 1764.

Truax, Charles B. and Carkhuff, Robert R. Client and therapist transparency in the therapeutic encounter. *Journal of Counseling Psychology,* 1965, *12,* 3-9.

Turoczi, John C. *The effects of interviewer evaluative statements and self-disclosure on the self-disclosing behavior of interviewees.* Unpublished doctoral dissertation, Lehigh University, 1972. *Dissertation Abstracts International,* 1973, *33* (11-A), 5990.

Weiner, Myron F. Self-exposure by the therapist as a therapeutic technique. *American Journal of Psychotherapy,* 1972, *26,* 42-51.

E1.2.1.1.5 *Effectiveness of therapist, counselor, and interviewer*

Allen, Jon G. *Adaptive function of affect in interpersonal interaction.* Unpublished doctoral dissertation, University of Rochester, 1973. *Dissertation Abstracts International,* 1973, *33* (12-B), 6069.

Allen, Thomas W. Effectiveness of counselor trainees as a function of psychological openness. *Journal of Counseling Psychology*, 1967, *14*, 35-40.

Anchor, Kenneth N.; Strassberg, Donald S.; and Elkins, David. Supervisors' perceptions of the relationship between therapist self-disclosure and clinical effectiveness. *Journal of Clinical Psychology*, 1976, *32*, 158.

Chaikin, Alan L. and Derlega, Valerian J. *Self-disclosure.* Morristown, New Jersey: General Learning Press, 1974.

Combs, Arthur W.; Avila, Donald L.; and Purkey, William W. *Helping relationships: Basic concepts for the helping professions.* Boston: Allyn and Bacon, 1971.

Graff, Robert W. Relationship of counselor self-disclosure to counselor effectiveness. *Journal of Experimental Education*, 1970, *38*, 19-22.

Ohlson, E. LaMonte and Rupiper, O. J. A preliminary investigation into the self-disclosing ability of school psychology trainees. *Psychology*, 1975, *12*, 36-40.

Shaffer, Warren S. *The effects of counselor self-disclosure, status, and length of time of intimacy on subject evaluation and selection of counselor.* Unpublished doctoral dissertation, University of Arkansas, 1976. *Dissertation Abstracts International,* 1976, *37* (5-A), 2650.

Thomas, Ivor J. *An investigation of the relationships among self-disclosure, self-concept, and counseling effectiveness.* Unpublished doctoral dissertation, University of Southern California, 1968. *Dissertation Abstracts International,* 1968, *29* (1-A), 130.

Zurflueh, Max. *An investigation of the relationship between self-disclosure, self-actualization, and counselor effectiveness.* Unpublished doctoral dissertation, Arizona State University, 1974. *Dissertation Abstracts International,* 1974, *34* (10-A), 6472-6473.

E1.2.1.2 *Client and interviewee dimensions*

E1.2.1.2.1 Interpersonal Dimensions

E1.2.1.2.1 *Characteristics of the client and interviewee (see also* E1.3.1.2 *Member* and H6. *Psychiatric Patients)*

. Becker, Jane F. and Munz, David C. Extroversion and reciprocation of interviewer disclosures. *Journal of Consulting and Clinical Psychology,* 1975, *43,* 593.

Cline, Rebecca J. *An experimental study of the effects of interviewee locus of evaluation and interviewer style on depth and amount of interviewee self-disclosure and other-disclosure.* Unpublished doctoral dissertation, Pennsylvania State University, 1975. *Dissertation Abstracts International,* 1976, *37* (2-A), 690.

Crapo, Steven E. *The influence of belief systems upon self-disclosure.* [dogmatism] Unpublished doctoral dissertation, Arizona State University, 1970. *Dissertation Abstracts International,* 1970, *31* (1-A), 144.

Doster, Joseph A. Sex role learning and interview communication. *Journal of Counseling Psychology,* 1976, *23,* 482-485.

Fischer, Michael J. and Apostal, Robert A. Selected vocal cues and counselor's perceptions of genuineness, self-disclosure, and anxiety. *Journal of Counseling Psychology,* 1975, *22,* 92-96.

Heilbrun, Alfred B. Jr. History of self-disclosure in females and early defection from psychotherapy. *Journal of Counseling Psychology,* 1973, *20,* 250-257.

Heilbrun, Alfred B. Jr. Interviewer style, client satisfaction, and premature termination following the initial counseling contact. *Journal of Counseling Psychology,* 1974, *21,* 346-350.

Hyink, Paul W. *The influence of client ego-strength, client sex and therapist sex on the frequency, depth, and focus of client self-disclosure.* Unpublished doctoral dissertation, Michigan State University, 1974. *Dissertation Abstracts International,* 1975, *35* (9-B), 4652.

Meares, Russell. The secret. *Psychiatry,* 1976, *39,* 258-265.

Peterson, Ronald E. *The effects of self-disclosure on self-concept in a group of low-income clients.* Unpublished doctoral dissertation, United States International University, 1975. *Dissertation Abstracts International,* 1975, *36* (6-B), 3127.

Sousa-Poza, Joaquin F. and Rohrberg, Robert. Communicational and interactional aspects of self-disclosure in psychotherapy: Differences related to cognitive style. *Psychiatry*, 1976,
39, 81-91.

Strassberg, Donald S. *Client self-disclosure in individual psychotherapy.* Unpublished doctoral dissertation, George Peabody
College for Teachers, 1975. *Dissertation Abstracts International*, 1976, *36* (8-B), 4182.

Strassberg, Donald S. and Anchor, Kenneth N. Ratings of client
self-disclosure and improvement as a function of sex of client and therapist. *Journal of Clinical Psychology*, in press.

Todd, Judy L. and Shapira, Ariella. U. S. and British self-disclosure, anxiety, empathy, and attitudes to psychotherapy.
Journal of Cross-Cultural Psychology, 1974, *5*, 364-369.

Wolkon, George H.; Moriwaki, Sharon; and Williams, Karen J.
Race and social class as factors in the orientation towards
psychotherapy. *Journal of Counseling Psychology*, 1973,
20, 312-316.

E1.2.1.2.2 *Expectations of the client and interviewee (see also* E1.3.1.2
Group member and E2.6 *Expectations)*

Baldwin, Bruce A. Self-disclosure and expectations for psychotherapy in repressors and sensitizers. *Journal of Counseling
Psychology*, 1974, *21*, 455-456.

Bradford, Eregina G. *Therapist self-disclosure and client expectations.* Unpublished doctoral dissertation, Kent State University, 1975. *Dissertation Abstracts International*, 1975, *36*
(6-B), 3024.

Donahue, Gerald E. *The relative effects of positive statements
regarding counselor ability and experience on self-disclosure
and relationship satisfaction with respect to selected personality variables.* Unpublished doctoral dissertation, University
of Mississippi, 1974. *Dissertation Abstracts International*,
1975, *35* (7-A), 4155.

Doster, Joseph A. Individual differences affecting interviewee
expectancies and perceptions of self-disclosure. *Journal of
Counseling Psychology*, 1975, *22*, 192-198.

E1.2.1.2.2 Interpersonal Dimensions

Doster, Joseph A. and Slaymaker, Judith. Need approval, uncertainty anxiety, and expectancies of interview behavior. *Journal of Counseling Psychology*, 1972, *19*, 522-528.

Gay, Evan G. *Interviewer role and self-disclosure level as determinants of interviewee self-disclosure level and reactions to an interview.* Unpublished doctoral dissertation, University of Minnesota, 1975. *Dissertation Abstracts International*, 1975, *36* (6-B), 3039.

Hayward, Richard H. *Process and outcome consequences of therapist self-disclosure.* Unpublished doctoral dissertation, University of Colorado, 1973. *Dissertation Abstracts International*, 1974, *34* (12-B), 6210.

Horner, Beverly M. *The effects of counselor similarity self-disclosure on clients with differing role expectations.* Unpublished doctoral dissertation, University of Iowa, 1974. *Dissertation Abstracts International*, 1975, *35* (7-A), 4158.

Kopfstein, Joan H. *Need for approval, expectancy for consequences, and behavior in Gestalt experiments.* Unpublished doctoral dissertation, Georgia State University, 1972. *Dissertation Abstracts International*, 1974, *34* (8-B), 4048.

Lee, Robert E. *Some effects of a protestant clergy stereotype on counselor preference, self-disclosure readiness, and desire for counseling among junior college students.* Unpublished doctoral dissertation, University of Florida, 1969. *Dissertation Abstracts International*, 1970, *31* (3-A), 1015.

Rabin, Marilyn S. *The effectiveness of helper self-disclosure as a function of role-expectations and levels of self-disclosure.* Unpublished doctoral dissertation, University of Cincinnati, 1975. *Dissertation Abstracts International*, 1975, *36* (4-B), 1929.

Silver, Robert J. Effects of subject status and interviewer response program on subject self-disclosure in standardized interviews. *Proceedings of the 78th Annual Convention of the American Psychological Association*, 1970, *5*, 539-540.

Silver, Robert J. *Effects of relative interviewer status and interviewer program upon subject self-disclosure in standardized interviews.* Unpublished doctoral dissertation, Indiana University, 1973. *Dissertation Abstracts International*, 1973, *33* (8-B), 3962.

Wilson, Melvin N. and Rappaport, Julian. Personal self-disclosure: Expectancy and situational effects. *Journal of Consulting and Clinical Psychology*, 1974, *42*, 901-908.

E1.2.1.2.3 *Pretherapy training (see also* G. MODIFICATION OF SELF-
DISCLOSING BEHAVIOR)

Braukmann, Curtis J.; Fixsen, Dean L.; Phillips, Elery L.; Wolf,
Montrose M.; and Maloney, Dennis M. An analysis of a selection interview training package for predelinquents at Achievement Place. *Criminal Justice and Behavior*, 1974, *1*, 30-42.

Fernandez, Edwin B. *A study of changes in measured self-concept, self-disclosure, and attitudes towards family life as a
result of the use of a socialization technique before and
during psychotherapy.* Unpublished doctoral dissertation,
Temple University, 1975. *Dissertation Abstracts International*, 1975, *36* (6-B), 3034.

Gadaleto, Angelo I. *Differential effects of fidelity in client pretraining on client anxiety, self-disclosure, satisfaction, and
outcome.* Unpublished doctoral dissertation, University of
Virginia, 1976. *Dissertation Abstracts International*, 1976,
37 (5-B), 2503.

Goldstein, Ronald. *The effect of inner circle strategy pretraining upon self-disclosure in the initial counseling session.* Unpublished doctoral dissertation, Temple University, 1972.
Dissertation Abstracts International, 1973, *33* (10-B), 5016.

Overcash, Stephen J. *The effects of vicarious counseling pretraining on client self-disclosure, concreteness, and satisfaction.* Unpublished doctoral dissertation, University of Virginia, 1974. *Dissertation Abstracts International*, 1975, *35*
(8-A), 5034.

Raque, David W. *The effects of a videotaped pretherapy training program on the behavior of clients during their initial
sessions.* Unpublished doctoral dissertation, Southern Illinois
University, Carbondale, 1973. *Dissertation Abstracts International*, 1974, *34* (9-B), 4673.

Scheiderer, Edwin G. *Effects of instructions and modeling in
producing self-disclosure in the initial clinical interview.*
Unpublished doctoral dissertation, University of Illinois,

Urbana, 1974. *Dissertation Abstracts International,* 1975, *35* (12-B), 6112.

Schnitz, Donald R. *Facilitating self-disclosure responses in a simulated counseling interview through the use of audiotape modeling, videotape modeling, and instruction.* Unpublished doctoral dissertation, Auburn University, 1973. *Dissertation Abstracts International,* 1974, *34* (10-A), 6391-6392.

Smith, Joyce A. and Lewis, William A. Effect of videotaped models on the communication of college students in counseling. *Journal of Counseling Psychology,* 1974, *21,* 78-80.

Stachowiak, Thaddeus I. *Effects of pretherapy modeling model status and therapist status on client self-disclosure: An analogue study.* Unpublished doctoral dissertation, Michigan State University, 1974. *Dissertation Abstracts International,* 1974, *35* (6-B), 3038.

Stone, Gerald L. and Stebbins, Larry W. Effect of differential pretraining on client self-disclosure. *Journal of Counseling Psychology,* 1975, *22,* 17-20.

Wuehler, Paul R. *A study of the effects of videotape modeling and counselor/client pre-counseling interaction upon self-disclosure in initial personal assessment feedback counseling interviews.* Unpublished doctoral dissertation, Brigham Young University, 1975. *Dissertation Abstracts International,* 1976, *36* (7-B), 3635.

E1.2.1.3 *Process dimensions in the therapeutic interview (see also E1.-2.1.1.4.2 Response style and E1.2.1.1.4.3 Self-disclosure of therapist)*

Anchor, Kenneth N. and Sandler, Howard M. Psychotherapy sabotage and avoidance of self-disclosure. *Proceedings of the 81st Annual Convention of the American Psychological Association.* 1973, *8,* 485-486.

Anchor, Kenneth N. and Sandler, Howard M. Psychotherapy sabotage revisited: The better half of individual psychotherapy. *Journal of Clinical Psychology,* 1976, *32,* 146-148.

Dudgeon, Thomas B. *The effect of status and task manipulations on the interview responsivity of sensitizing and repressing juvenile delinquents.* Unpublished doctoral dissertation, Indiana University, 1972. *Dissertation Abstracts International,* 1973, *33* (8-B), 3933-3934.

Edelman, Robert I. and Snead, Roderick. Self-disclosure in a simulated psychiatric interview. *Journal of Consulting and Clinical Psychology,* 1972, *38,* 354-358.

Exline, Ralph V.; Gray, David; and Schuette, Dorothy. Visual behavior in a dyad as affected by interview content and sex of respondent. *Journal of Personality and Social Psychology,* 1965, *1,* 201-209.

Fischer, Michael J. and Apostal, Robert A. Selected vocal cues and counselor's perceptions of genuineness, self-disclosure, and anxiety. *Journal of Counseling Psychology,* 1975, *22,* 92-96.

Forrest, Gary G. *Transparency as a prognostic variable in psychotherapy.* Unpublished doctoral dissertation, University of North Dakota, 1970. *Dissertation Abstracts International,* 1971, *31* (9-A), 4457.

Goodman, G. M. Findings from a study of emotional disclosure in psychotherapy relationships. *Counseling Center Discussion Papers,* University of Chicago, 1962, *8* (13). [see A1. Breed and Jourard, 1970, p. 11]

Heller, Kenneth. Laboratory interview research as analogue to treatment. In Allen E. Bergin and Sol L. Garfield (Eds.), *Handbook of psychotherapy and behavior change: An empirical analysis.* New York: John Wiley and Sons, 1971.

Hill, Clara E. *An investigation of the effects of therapist and client variables on the psychotherapy process.* Unpublished doctoral dissertation, Southern Illinois University, Carbondale, 1973. *Dissertation Abstracts International,* 1975, *35* (12-B), 6095.

James, Charles R. *The socialization process of psychotherapy training: Self-disclosure, self-concept and conformity of value orientation as mediated by trainer influence.* Unpublished doctoral dissertation, George Peabody College for Teachers, 1973. *Dissertation Abstracts International,* 1973, *34* (7-B), 3498.

Jourard, Sidney M. I-thou relationship versus manipulation in counseling and psychotherapy. *Journal of Individual Psychotherapy,* 1959, *15,* 174-179.

E1.2.1.3 Interpersonal Dimensions

Jourard, Sidney M. The phenomenon of resistance in the psycho-therapist. *Counseling Center Discussion Papers,* University of Chicago, 1961, 7 (13).

Jourard, Sidney M. Counseling for authenticity. In Carlton E. Beck (Ed.), *Guidelines for guidance.* Dubuque, Iowa: W. C. Brown, 1966.

Jourard, Sidney M. The beginnings of self-disclosure. *Voices: The Art and Science of Psychotherapy,* 1970, *6,* 42-51.

Krohn, Marvin; Waldo, Gordon P., and Chiricos, Theodore G. Self-reported delinquency: A comparison of structured inter-views and self-administered checklists. *Journal of Criminal Law and Criminology,* 1974, *65,* 545-553.

Liberman, Bernard L. *The effect of modeling procedures on attraction and disclosure in a psychotherapy analogue.* Unpub-lished doctoral dissertation, Syracuse University, 1970. *Disser-tation Abstracts International,* 1970, *32* (1-B), 564.

Mann, Brenda and Murphy, Kevin C. Timing of self-disclosure, reciprocity of self-disclosure, and reactions to an initial inter-view. *Journal of Counseling Psychology,* 1975, *22,* 304-308.

McGuire, Dennis; Thelen, Mark H.; and Amolsch, Thomas. Inter-view self-disclosure as a function of length of modeling and descriptive instructions. *Journal of Consulting and Clinical Psychology,* 1975, *43,* 356-362.

Nosanchuk, Melvin F. *The comparative effects of different methods of interviewing on self-disclosing behavior.* Unpub-lished doctoral dissertation, University of Utah, 1972. *Disser-tation Abstracts International,* 1973, *33* (10-A), 5498.

O'Hare, Christopher. *Impact of intimacy and temporal orienta-tion of helper self-disclosure on the helping process.* Unpub-lished doctoral dissertation, University of California, Los Angeles, 1975. *Dissertation Abstracts International,* 1976, *36* (7-B), 3618.

Ohlson, Ronald W. *The effects of video-tape modeling of self-dis-closure upon client revealingness and personality change.* Un-published doctoral dissertation, Fuller Theological Seminary, 1970. *Dissertation Abstracts International,* 1972, *32* (12-B), 7320.

Polansky, Norman A. The concept of verbal accessibility. *Smith College Studies in Social Work,* 1965, *36,* 1-46.

Shaffer, Warren S. *The effects of counselor self-disclosure, status, and length of time of intimacy on subject evaluation and selection of counselor.* Unpublished doctoral dissertation, University of Arkansas, 1976. *Dissertation Abstracts International,* 1976, *37* (5-A), 2650.

Sinha, Virendra. Self-disclosure: Its clinical importance. *Indian Journal of Clinical Psychology,* 1974, *1,* 81-83.

Strassberg, Donald S.; Anchor, Kenneth N.; Gabel, Harris; and Cohen, B. Self-disclosure in individual psychotherapy. *Psychotherapy: Theory, Research, and Practice,* in press.

Strassberg, Donald S.; Roback, Howard B.; D'Antonio, M.; and Gabel, Harris. Self-disclosure: A critical and selective review of the clinical literature. *Comprehensive Psychiatry,* in press.

Vann, Patrick R. *Differential treatment effects and self-disclosing behavior: A psychotherapy analogue study.* Unpublished doctoral dissertation, University of Rochester, 1975. *Dissertation Abstracts International,* 1975, *36* (3-B), 1463.

E1.2.1.4   *Situational dimensions (see also* F. SITUATIONAL DIMENSIONS)

Chaikin, Alan L.; Derlega, Valerian J.; and Miller, Sarah J. Effects of room environment on self-disclosure in a counseling analogue. *Journal of Counseling Psychology,* 1976, *23,* 479-481.

Cogan, James M. *The effect of the presence or absence of another person on the verbalizations of schizophrenics under a demand for intimate self-disclosure.* Unpublished doctoral dissertation, University of Missouri, Columbia, 1975. *Dissertation Abstracts International,* 1976, *36* (7-B), 3594.

Feigenbaum, William M. *Self-disclosure in the psychological interview as a function of interviewer self-disclosure, sex of subjects, and seating arrangements.* Unpublished doctoral dissertation, University of South Carolina, 1974. *Dissertation Abstracts International,* 1975, *35* (10-B), 5108.

Janofsky, Annelies I. *A study of affective self-references in telephone vs. face to face interviews.* Unpublished doctoral dissertation, University of Oregon, 1970. *Dissertation Abstracts International*, 1971, *31* (10-B), 6258.

Janofsky, Annelies I. Affective self-disclosure in telephone vs. face-to-face interviews. *Journal of Humanistic Psychology*, 1971, *11*, 93-103.

Lassen, Carol L. Effect of proximity on anxiety and communication in the initial psychiatric interview. *Journal of Abnormal Psychology*, 1973, *81*, 226-232.

Sims, Gregory K. and Sims, Janet M. Does face-to-face contact reduce counselee responsiveness with emotionally insecure youth? *Psychotherapy: Theory, Research, and Practice*, 1973, *10*, 348-351.

Weber, Judy W. *The effects of physical proximity and body boundary size on the self-disclosure interview.* Unpublished doctoral dissertation, University of Southern California, 1972. *Dissertation Abstracts International*, 1973, *33* (7-B), 3327.

E1.2.2 *Laboratory relationships: experimenter-subject and experimental dyads*

Allen, Jon G. When does exchanging personal information constitute self-disclosure? *Psychological Reports*, 1974, *35*, 195-198.

Burkhalter, Sandra L. *The effect of interviewer verbal and nonverbal activity level on interviewee verbal and nonverbal activity level and the assessment of the relationship between verbal activity and self-disclosure.* Unpublished doctoral dissertation, Emory University, 1975. *Dissertation Abstracts International*, 1976, *36* (12-B), 6373.

Dawson, Carolyn. *Affect and self-disclosure as a function of touch in an interview between strangers.* Unpublished doctoral dissertation, Columbia University, 1973. *Dissertation Abstracts International*, 1973, *34* (6-B), 2925.

Derlega, Valerian J.; Chaikin, Alan L.; and Herndon, James. Demand characteristics and disclosure reciprocity. *Journal of Social Psychology*, 1975, *97*, 301-302.

Donderio, Rene A. *The effect of examiner variables on self-disclosure in TAT stories.* Unpublished doctoral dissertation, State University of New York at Buffalo, 1969. *Dissertation Abstracts International*, 1969, *30* (6-B), 2904.

Drag, Lee R. *Experimenter-subject interaction: A situational determinant of differential levels of self-disclosure.* Unpublished master's thesis, University of Florida, 1968. [summary in Charles D. Spielberger (Ed.), *Current topics in psychology* (Vol. 1). New York: Academic Press, 1969, pp. 117-120.]

Drag, Richard M. *Experimenter behavior and group size as variables influencing self-disclosure.* Unpublished doctoral dissertation, University of Florida, 1968. *Dissertation Abstracts International,* 1969, *30* (5-B), 2416.

Frey, Marshall. *The effects of self-disclosure and social reinforcement on performance in paired-associate learning.* Unpublished honors paper, University of Florida, 1967. [summary in Charles D. Spielberger (Ed.), *Current topics in psychology* (Vol. 1). New York: Academic Press, 1969, pp. 120-123.]

Gilbert, Carol J. *The relationship of locus of control, experimenter disclosure, and repeated encounters to "actual" disclosure, subject-perceived disclosure, anxiety, neuroticism, and social desirability.* Unpublished doctoral dissertation, University of Kansas, 1972. *Dissertation Abstracts International,* 1973, *33* (9-B), 4487.

Heifitz, M. L. *Experimenter effect upon openness of response to the Rotter Incomplete Sentence Blank.* Unpublished honors paper, University of Florida, 1967. [summary in Charles D. Spielberger (Ed.), *Current topics in psychology* (Vol. 1). New York: Academic Press, 1969, pp, 113-117.]

Hood, Thomas C. and Back, Kurt W. Self-disclosure and the volunteer: A source of bias in laboratory experiments. *Journal of Personality and Social Psychology,* 1971, *17*, 130-136.

Johnson, Carl F. and Dabbs, James M. Jr. Self-disclosure in dyads as a function of distance and the subject-experimenter relationship. *Sociometry,* 1976, *39*, 257-263.

Jongsma, Arthur E. Jr. *The effects of experimenter trust and trustworthiness on subject's reciprocal self-disclosure.* Unpublished doctoral dissertation, Northern Illinois University, 1973. *Dissertation Abstracts International,* 1973, *34* (3-B), 1277.

Jourard, Sidney M. *Disclosing man to himself.* Princeton: D. Van Nostrand Company, 1968.

Jourard, Sidney M. The effects of experimenters' self-disclosure on subjects' behavior. In Charles D. Spielberger (Ed.), *Current topics in psychology* (Vol. 1). New York: Academic Press, 1969.

Jourard, Sidney M. *Self-disclosure: An experimental analysis of the transparent self.* New York: Wiley-Interscience, 1971.

Jourard, Sidney M. and Friedman, Robert. Experimenter-subject "distance" and self-disclosure. *Journal of Personality and Social Psychology,* 1970, *15,* 278-282.

Jourard, Sidney M. and Kormann, Leo A. Getting to know the experimenter and its effect on psychological test performance. *Journal of Humanistic Psychology,* 1968, *8,* 155-159.

Kormann, Leo A. *Getting to know the experimenter and its effect on EPPS test performance.* Unpublished master's thesis, University of Florida, 1967. [summary in Charles D. Spielberger (Ed.), *Current topics in psychology* (Vol. 1). New York: Academic Press, 1969, pp. 112-113.]

Kutner, David H. Jr. *Ecological aspects of immediacy and self-disclosure in an interview setting.* Unpublished doctoral dissertation, Yale University, 1975. *Dissertation Abstracts International,* 1976, *36* (12-B), 6447.

Marshall, Marilyn J. *The effects of two interviewer variables on self-disclosure in an experimental interview situation.* Unpublished master's thesis, Pennsylvania State University, 1970.

McAllister, Ann D. *Interviewee self-disclosure as a function of level and identity of self-disclosing models.* Unpublished doctoral dissertation, Emory University, 1973. *Dissertation Abstracts International,* 1974, *34* (7-B), 161.

McAllister, Ann and Kiesler, Donald J. Interpersonal disclosure as a function of interpersonal trust, task modeling, and interviewer self-disclosure. *Journal of Consulting and Clinical Psychology,* 1975, *43,* 428.

Mouton, Jane S.; Blake, Robert R.; and Olmstead, Joseph A. The relationship between frequency of yielding and the disclosure of personal identity. *Journal of Personality,* 1956, *24,* 339-347.

Powell, W. J. Jr. Differential effectiveness of interviewer interventions in an experimental interview. *Journal of Consulting and Clinical Psychology,* 1968, *32,* 210-215.

Sousa-Poza, Joaquin F.; Rohrberg, Robert; and Mercure, André. *Kinesic behavior accompanying person-oriented and non-person oriented verbal content: A preliminary report.* Paper presented at First International Symposium on Non-Verbal Aspects and Techniques of Psychotherapy, Vancouver, July, 1974.

Suchman, David I. *Responses of subjects to two types of interviews.* Unpublished doctoral dissertation, Ohio State University, 1966. *Dissertation Abstracts International,* 1967, *27* (9-B), 3297.

Switkin, Linda R. *Self-disclosure as a function of sex roles, experimenter-subject distance, sex of experimenter and intimacy of topics.* Unpublished doctoral dissertation, St. Louis University, 1974. *Dissertation Abstracts International,* 1974, *35* (5-B), 2451.

Tognoli, Jerome J. *Reciprocal behavior in interpersonal information exchange.* Unpublished doctoral dissertation, University of Delaware, 1967. *Dissertation Abstracts International,* 1968, *29* (3-B), 1193.

Tognoli, Jerome. Response matching in interpersonal information exchange. *British Journal of Social and Clinical Psychology,* 1969, *8,* 116-123.

Vondracek, Fred W. *The manipulation of self-disclosure in an experimental interview situation.* Unpublished doctoral dissertation, Pennsylvania State University, 1968. *Dissertation Abstracts International,* 1969, *30* (3-B), 1350.

Vondracek, Fred W. The study of self-disclosure in experimental interviews. *Journal of Psychology,* 1969, *72,* 55-59.

Zoberi, Seemie. *Rapport by operant conditioning.* Unpublished doctoral dissertation, University of South Dakota, 1973. *Dissertation Abstracts International,* 1974, *34* (5-B), 2324.

E1.3   *Professional relationships: group*

E1.3.1   *Therapeutic groups*

E1.3.1.1   *Group leader, facilitator, and therapist dimensions*

Armstrong, Renate G. A comparison between group therapists and members of the desired degree of self-disclosure by therapists. *Newsletter for Research in Mental Health and Behavioral Sciences,* 1974, *16,* 20-21.

Bean, Howard B. *The effects of a role-model and instructions on group interpersonal openness and cohesiveness.* Unpublished doctoral dissertation, West Virginia University, 1971. *Dissertation Abstracts International,* 1972, *32* (7-B), 4201.

Bolman, Lee. Some effects of trainers on their T groups. *Journal of Applied Behavioral Science,* 1971, *7,* 309-326.

Carlson, Christopher R. *The relationship of anxiety, openness, and group psychotherapy experience with perceptions of therapist self-disclosure among psychiatric patients.* Unpublished doctoral dissertation, University of Texas, Austin, 1975. *Dissertation Abstracts International,* 1976, *37* (1-B), 453.

Cohen, Howard K. *Group methods in undergraduate education: An evaluation of student led discussion groups in sex education.* Unpublished doctoral dissertation, University of Rochester, 1974. *Dissertation Abstracts International,* 1974, *35* (1-B), 497-498.

Cooper, Cary L. The influence of the trainer on participant change in T-groups. *Human Relations,* 1969, *22,* 515-530.

Copeland, Edna D. *Leadership status, leadership style and self-disclosure.* Unpublished doctoral dissertation, Georgia State University, 1970. *Dissertation Abstracts International,* 1971, *32* (1-B), 553.

Culbert, Samuel A. *Trainer self-disclosure and member growth in a T-group.* Unpublished doctoral dissertation, University of California, Los Angeles, 1966. *Dissertation Abstracts International,* 1966, *27* (6-B), 2131.

Culbert, Samuel A. Trainer self-disclosure and member growth in a T-group. *Journal of Applied Behavioral Science,* 1968, *4,* 47-73.

Dies, Robert R. Group therapist self-disclosure: An evaluation by clients. *Journal of Counseling Psychology,* 1973, *20,* 344-348.

Dies, Robert R.; Cohen, Lauren; and Pines, Sharon. Content considerations in group therapist self-disclosure. *Proceedings of the 81st Annual Convention of the American Psychological Association,* 1973, *8,* 481-482.

Eisman, Elena J. *The effect of leader sex and self-disclosure on member self-disclosure in marathon encounter groups.* Unpublished doctoral dissertation, Boston University, 1975. *Dissertation Abstracts International,* 1975, *36* (3-B), 1429.

Fuller, James B. *An investigation of self-disclosing behavior and the affective response within a T-group setting.* Unpublished doctoral dissertation, West Virginia University, 1971. *Dissertation Abstracts International,* 1971, *32* (4-A), 1852.

Gould, Victor A. *Self-disclosure in small interaction groups in relation to the self-disclosure of the group leader.* Unpublished doctoral dissertation, Boston University, 1975. *Dissertation Abstracts International,* 1975, *36* (3-A), 1304.

Hayalian, Thomas. *The effect of trainer's level of self-disclosure and participants' inclusion orientation on participants' self-disclosures in an encounter group.* Unpublished doctoral dissertation, University of Kansas, 1975. *Dissertation Abstracts International,* 1976, *36* (7-B), 3674.

Hodge, M. B. *Management of the fear of self-disclosure in therapy groups.* Paper presented at the Meeting of the Western Psychological Association, San Diego, 1968.

Kangas, Jon A. Group members' self-disclosure: A function of preceding self-disclosure by leader or other group member. *Comparative Group Studies,* 1971, *2,* 65-70.

Kovan, Robert A. Resistance of the marathon facilitator to becoming an intimate member of the group. *Psychosomatics,* 1968, *9,* 286.

Lakin, Martin. *Interpersonal encounter: Theory and practice in sensitivity training.* New York: McGraw-Hill, 1972.

Lieberman, Morton A.; Yalom, Irvin D.; and Miles, Matthew B. *Encounter groups: First facts.* New York: Basic Books, 1973.

Lund, R. D. *Therapist self-reference as a group therapy technique.* Unpublished master's thesis. University of Colorado, 1964.

May, Orlan P. *Self-disclosure and mental health: A study of encounter-group members' perceptions of group leaders.* Unpublished doctoral dissertation, University of Tennessee, 1972. *Dissertation Abstracts International,* 1973, *33* (8-A), 4092.

E1.3.1.1 Interpersonal Dimensions

May, Orlan P. and Thompson, Charles L. Perceived levels of self-disclosure, mental health, and helpfulness of group leaders. *Journal of Counseling Psychology,* 1973, *20,* 349-352.

Moss, Carolyn J. *Effects of leader behavior in personal growth groups: Self-disclosure and experiencing.* Unpublished doctoral dissertation, Southern Illinois University, Carbondale, 1975. *Dissertation Abstracts International,* 1976, *36* (12-B), 6361.

Moss, Carolyn J. and Harren, Vincent A. Effects of leader disclosure on member disclosure in personal growth groups. *Small Group Behavior,* in press.

Psathas, George and Hardert, R. Trainer intervention and normative patterns in the T group. *Journal of Applied Behavioral Science,* 1966, *2,* 149-170.

Rodriguez, Richard M. *The effect of a group leader's cultural identity upon self-disclosure.* Unpublished doctoral dissertation, Arizona State University, 1971. *Dissertation Abstracts International,* 1972, *32* (6-A), 3039.

Truax, Charles B. The process of group psychotherapy. *Psychological Monographs,* 1961, *75* (7, whole No. 511).

Truax, Charles B. Counselor interpersonal reinforcement of client self-exploration and therapeutic outcome in group counseling. *Journal of Counseling Psychology,* 1968, *15,* 225-231.

Shaffer, John B. and Galinsky, M. David. *Models of group therapy and sensitivity training.* Englewood Cliffs, New Jersey: Prentice-Hall, 1974.

Wile, Daniel B.; Bron, Gary D.; and Pollack, Herbert B. The Group Therapy Questionnaire: An instrument for study of leadership in small groups. *Psychological Reports,* 1970, *27,* 263-273.

E1.3.1.2 *Group member dimensions*

Anchor, Kenneth N.; Vojtisek, John E.; and Berger, Stephen E. Social desirability as a predictor of self-disclosure in groups. *Psychotherapy: Theory, Research, and Practice,* 1972, *9,* 262-264.

Anchor, Kenneth N.; Vojtisek, John E.; and Patterson, Roger L. Trait anxiety, initial structuring, and self-disclosure in groups of schizophrenic patients. *Psychotherapy: Theory, Research, and Practice,* 1973, *10,* 155-158.

Clark, William H. *A study of the relationships between the client personality traits of dogmatism, empathy, self-disclosure, and the behavioral changes resulting from a therapeutic group experience.* Unpublished doctoral dissertation, The American University, 1972. *Dissertation Abstracts International,* 1973, *33* (10-A), 5488.

Davis, Terry B.; Frye, Roland L.; and Joure, Sylvia. Perceptions and behaviors of dogmatic subjects in a T-group setting. *Perceptual and Motor Skills,* 1975, *41,* 375-381.

Doyne, Stephen E. *The relationship between self-disclosure and self-esteem in encounter groups.* Unpublished doctoral dissertation, George Peabody College for Teachers, 1972. *Dissertation Abstracts International,* 1972, *33* (4-B), 1786.

Ganter, Grace and Polansky, Norman A. Predicting a child's accessibility to individual treatment from diagnostic groups. *Social Work,* 1964, *9,* 56-63.

Ganter, Grace; Yeakel, Margaret; and Polansky, Norman A. Intermediary group treatment of inaccessible children. *American Journal of Orthopsychiatry,* 1965, *35,* 739-746.

Harren, Vincent A. *Videotape pretraining program for encounter group members: A training manual for encounter group cofacilitators.* Unpublished manuscript, Southern Illinois University, 1975.

Kelber, Sister Mary B. *Exploration of group sessions with rehabilitating post-myocardial infarction males regarding self-disclosure and cardiac adjustment with objective and subjective evaluations of group sessions.* Unpublished doctoral dissertation, The Catholic University of America, 1976. *Dissertation Abstracts International,* 1976, *37* (3-B), 1408.

Kuiken, Don; Rasmussen, R. V.; and Cullen, Dallas. Some predictors of volunteer participation in human relations training groups. *Psychological Reports,* 1974, *35,* 499-504.

Millard, Edward R. *The effects of writing assignments upon rational thinking and level of self-disclosure in group counseling.*

Unpublished doctoral dissertation, Fordham University, 1976. *Dissertation Abstracts International,* 1976, *37* (2-A), 813.

Pearson, Richard E. *Verbal behavior in the training group setting of individuals differing in conceptual style.* New York: Syracuse University, 1966. (ERIC Document Reproduction Service No. ED 050 420)

Petersen, Dwight J. *The relationship between self-concept and self-disclosure of underachieving college students in group counseling.* Unpublished doctoral dissertation, Brigham Young University, 1972. *Dissertation Abstracts International,* 1972, *33* (5-B), 2354.

Rothenberg, Eugenia. *The effect of self-disclosure and pseudo-self-disclosure on social adjustment of institutionalized delinquent girls.* Unpublished doctoral dissertation, University of New Mexico, 1969. *Dissertation Abstracts International,* 1970, *30* (12-A), 5246.

E1.3.1.3 *Process and outcome dimensions*

Althouse, Richard H. *Enhancing self-disclosure and cohesiveness in psychotherapy groups: An analogue study.* Unpublished doctoral dissertation, Pennsylvania State University, 1975. *Dissertation Abstracts International,* 1976, *36* (7-B), 3668.

Anchor, Kenneth N. *Interaction patterns in experimental, marathon, and traditionally spaced groups.* Unpublished master's thesis, University of Connecticut, 1970.

Anchor, Kenneth N. *High and low risk self-disclosure in group psychotherapy.* Paper presented at the Meeting of the Midwestern Psychological Association, Chicago, 1974. (ERIC Document Reproduction Service No. ED 099 746)

Ashcraft, Carolyn. *Effects of laboratory training on self-concept, self-disclosure, and locus of control.* Paper presented at the Meeting of the Southeastern Psychological Association, New Orleans, 1969.

Bailey, Roger L. *The effects of temporal sequence variation on self-directed small groups in a college environment.* Unpublished doctoral dissertation, United States International University, 1971. *Dissertation Abstracts International,* 1971, *32* (6-B), 3614.

Barbour, Alton. The self-disclosure aspect of the psychodrama sharing session. *Group Psychotherapy and Psychodrama*, 1972, *25*, 132-138.

Baum, Ronald C. *Self-disclosure in small groups as a function of group composition.* Unpublished doctoral dissertation, University of Cincinnati, 1971. *Dissertation Abstracts International*, 1972, *32* (7-B), 4200.

Beach, Wayne A. *Personalizing group environments: A conceptual approach toward more effective small group functioning.* Paper presented at the Annual Meeting of the Western Speech Communication Association, Newport Beach, California, 1974. (ERIC Document Reproduction Service No. ED 099 937)

Bednar, Richard L.; Melnick, Joseph; and Kaul, Theodore J. Risk, responsibility, and structure: A conceptual framework for initiating group counseling and psychotherapy. *Journal of Counseling Psychology*, 1974, *21*, 31-37.

Berger, Stephen E. and Anchor, Kenneth N. Disclosure process in group interaction. *Proceedings of the 78th Annual Convention of the American Psychological Association*, 1970, *5*, 529-530.

Brasfield, Charles R. and Cubitt, Anne. Changes in self-disclosure behavior following an intensive "encounter" group experience. *Canadian Counselor*, 1974, *8*, 12-21.

Callan, Joanne E. *A measure of self-disclosure in intensive small groups.* Unpublished doctoral dissertation, University of Texas at Austin, 1970. *Dissertation Abstracts International*, 1971, *31* (7-B), 4306.

Canino-Stolberg, Glorisa. *The effects of physical contact exercises on marathon encounter leaderless groups on dimensions of self-concept, self-disclosure and touching behavior.* Unpublished doctoral dissertation, Temple University, 1975. *Dissertation Abstracts International*, 1976, *36* (7-B), 3592.

Clark, James V. Authentic interaction and personal growth in sensitivity training groups. *Journal of Humanistic Psychology*, 1963, *3*, 1-13.

Cleland, Robert S. and Carnes, G. Derwood. Emotional vs. ideational emphasis during group counseling with student nurses. *Journal of Counseling Psychology*, 1965, *12*, 282-286.

E1.3.1.3 Interpersonal Dimensions

Conyne, Robert K. Effects of facilitator-directed and self-directed group experiences. *Counselor Education and Supervision,* 1974, *13,* 184-189.

Cooper, Cary L. and Bowles, David. Physical encounter and self-disclosure. *Psychological Reports,* 1973, *33,* 451-454.

Corsini, Raymond J. Issues in encounter groups. *The Counseling Psychologist,* 1970, *2,* 28-34.

Coulson, William. Inside a basic encounter group. *The Counseling Psychologist,* 1970, *2,* 1-27.

Crews, Catherine Y. and Melnick, Joseph. Use of initial and delayed structure in facilitating group development. *Journal of Counseling Psychology,* 1976, *23,* 92-98.

Cutter, Henry S.; Samaraweera, Albert B.; Fish, Richard A.; Morris, Louis; and Merritt, Repton. Emotional openness and mood change in marathon group psychotherapy. *International Journal of the Addictions,* 1974, *9,* 741-748.

D'Augelli, Anthony R. *The effects of interpersonal skills and pretraining on group interaction.* Unpublished doctoral dissertation, University of Connecticut, 1973. *Dissertation Abstracts International,* 1973, *33* (10-B), 5010. (a)

D'Augelli, Anthony R. Group composition using interpersonal skills: An analogue study on the effects of members interpersonal skills on peer ratings and group cohesiveness. *Journal of Counseling Psychology,* 1973, *6,* 531-534. (b)

D'Augelli, Anthony R. and Chinsky, Jack M. Interpersonal skills and pretraining: Implications for the use of group procedures for interpersonal learning and for the selection of nonprofessional mental health workers. *Journal of Consulting and Clinical Psychology,* 1974, *42,* 65-72.

D'Augelli, Anthony R.; Chinsky, Jack M.; and Getter, Herbert. The effect of group composition and duration on sensitivity training. *Small Group Behavior,* 1974, *5,* 56-64.

Delbam, Andrew R. *The effect of intragroup distance on self-disclosure.* Unpublished doctoral dissertation, Indiana University, 1974. *Dissertation Abstracts International,* 1975, *35* (7-B), 3645.

Dies, Robert R. and Sadowsky, Richard. A brief encounter group experience and social relationships in a dormitory. *Journal of Counseling Psychology,* 1974, *21,* 112-115.

Diethelm, Daniel R. *Changes in levels of self-disclosure and perceived self-disclosure between partners following participation in a weekend encounter group for couples.* Unpublished doctoral dissertation, University of Connecticut, 1974. *Dissertation Abstracts International,* 1974, *34* (9-A), 5622.

Egan, Gerald. *Encounter: Group processes for interpersonal growth.* Belmont, California: Brooks/Cole Publishing Company, 1970.

Egan, Gerald (Ed.). *Encounter groups: Basic readings.* Belmont, California: Brooks/Cole Publishing Company, 1971.

Egan, Gerald. *Face to face: The small group experience and interpersonal growth.* Belmont, California: Brooks/Cole Publishing Company, 1973.

Ehrentheil, Otto F.; Chase, Stanley J.; and Hyde, Mary R. Revealing and body display. *Archives of General Psychiatry,* 1973, *29,* 363-367.

Esposito, Ronald P.; McAdoo, Harriette; and Scher, Linda. The Johari Window as an evaluative instrument for group process. *Interpersonal Development,* 1975/76, *6,* 25-37.

Goldman, Andrew P. *Empathy, self-disclosure, confrontation and cohesiveness in marathon-groups and conventional encounter-groups.* Unpublished doctoral dissertation, Syracuse University, 1972. *Dissertation Abstracts International,* 1973, *34* (3-B), 1275.

Goodstein, Leonard D.; Goldstein, Joel J.; D'Orta, Carolyn V.; and Goodman, Margaret A. Measurement of self-disclosure in encounter groups: A methodological study. *Journal of Counseling Psychology,* 1976, *23,* 142-146.

Gottlieb, Marvin R. *The effects of laboratory training methods on highly stable variables such as self-esteem and self-disclosure.* Paper presented at the Annual Meeting of the International Communication Association, Montreal, Canada, 1973. (ERIC Document Reproduction Service No. ED 085 788)

E1.3.1.3 Interpersonal Dimensions

Gottschalk, Louis A. and Pattison, E. Mansell. Psychiatric perspectives on T-groups and the laboratory movement: An overview. *American Journal of Psychiatry,* 1969, *126,* 823.

Grencik, Judith A. *The effects of a model on verbal behavior in group counseling.* Unpublished doctoral dissertation, University of Maryland, 1971. *Dissertation Abstracts International,* 1972, *32* (12-A), 6807.

Higbee, Kenneth L. Group influence on self-disclosure. *Psychological Reports,* 1973, *32,* 903-909.

Hrubetz, Joan. *Measurement of changes in nursing students' levels of empathy, self-disclosure, and confrontation as outcomes of systematic human relations training.* Unpublished doctoral dissertation, St. Louis University, 1975. *Dissertation Abstracts International,* 1975, *36* (6-B), 2725.

Hurley, Shirley J. *Self-disclosure in counseling groups as influenced by structured confrontation and interpersonal process recall.* Unpublished doctoral dissertation, Michigan State University, 1967. *Dissertation Abstracts International,* 1968, *29* (1-A), 123.

Johnson, David L. and Ridener, Larry R. Self-disclosure, participation, and perceived cohesiveness in small group interaction. *Psychological Reports,* 1974, *35,* 361-362.

Kahn, Michael H. and Rudestam, Kjell E. The relationship between liking and perceived self-disclosure in small groups. *Journal of Psychology,* 1971, *78,* 81-85.

Kessel, Elizabeth V. *Interpersonal trust and attitude toward the expression of positive and negative affect within the T-group.* Unpublished doctoral dissertation, West Virginia University, 1971. *Dissertation Abstracts International,* 1971, *32* (4-A), 1855-1856.

Kinder, Billy N. *The relationship of pre-therapy self-disclosure, the structure of group therapy, and locus-of-control on therapeutic outcome.* Unpublished doctoral dissertation, University of South Carolina, 1975. *Dissertation Abstracts International,* 1976, *37* (1-B), 465.

Kirshner, Barry J. *The effects of experimental manipulation of self-disclosure on group cohesivesness.* Unpublished doctoral dissertation, University of Maryland, 1976. *Dissertation Abstracts International,* 1976, *37* (6-B), 3081.

Koch, Sigmund. The image of man implicit in encounter group therapy. *Journal of Humanistic Psychology*, 1971, *11*, 109-128.

Kraft, Lee W. and Vraa, Calvin W. Sex composition of groups and patterns of self-disclosure by high school females. *Psychological Reports*, 1975, *37*, 733-734.

Kuppersmith, Joel H. *The relative effects of here-and-now versus there-and-then self-disclosure upon personality and cohesiveness in marathon encounter groups.* Unpublished doctoral dissertation, University of Mississippi, 1975. *Dissertation Abstracts International*, 1975, *36* (4-A), 2028.

Lakin, Martin. *Interpersonal encounter: Theory and practice in sensitivity training.* New York: McGraw-Hill Book Company, 1972.

Levy, Stephen J. *An empirical study of disclosing behavior in a verbal encounter group.* Unpublished doctoral dissertation, Yeshiva University, 1971. *Dissertation Abstracts International*, 1972, *32* (10-A), 5896-5897.

Lieberman, Morton A.; Yalom, Irvin D.; and Miles, Matthew B. *Encounter groups: First facts.* New York: Basic Books, 1973.

Lubin, Bernard J. A modified version of the self-disclosure inventory. *Psychological Reports*, 1965, *17*, 498.

Lubin, Bernard and Harrison, Roger L. Predicting small group behavior with the self-disclsoure inventory. *Psychological Reports*, 1964, *15*, 77-78.

Luft, Joseph. *Group processes: An introduction to group dynamics.* Palo Alto, California: National Press Books, 1970.

MacDoniels, Joseph W. *Factors related to the level of open expression in small group laboratory learning experiences.* Unpublished doctoral dissertation, University of Kansa, 1972. *Dissertation Abstracts International*, 1973, *33* (11-A), 6488-6489.

Miller, Sherod L. *The effects of communication training in small groups upon self-disclosure and openness in engaged couples' systems of interaction: A field experiment.* Unpublished doctoral dissertation, University of Minnesota, 1971. *Dissertation Abstracts International*, 1971, *32* (5-A), 2819.

E1.3.1.3 Interpersonal Dimensions

Morris, Kenneth T. and Cinnamon, Kenneth M. (Eds.). *Controversial issues in human relations training groups.* Springfield, Illinois: Charles C. Thomas, 1976.

Mowrer, O. Hobart. *The new group therapy.* Princeton: D. Van Nostrand Company, 1964.

Neff, Richard. The group constellation. *Psychotherapy: Theory, Research, and Practice,* 1974, *11,* 80-82.

Ollerman, Thomas E. *The effect of group counseling upon self-actualization, self-disclosure, and the development of interpersonal trust among prison inmates.* Unpublished doctoral dissertation, New Mexico State University, 1975. *Dissertation Abstracts International,* 1975, *36* (6-A), 3415.

Pino, Christopher J. Relation of a trainability index to T-group outcomes. *Journal of Applied Psychology,* 1971, *55,* 439-442.

Piper, William E. *Evaluation of the effects of sensitivity training and the effects of varying group composition according to interpersonal trust.* Unpublished doctoral dissertation, University of Connecticut, 1972. *Dissertation Abstracts International,* 1972, *33* (6-B), 2819.

Query, William T. Jr. *An experimental investigation of self-disclosure and its effect upon some properties of psychotherapeutic groups.* Unpublished doctoral dissertation, University of Kentucky, 1961. *Dissertation Abstracts International,* 1970, *31* (4-B), 2263.

Query, William T. Jr. Self-disclosure as a variable in group psychotherapy. *The International Journal of Group Psychotherapy,* 1964, *14,* 107-116.

Quimby, Scott L. *An experimental analysis of a proposed methodology for investigating self-disclosure, feedback, leads, and impersonal communication in a T-group setting.* Unpublished doctoral dissertation, Purdue University, 1975. *Dissertation Abstracts International,* 1976, *36* (10-A), 6484.

Reisel, Jerome. *A search for behavior patterns in sensitivity training groups.* Unpublished doctoral dissertation, University of California, Los Angeles, 1959. [not abstracted by *Dissertation Abstracts*]

Ribner, Neil G. *The effects of an explicit group contract on self-disclosure and group cohesiveness.* Unpublished doctoral dissertation, University of Cincinnati, 1971. *Dissertation Abstracts International,* 1972, *32* (7-B), 4226.

Ribner, Neil G. Effects of an explicit group contract on self-disclosure and group cohesiveness. *Journal of Counseling Psychology,* 1974, *21,* 116-120.

Robbins, Ronald B. *The effects of cohesiveness and anxiety on self-disclosure under threatening conditions.* Unpublished doctoral dissertation, University of Missouri, Columbia, 1965. *Dissertation Abstracts International,* 1965, *27* (6-B), 2145.

Roberts, Arthur H. *Self-disclosure and personal change in encounter groups.* Unpublished doctoral dissertation, University of Chicago, 1971. [not abstracted in *Dissertation Abstracts*]

Rogers, Carl L. Process of the basic encounter group. In James F. T. Bugental (Ed.), *Challenges of humanistic psychology.* New York: McGraw-Hill, 1967.

Rogers, Carl L. *Carl Rogers on encounter groups.* New York: Harper and Row, 1970.

Scherz, Malcolm E. *Changes in self-esteem following experimental manipulation of self-disclosure and feedback conditions in a sensitivity laboratory.* Unpublished doctoral dissertation, George Peabody College for Teachers, 1972. *Dissertation Abstracts International,* 1972, *33* (4-B), 1805.

Schrum, Jerry D. *The effects of empathy, self-disclosure, and the social desirability response set on the development of interpersonal relationships within growth-oriented psychotherapy groups.* Unpublished doctoral dissertation, Southern Illinois University, Carbondae, 1971. *Dissertation Abstracts International,* 1972, *33* (2-B), 922.

Schwartz, Robert I. *An experimental study of massed and spaced encounter.* Unpublished doctoral dissertation, State University of New York, Albany, 1971. *Dissertation Abstracts International,* 1972, *33* (6-A), 2723.

Scott, Alvin G. *Self-disclosure as personalized risk taking in sensitivity training.* Unpublished doctoral dissertation, Harvard University, 1970. [not abstracted in *Dissertation Abstracts*]

Shaffer, John B. and Galinsky, M. David. *Models of group therapy and sensitivity training.* Englewood Cliffs, New Jersey: Prentice-Hall, Inc., 1974.

Strassberg, Donald; Roback, Howard B.; Anchor, Kenneth N.; and Abramowitz, Stephen I. Self-disclosure in group therapy with schizophrenics. *Archives of General Psychiatry,* 1975, *32,* 1259-1261.

Steele, Dennis D. *Self-disclosure and peak experience in intensive small groups.* Unpublished doctoral dissertation, University of Utah, 1973. *Dissertation Abstracts International,* 1973, *34* (7-B), 3476.

Stein, Donald K. *Expectation and modeling in sensitivity groups.* Unpublished doctoral dissertation, University of Connecticut, 1971. *Dissertation Abstracts International,* 1971, *32* (1-B), 571-572.

Trafton, Richard. *Encounter group process: A descriptive analysis.* Unpublished master's thesis, Southern Illinois University, Carbondale, 1974.

Truax, Charles B. The process of group psychotherapy. *Psychological Monographs,* 1961, *75* (7, whole No. 511).

Vannote, Vance G. *An investigation of the effects of physical contact upon self-disclosure in marathon groups.* Unpublished doctoral dissertation, University of North Dakota, 1974. *Dissertation Abstracts International,* 1975, *35* (10-B), 5143.

Walker, R. E.; Shack, J. R.; Egan, G.; Sheridan, K. and Sheridan, E. *The development of self-disclosure.* Unpublished manuscript. [*see* A1. Breed and Jourard, 1970, p. 50]

Weigel, Richard; Dinges, Norman; Dyer, Robert; and Straumfjord, A. A. Perceived self-disclosure, mental health, and who is liked in group treatment. *Journal of Counseling Psychology,* 1972, *19,* 47-52.

Weigel, Richard G. and Warnath, Charles F. The effects of group therapy on reported self-disclosure. *The International Journal of Group Psychotherapy,* 1968, *18,* 31-41.

West, Lloyd W. Some implications of self-disclosure studies for group counseling with adolescents. *Canadian Counselor,* 1970, *4,* 57-62.

Whitaker, Dorothy S. and Lieberman, Morton A. Assessing interpersonal behavior in group therapy. *Perceptual and Motor Skills,* 1964, *18,* 763-764.

E1.3.2 *Classroom groups (see also* H1. *Children and Preadolescents;* H2. *Adolescents;* H3. *College students)*

Bloom, Melanie M. *A study of self-disclosing communication in two different approaches to the basic speech course.* Unpublished doctoral dissertation, Ohio University, 1975. *Dissertation Abstracts International,* 1976, *36* (10-A), 6364.

Carich, Pete A. *Teacher self-disclosure: A study of student perceptions of teacher behavior.* Unpublished doctoral dissertation, St. Louis University, 1973. *Dissertation Abstracts International,* 1974, *34* (8-A), 4730.

Hackett, Jay K. *An investigation of the correlation between teacher observed and self-reported affective behavior toward science.* Unpublished doctoral dissertation, University of Northern Colorado, 1972. *Dissertation Abstracts International,* 1973, *49,* 3183.

Himelstein, Philip and Kimbrough, Wilson W. Jr. A study of self-disclosure in the classroom. *Journal of Psychology,* 1963, *55,* 437-440.

Kuiper, H. Peter. *Teacher self-disclosure and advocacy, compared to neutrality, their effect on learning, with special reference to religious studies.* (ERIC Document No. ED 111 463)

Myers, Raymond A. *The role of self-disclosure as related to selected professional and predictive variables in a graduate humanistic teacher education program.* Unpublished doctoral dissertation, George Washington University, 1975. *Dissertation Abstracts International,* 1976, *36* (11-A), 7358.

Reck, Jon J. *Psychological tests as invasions of privacy in personnel settings: Students' reactions, approval motivation, and self-disclosure patterns.* Unpublished doctoral dissertation, University of Houston, 1967. *Dissertation Abstracts International,* 1967, *28* (6-B), 2630.

Woolfolk, Anita E. and Woolfolk, Robert L. Student response to teacher verbal and nonverbal behavior. *Journal of Experimental Education,* 1975, *44,* 36-40.

E1.3.3 Interpersonal Dimensions

E1.3.3 *Industrial and occupational groups*

Plym, Donald L. *Employee self-disclosure as related to illness, absenteeism, self-perceived wellness, and job satisfaction.* Unpublished doctoral dissertation, University of Arizona, 1966. *Dissertation Abstracts International,* 1967, *27* (8-A), 2617.

Slobin, Dan I.; Miller, Stephen H.; and Porter, Lyman W. Forms of address and social relations in a business organization. *Journal of Personality and Social Psychology,* 1968, *8,* 289-293.

Tubbs, Stewart L. and Baird, John W. *The open person . . . Self-disclosure and personal growth.* Columbus, Ohio: Charles E. Merrill Publishing Company, 1976.

E2. *Interpersonal Processes (see also B1.8 Interpersonal dimensions)*

E2.1 *Reciprocity, dyadic effect: social norm, social exchange, and role differentiation (see also E1.2.1.1.4.3 Therapist self-disclosure; E1.-2.1.2.1 Characteristics of the client; E1.2.2 Laboratory relationships; E1.3.1.1 Group leader and E1.3.1.2 Group member)*

Altman, Irwin. Reciprocity of interpersonal exchange. *Journal for the Theory of Social Behavior,* 1973, *3,* 249-261.

Certner, Barry C. *The exchange of self-disclosures in same-sexed and heterozexual groups of strangers.* Unpublished doctoral dissertation, University of Cincinnati, 1970. *Dissertation Abstracts International,* 1971, *31* (9-A), 4885.

Certner, Barry C. Exchange of self-disclosures in same-sexed groups of strangers. *Journal of Consulting and Clinical Psychology,* 1973, *40,* 292-297.

Chaikin, Alan L. and Derlega, Valerian J. Liking for the norm-breaker in self-disclosure. *Journal of Personality,* 1974, *42,* 117-129.

Chaikin, Alan L.; Derlega, Valerian L.; Bayma, Benjamin; and Shaw, Jacqueline. Neuroticism and disclosure reciprocity. *Journal of Consulting and Clinical Psychology,* 1975, *43,* 13-19.

Chittick, Eldon V. and Himelstein, Philip. The manipulation of self-disclosure. *Journal of Psychology,* 1967, *65,* 117-121.

Cozby, Paul C. Self-disclosure, reciprocity and liking. *Sociometry,* 1972, *35,* 151-160.

Cozby, Paul C. Self-disclosure: A literature review. *Psychological Bulletin,* 1973, *79,* 73-91.

Culbert, Samuel A. The interpersonal process of self-disclosure: It takes two to see one. *Explorations in Applied Behavioral Science,* 1967, *3,* 2-31.

Daher, Douglas M. *Types of self-disclosure content, similarity and interpersonal attraction.* Unpublished doctoral dissertation, University of Notre Dame, 1975. *Dissertation Abstracts International,* 1975, *36* (6-B), 3118.

Daher, Douglas M. and Banikiotes, Paul G. Interpersonal attraction and rewarding aspects of disclosure content and level. *Journal of Personality and Social Psychology,* 1976, *33,* 492-496.

Davis, John D. Self-disclosure in an acquaintance exercise: Responsibility for level of intimacy. *Journal of Personality and Social Psychology,* 1976, *33,* 787-792.

Derlega, Valerian J. and Chaikin, Alan L. *Sharing intimacy: What we reveal to others and why.* Englewood Cliffs, New Jersey: Prentice-Hall, Inc., 1975.

Derlega, Valerian J.; Chaikin, Alan L.; and Herndon, James. Demand characteristics and disclosure reciprocity. *Journal of Social Psychology,* 1975, *97,* 301-302.

Derlega, Valerian J.; Harris, Marian S. and Chaikin, Alan L. Self-disclosure reciprocity, liking and the deviant. *Journal of Experimental Social Psychology,* 1973, *9,* 277-284.

Derlega, Valerian J.; Walmer, James; and Furman, Gail. Mutual disclosure in social interactions. *Journal of Social Psychology,* 1973, *90,* 159-160.

Derlega, Valerian J.; Wilson, Midge; and Chaikin, Alan L. Friendship and disclosure reciprocity. *Journal of Personality and Social Psychology,* 1976, *34,* 578-582.

Ehrlich, Howard J. and Graeven, David B. Reciprocal self-disclosure in a dyad. *Journal of Experimental Social Psychology,* 1971, *7,* 389-400.

Gaebelein, Jacquelyn W. Self-disclosure among friends, acquaintances, and strangers. *Psychological Reports,* 1976, *38,* 967-970.

Gouldner, Alvin W. The norm of reciprocity: A preliminary statement. *American Sociological Review*, 1960, *25*, 161-178. [background on social norm]

Hamilton, Larry K. *The relationship between self-disclosure and neuroticism*. Unpublished doctoral dissertation, Northwestern University, 1971. *Dissertation Abstracts International*, 1971, *32* (6-B), 3635.

Hick, Kenneth W.; Mitchell, Terence R.; Bell, Cecil H.; and Carter, William B. Determinants of interpersonal disclosure: Some competitive tests. *Personality and Social Psychology Bulletin*, 1975, *1*, 620-623.

Himelstein, Philip and Kimbrough, Wilson W. Jr. A study of self-disclosure in the classroom. *Journal of Psychology*, 1963, *55*, 437-440.

Homans, George C. Social behavior as exchange. *American Journal of Sociology*, 1958, *63*, 597-606. [background on social exchange]

Huesmann, L. Rowell and Levinger, George. Incremental exchange theory: A formal model for progression in dyadic interaction. *Proceedings of the 80th Annual Meeting of the American Psychological Association*, 1972, 7, 903-904. [program summary]

Johnson, David W. and Noonan, M. Patricia. Effects of acceptance and reciprocation of self-disclosures on the development of trust. *Journal of Counseling Psychology*, 1972, *19*, 411-416.

Jones, Edward E. and Archer, Richard L. Are there special effects of personalistic self-disclosure? *Journal of Experimental Social Psychology*, 1976, *12*, 180-193.

Jourard, Sidney M. Self-disclosure and other-cathexis. *Journal of Abnormal Social Psychology*, 1959, *59*, 428-431.

Jourard, Sidney M. *Self-disclosure: An experimental analysis of the transparent self*. New York: Wiley-Interscience, 1971.

Jourard, Sidney M. and Landsman, Murray J. Cognition, cathexis and the "dyadic effect" in men's self-disclosing behavior. *Merrill-Palmer Quarterly*, 1960, *6*, 178-186.

Jourard, Sidney M. and Richman, Patricia. Disclosure output and input in college students. *Merrill-Palmer Quarterly*, 1963, *9*, 141-148.

Kohen, Janet A. *Self-disclosing behavior in cross sex dyads.* Unpublished doctoral dissertation, University of Iowa, 1972. *Dissertation Abstracts International*, 1972, *33* (4-A), 1851.

Kohen, Janet A. The development of reciprocal self-disclosure in opposite-sex interaction. *Journal of Counseling Psychology*, 1975, *22*, 404-410.

Levinger, George and Senn, David J. Disclosure of feelings in marriage. *Merrill-Palmer Quarterly*, 1967, *13*, 237-249.

Lum, Kenneth. Towards multicentered marital therapy. *Psychotherapy: Theory, Research, and Practice*, 1973, *10*, 208-211.

Lynn, Steven J. *An experimental test of the reciprocity norm, social attraction, and normative standard theories of self-disclosure reciprocity.* Unpublished doctoral dissertation, Indiana University, 1976. *Dissertation Abstracts International*, 1976, *37* (4-B), 1911.

Mann, Brenda and Murphy, Kevin C. Timing of self-disclosure, reciprocity of self-disclosure, and reactions to an initial interview. *Journal of Counseling Psychology*, 1975, *22*, 304-308.

Mayo, P. R. Self-disclosure and neurosis. *British Journal of Social and Clinical Psychology*, 1968, 7, 140-148.

Moss, Carolyn J. *Effects of leader behavior in personal growth groups: Self-disclosure and experiencing.* Unpublished doctoral dissertation, Southern Illinois University, Carbondale, 1975. *Dissertation Abstracts International*, 1976, *36* (12-B), 6361.

Moss, Carolyn J. and Harren, Vincent A. Effects of leader disclosure on member disclosure in personal growth groups. *Small Group Behavior,* in press.

Pearce, W. Barnett and Sharp, Stewart M. Self-disclosing communication. *Journal of Communication*, 1973, *23*, 409-425.

Pearce, W. Barnett; Wright, Paul H.; Sharp, Stewart M.; and Slama, Katherine M. Affection and reciprocity in self-disclosing communication between same-sexed friends. *Human Communication Research*, 1974, *1*, 5-14.

Resnick, Jaquelyn L. *The effect of high revealing subjects on the self-disclosure of low revealing subjects.* Paper presented at the

Meeting of the Southeastern Psychological Association, Louisville, 1970. [see A1. Breed and Jourard, 1970, pp. 36-37]

Rubin, Zick. Lovers and other strangers: The development of intimacy in encounters and relationships. *American Scientist,* 1974, *62,* 182-190.

Rubin, Zick. Disclosing oneself to a stranger: Reciprocity and its limits. *Journal of Experimental Social Psychology,* 1975, *11,* 223-260.

Rubin, Zick. Naturalistic studies of self-disclosure. *Personality and Social Psychology Bulletin,* 1976, *2,* 260-263.

Savicki, Victor and the Oregon College of Education. Outcomes of nonreciprocal self-disclosure strategies. *Journal of Personality and Social Psychology,* 1972, *23,* 271-276.

Schutte, Jerald G. *The effects of power and trust on self-disclsoure in social interaction.* Unpublished doctoral dissertation, University of California, Los Angeles, 1974. *Dissertation Abstracts International,* 1974, *35* (5-B), 2484.

Sermat, Vello and Smyth, Michael. Content analysis of verbal communication in the development of a relationship: Conditions influencing self-disclosure. *Journal of Personality and Social Psychology,* 1973, *26,* 332-346.

Strassberg, Donald S.; Gabel, Harris; and Anchor, Kenneth. Patterns of self-disclosure in parent discussion groups. *Small Group Behavior,* 1976, *7,* 369-378.

Taylor, Dalmas A. *Self-disclosure as an exchange process: Reinforcement effects.* Paper presented at the Meeting of the American Psychological Association, Montreal, Canada, 1973. (ERIC Document Reproduction Service No. ED 083 521)

Taylor, Dalmas A. and Altman, Irwin. Self-disclosure as a function of reward-cost outcomes. *Sociometry,* 1975, *38,* 18-31.

Taylor, Dalmas A.; Altman, Irwin; and Sorrentino, Richard. Interpersonal exchange as a function of rewards and costs and situational factors: Expectancy confirmation-disconfirmation. *Journal of Experimental Social Psychology,* 1969, *5,* 324-339.

Taylor, Dalmas A. and Kleinhans, Bruce. *Beyond words: Other aspects of self-disclosure.* Paper presented at the meeting of the

American Psychological Association, New Orleans, 1974. (ERIC Document Reproduction Service No. ED 099 757)

Tognoli, Jerome J. *Reciprocal behavior in interpersonal information exchange.* Unpublished doctoral dissertation, University of Delaware, 1967. *Dissertation Abstracts International,* 1968, *29* (3-B), 1193.

Tognoli, Jerome J. Response matching in interpersonal information exchange. *British Journal of Social and Clinical Psychology,* 1969, *8,* 116-123.

Vondracek, Sarah I. *The measurement and correlates of self-disclosure in preadolescents.* Unpublished doctoral dissertation, Pennsylvania State University, 1969. *Dissertation Abstracts International,* 1970, *30* (11-B), 5230.

Wolff, Leanne O. *Self-disclosure in the marital .dyad.* Unpublished doctoral dissertation, Bowling Green State University, 1976. *Dissertation Abstracts International,* 1976, *37* (5-B), 2581.

Worthy, Morgan; Gary, Albert L.; and Kahn, Gay M. Self-disclosure as an exchange process. *Journal of Personality and Social Psychology,* 1969, *13,* 59-63.

E2.1.1 *Modeling of self-disclosure (see also* E1.2.1.1.4.3 *self-disclosure of therapist* and E1.3.1.1 *Group leader)*

Bean, Howard B. *The effects of a role-model and instructions on group interpersonal openness and cohesiveness.* Unpublished doctoral dissertation, West Virginia University, 1971. *Dissertation Abstracts International,* 1972, *32* (7-B), 4201.

Blackburn, James R. *The efficacy of modeled self-disclosure on subjects response in an interview situation.* Unpublished doctoral dissertation, University of Arkansas, 1970. *Dissertation Abstracts International,* 1970, *31* (3-B), 1529.

Bliss, Beverly. *The effect of modeling and behavior rehearsal upon the modification of self-disclosing behavior in children.* Unpublished doctoral dissertation, University of Wisconsin, Madison, 1973. *Dissertation Abstracts International,* 1974, *34* (10-B), 5182.

Cone, Harles E. *The effects of video-tape modeling on self-disclosing behaviors of clients in a clinical setting.* Unpublished doctoral dissertation, University of Missouri, Kansas City, 1976. *Dissertation Abstracts International,* 1976, *37* (5-A), 2630.

Crowley, Thomas J. and Ivey, Allen E. Dimensions of effective interpersonal communications: Specifying behavioral components. *Journal of Counseling Psychology,* 1976, *23,* 267-271.

Davis, John D. and Skinner, Adrian E. Rciprocity of self-disclosure in interviews: Modeling or social exchange? *Journal of Personality and Social Psychology,* 1974, *29,* 779-784.

Doster, Joseph A. and Brooks, Samuel J. Interviewer disclosure modeling, information revealed, and interviewee verbal behavior. *Journal of Consulting and Clinical Psychology,* 1974, *42,* 420-426.

Fantasia, Saverio C. *The effects of a moderate disclosing model on the subsequent disclosure level of high and low disclosers.* Unpublished master's thesis, SUNY College at Cortland, New York, 1974.

Fantasia, Saverio C.; Lombardo, John P.; and Wolf, Thomas M. Modification of self-disclosing behaviors through modeling and vicarious reinforcement. *Journal of General Psychology,* 1976, *95,* 209-218.

Gadaleto, Angelo I. *Differential effects of fidelity in client pretraining on client anxiety, self-disclosure, satisfaction and outcome.* Unpublished doctoral dissertation, University of Virginia, 1976. *Dissertation Abstracts International,* 1976, *37* (5-B), 2503.

Garrigan, James J. *Effects of modeling on self-disclosure of emotionally disturbed preadolescent boys.* Unpublished doctoral dissertation, Lehigh University, 1975. *Dissertation Abstracts International,* 1975, *36* (5-B), 2467.

Green, Alan H. *The effect of various forms of modeling and instructional procedures upon the modification of self-disclosing verbal behavior.* Unpublished doctoral dissertation, University of Wisconsin, 1972. *Dissertation Abstracts International,* 1972, *33* (8-B), 3938.

Green, Alan H. and Marlatt, G. Alan. Effects of instructions and modeling upon affective and descriptive verbalization. *Journal of Abnormal Psychology,* 1972, *80,* 189-196.

Grencik, Judith A. *The effects of a model on verbal behavior in group counseling.* Unpublished doctoral dissertation, University of Maryland, 1971. *Dissertation Abstracts International, 1972, 32* (12-A), 6807.

Heller, Kenneth. Laboratory interview research as analogue to treatment. In Allen E. Bergin and Sol L. Garfield (Eds.), *Handbook of psychotherapy and behavior change: An empirical analysis.* New York: John Wiley and Sons, 1971.

Highlen, Pamela S. *Effects of social modeling and cognitive structuring strategies on affective self-disclosure of single undergraduate college males.* Unpublished doctoral dissertation, Michigan State University, 1975. *Dissertation Abstracts International, 1976, 36* (9-A), 5823.

Jaffe, Peggy E. . *Self-disclosure: An example of imitative behavior.* Unpublished master's thesis, University of Florida, 1969.

James, Charles R. *The socialization process of psychotherapy training: Self-disclosure, self-concept, and conformity of value orientation as mediated by trainer influence.* Unpublished doctoral dissertation, George Peabody College for Teachers, 1973. *Dissertation Abstracts International, 1973, 34* (7-B), 3498.

Jones, Lawrence K. *Relationship between self-disclosure and positive mental health, modeled self-disclosure, and socio-economic status.* Unpublished doctoral dissertation, University of Missouri, 1971. *Dissertation Abstracts International, 1972, 32* (9-A), 4953.

Kaplan, Sheila J. *The effects of a self-instructing model, behavior rehearsal, and internal-external instructions upon self-disclosure.* Unpublished doctoral dissertation, University of Wisconsin, Madison, 1972. *Dissertation Abstracts International, 1973, 34* (10-B), 5196.

Leaman, David Ray. *The effects of modeling on self-disclosure.* Unpublished doctoral dissertation, Ball State Teachers College, 1975. *Dissertation Abstracts International, 1976, 36* (8-A), 5049.

Lee, La Mont R. *The effect of modeling on the persistence of change in self-disclosure among ministerial students.* Unpublished doctoral dissertation, Fuller Theological Seminary, 1974. *Dissertation Abstracts International, 1975, 36* (1-B), 448.

E2.1.1 Interpersonal Dimensions

Liberman, Bernard L. *The effect of modeling procedures on attraction and disclosure in a psychotherapy analogue.* Unpublished doctoral dissertation, Syracuse University, 1970. *Dissertation Abstracts International,* 1970, *32* (1-B), 564.

Marcus, Bette B. *Self-disclosure as a function of attitude similarity and physical attractiveness.* Unpublished doctoral dissertation, University of Maryland, 1976. *Dissertation Abstracts International,* 1976, *37* (6-B), 3155.

Marlatt, G. Alan. *Vicarious and direct reinforcement control of verbal behavior in an interview setting.* Unpublished doctoral dissertation, Indiana University, 1968. *Dissertation Abstracts International,* 1968, *29* (5-B), 1845-1846.

Marlatt, G. Alan. Comparison of vicarious and direct reinforcement control of verbal behavior in an interview setting. *Journal of Personality and Social Psychology,* 1970, *16,* 695-703.

Marlatt, G. Alan; Jacobson, Edward A.; Johnson, Donald L.; and Morrice, D. James. Effects of exposure to a model receiving evaluative feedback upon subsequent behavior in an interview. *Journal of Consulting and Clinical Psychology,* 1970, *34,* 104-112.

McAllister, Ann D. *Interviewee self-disclosure as a function of level and identity of self-disclosing models.* Unpublished doctoral dissertation, Emory University, 1973. *Dissertation Abstracts International,* 1974, *34* (7-B), 161.

McAllister, Ann D. and Kiesler, Donald J. Interpersonal disclosure as a function of interpersonal trust, task modeling, and interviewer self-disclosure. *Journal of Consulting and Clinical Psychology,* 1975, *43,* 428.

McGuire, Dennis; Thelen, Mark H.; and Amolsch, Thomas. Interview self-disclosure as a function of length of modeling and descriptive instructions. *Journal of Consulting and Clinical Psychology,* 1975, *43,* 356-362.

Moore, Dana L. *The effects of a model presented in two different media upon two measures of self-disclosure.* Unpublished doctoral dissertation, West Virginia University, 1976. *Dissertation Abstracts International,* 1976, *37* (4-B), 1918.

Noel, Joseph R. and De Chenne, Timothy K. Three dimensions of psychotherapy: I-we-thou. In David A. Wexler and Laura N.

Rice (Eds.). *Innovations in client-centered therapy.* New York: John Wiley and Sons, 1974.

Ohlson, Ronald W. *The effects of video-tape modeling of self-disclosure upon client revealingness and personality change.* Unpublished doctoral dissertation, Fuller Theological Seminary, 1970. *Dissertation Abstracts International,* 1972, *32* (12-B), 7320.

Post, Barbara J. *The effectiveness of modeling, vicarious reinforcement, behavior rehearsal and self-instruction in facilitating self-disclosure by preadolescent children.* Unpublished doctoral dissertation, University of Wisconsin, Madison, 1975. *Dissertation Abstracts International,* 1975, *36* (3-B), 1452.

Rubin, Zick. Lovers and other strangers: The development of intimacy in encounters and relationships. *American Scientist,* 1974, *62,* 182-190.

Rubin, Zick. Disclosing oneself to a stranger: Reciprocity and its limits. *Journal of Experimental Social Psychology,* 1975, *11,* 233-260.

Rubin, Zick. Naturalistic studies of self-disclosure. *Personality and Social Psychology Bulletin,* 1976, *2,* 260-263.

Sarason, Irwin G. Test anxiety and the self-disclosing coping model. *Journal of Consulting and Clinical Psychology,* 1975, *43,* 148-153.

Sarason, Irwin G.; Ganzer, Victor; and Singer, Michael. Effects of modeled self-disclosure on the verbal behavior of persons differing in defensiveness. *Journal of Counsulting and Clinical Psychology,* 1972, *39,* 483-490.

Scheiderer, Edwin G. *Effects of instructions and modeling in producing self-disclosure in the initial clinical interview.* Unpublished doctoral dissertation, Univeristy of Illinois, Urbana, 1974. *Dissertation Abstracts International,* 1975, *35* (12-B), 6112.

Schnitz, Donald R. *Facilitating self-disclosure responses in a simulated counseling interview through the use of audiotape modeling, videotape modeling, and instruction.* Unpublished doctoral dissertation, Auburn University, 1973. *Dissertation Abstracts International,* 1974, *34* (10-A), 6391-6392.

Sherman, Richard M. *The effects of peer modeling and instructions on self-disclosure of internally and externally controlled male college students: An interview-analogue situation.* Unpublished doctoral dissertation, University of Georgia, 1975. *Dissertation Abstracts International,* 1976, *36* (9-B), 4708.

Smith, Joyce A. and Lewis, William A. Effect of videotaped models on the communication of college students in counseling. *Journal of Counseling Psychology,* 1974, *21,* 78-80.

Stachowiak, Thaddeus I. *Effects of pretherapy modeling, model status, and therapist status on client self-disclosure: An analogue study.* Unpublished doctoral dissertation, Michigan State University, 1974. *Dissertation Abstracts International,* 1974, *35* (6-B), 3038.

Stein, Donald K. *Expectation and modeling in sensitivity groups.* Unpublished doctoral dissertation, University of Connecticut, 1971. *Dissertation Abstracts International,* 1971, *32* (1-B), 571-572.

Stone, Gerald L. and Gotlib, Ian. Effect of instructions and modeling on self-disclosure. *Journal of Counseling Psychology,* 1975, *22,* 288-293.

Stone, Gerald L. and Jackson, Ted. Internal-external control as a determinant of the effectiveness of modeling and instructions. *Journal of Counseling Psychology,* 1975, *22,* 294-298.

Stone, Gerald L. and Stebbins, Larry W. Effect of differential pretraining on client self-disclosure. *Journal of Counseling Psychology,* 1975, *22,* 17-20.

Sykes, John D. Jr. *A study of self-disclosure prediction and two types of interviewer modeling in the counseling interview.* Unpublished doctoral dissertation, The College of William and Mary in Virginia, 1976. *Dissertation Abstracts International,* 1976, *37* (6-A), 3431.

Wagner, Stephen C. *The effects of pretraining and intimacy level of topic and depth of self-disclosure.* Unpublished doctoral dissertation, Ohio State University, 1976. *Dissertation Abstracts International,* 1976, *37* (6-B), 3101.

E2.2 *Attraction, liking, and sociometric choice*

Barrell, James and Jourard, Sidney. Being honest with persons we like. *Journal of Individual Psychology,* 1976, *32,* 185-193.

Bolman, Lee. Some effects of trainers on their T-groups. *Journal of Applied Behavioral Science*, 1971, 7, 309-326.

Brasfield, Charles R. *Intimacy of self-disclosure, availability of reaction to disclosure, and formation of interpersonal relationships.* Unpublished doctoral dissertation, University of British Columbia, Canada, 1971. *Dissertation Abstracts International*, 1972, 32 (10-B), 6043.

Breed, George R. Nonverbal communication and interpersonal attraction in dyads. Unpublished doctoral dissertation, University of Florida, 1969. *Dissertation Abstracts International*, 1970, 31 (3-A), 1369.

Brockner, Joel B. and Swap, Walter C. Effects of repeated exposure and attitudinal similarity on self-disclosure and interpersonal attraction. *Journal of Personality and Social Psychology*, 1976, 33, 531-540.

Certner, Barry C. *The exchange of self-disclosures in same sexed and heterosexual groups of strangers.* Unpublished doctoral dissertation, University of Cincinnati, 1970. *Dissertation Abstracts International*, 1971, 31 (9-A), 4885.

Certner, Barry C. Exchange of self-disclosures in same-sexed group of strangers. *Journal of Consulting and Clinical Psychology*, 1973, 40, 292-297.

Chaikin, Alan L. and Derlega, Valerian J. Liking for the norm-breaker in self-disclosure. *Journal of Personality*, 1974, 42, 117-129. (a)

Chaikin, Alan L. and Derlega, Valerian J. *Self-disclosure.* Morristown, New Jersey: General Learning Press, 1974. (b)

Cozby, Paul C. Self-disclosure, reciprocity and liking. *Sociometry*, 1972, 35, 151-160.

Cozby, Paul C. Self-disclosure: A literature review. *Psychological Bulletin*, 1973, 79, 73-91.

Daher, Douglas M. *Types of self-disclosure content, similarity and interpersonal attraction.* Unpublished doctoral dissertation, University of Notre Dame, 1975. *Dissertation Abstracts International*, 1975, 36 (6-B), 3118.

Daher, Douglas M. and Banikiotes, Paul G. Interpersonal attraction and rewarding aspects of disclosure content and level. *Journal of Personality and Social Psychology*, 1976, 33, 492-496.

Derlega, Valerian J. and Chaikin, Alan L. *Sharing intimacy: What we reveal to others and why.* Englewood Cliffs, New Jersey: Prentice-Hall, Inc., 1975.

Derlega, Valerian J.; Harris, Marian S.; and Chaikin, Alan L. Self-disclosure, reciprocity, liking, and the deviant. *Journal of Experimental Social Psychology,* 1973, *9,* 277-284.

Derlega, Valerian J.; Walmer, James; and Furman, Gail. Mutual disclosure in social interactions. *Journal of Social Psychology,* 1973, *90,* 159-160.

Ehrlich, Howard J. and Graeven, David B. Reciprocal self-disclosure in a dyad. *Journal of Experimental Social Psychology,* 1971, *7,* 389-400.

Fitzgerald, Maureen P. *Relationship between expressed self-esteem, assumed similarity and self-disclosure.* Unpublished doctoral dissertation, Fordham University, 1961. *Dissertation Abstracts International,* 1962, *22* (12), 4402.

Fitzgerald, Maureen P. Self-disclosure and expressed self-esteem, social distance and areas of the self revealed. *Journal of Social Psychology,* 1963, *56,* 405-412.

Gilbert, Shirley J. *A study of the effects of self-disclosure on interpersonal attraction and trust as a function of situational appropriateness and the self-esteem of the recipient.* Unpublished doctoral dissertation, University of Kansas, 1972. *Dissertation Abstracts International,* 1973, *33* (8-A), 4566.

Hall, Jon A. *The effect of interviewer expectation and level of self-disclosure on interviewee self-disclosure in a dyadic situation.* Unpublished doctoral dissertation, University of Arkansas, 1976. *Dissertation Abstracts International,* 1976, *37* (5-B), 2506.

Horenstein, David and Gilbert, Shirley. Anxiety, likeability, and avoidance as responses to self-disclosing communication. *Small Group Behavior,* 1976, *7,* 423-432.

Jones, Edward E. and Archer, Richard L. Are there special effects of personalistic self-disclosure? *Journal of Experimental Social Psychology,* 1976, *12,* 180-193.

Jones, Edward E. and Gordon, Eric M. Timing of self-disclosure and its effects on personal attraction. *Journal of Personality and Social Psychology,* 1972, *24,* 358-365.

Jourard, Sidney M. Self-disclosure and other-cathexis. *Journal of Abnormal Social Psychology,* 1959, *59,* 428-431.

Jourard, Sidney M. *Self-disclosure: An experimental analysis of the transparent self.* New York: Wiley-Interscience, 1971.

Kahn, M. H. and Rudestam, K. E. The relationship between liking and perceived self-disclosure in small groups. *Journal of Psychology,* 1971, *78,* 81-85.

Kaplan, Kalman J.; Firestone, Ira J.; Degnore, Roberta; and Moore, Michael. Gradiants of attraction as a function of disclosure probe intimacy and setting formality: On distinguishing attitude oscillation from attitude change—study one. *Journal of Personality and Social Psychology,* 1974, *30,* 638-646.

Kimble, Charles E. *The effects of acquaintanceship, disclosure level, and attributional variables on attraction and self-disclosure.* Unpublished doctoral dissertation, University of Texas, Austin, 1972. *Dissertation Abstracts International,* 1973, *34* (2-A), 862.

Klepper, Irwin L. *The effects of pre-interview exposure to vicarious reinforcement on disclosure and attraction in alcoholics: A psychotherapy analogue.* Unpublished doctoral dissertation, Syracuse University, 1971. *Dissertation Abstracts International,* 1971, *32* (1-B), 563-564.

Knecht, Laura; Lippman, Daniel; and Swap, Walter. Similarity, attraction, and self-disclosure. *Proceedings of the 81st Annual Convention of the American Psychological Association,* 1973, *8,* 205-206.

Kohen, Janet A. *Self-disclosing behavior in cross-sex dyads.* Unpublished doctoral dissertation, University of Iowa, 1972. *Dissertation Abstracts International,* 1972, *33* (4-A), 1851.

Kohen, Janet A. The development of reciprocal self-disclosure in opposite-sex interaction. *Journal of Counseling Psychology,* 1975, *22,* 404-410. (a)

Kohen, Janet A. Liking and self-disclosure in opposite sex dyads. *Psychological Reports,* 1975, *36,* 695-698. (b)

Krause, Fred. *An investigation of verbal exchanges between strangers.* Unpublished doctoral dissertation, Yeshiva University, 1969. *Dissertation Abstracts International,* 1969, *30* (3-A), 1235.

Lawless, Walter and Nowicki, Stephen. Role of self-disclosure in interpersonal attraction. *Journal of Consulting and Clinical Psychology,* 1972, *38,* 300.

Leuchtmann, Hanna. *Self-disclosure, attitudes, and sociometric choice.* Unpublished doctoral dissertation, Yeshiva University, 1968. *Dissertation Abstracts International,* 1969, *30* (1-B), 371.

Levin, Fredrica and Gergen, Kenneth J. Revealingness, ingratiation, and the disclosure of self. *Proceedings of the 77th Annual Convention of the American Psychological Association,* 1969, *4,* 447-448.

McAllister, Hunter A. Jr. *Effects of the self-disclosure process on interpersonal attraction.* Unpublished doctoral dissertation, University of North Carolina, Chapel Hill, 1974. *Dissertation Abstracts International,* 1975, *35* (8-B), 4259.

Mesch, Joyce C. *Interpersonal attraction and self-disclosure in interaction between orthopedically disabled and nondisabled male college students.* Unpublished doctoral dissertation, New York University, 1974. *Dissertation Abstracts International,* 1974, *35* (2-A), 894.

Mulligan, William L. *The effects of induced self-disclosure and interviewer feedback on compliance and liking.* Unpublished doctoral dissertation, Yale University, 1973. *Dissertation Abstracts International,* 1973, *34* (2-B), 878.

Nelson-Jones, Richard and Strong, Stanley R. Positive and negative self-disclosure, timing, and personal attraction. *The British Journal of Social and Clinical Psychology,* 1976, *15,* 323-325.

Pearce, W. Barnett; Wright, Paul H.; Sharp, Stewart M.; and Slama, Katherine M. Affection and reciprocity in self-disclosing communication between same-sexed friends. *Human Communication Research,* 1974, *1,* 5-14.

Persons, Roy W. and Marks, Philip A. Self-disclosure with recidivists: Optimum interviewer-interviewee matching. *Journal of Abnormal Psychology,* 1970, *76,* 387-391.

Petzelt, John A. *Self-disclosure and interpersonal attraction: The intimacy value and attitudinal similarity of the content of the disclosure.* Unpublished doctoral dissertation, Georgia State University, 1973. *Dissertation Abstracts International,* 1974, *34* (8-B), 4026.

Query, William T. Jr. *An experimental investigation of self-disclosure and its effect upon some properties of psychotherapeutic groups.*

Unpublished doctoral dissertation, University of Kentucky, 1961. *Dissertation Abstracts International*, 1970, *31* (4-B), 2263.

Query, William T. Jr. Self-disclosure as a variable in group psychotherapy. *The International Journal of Group Psychotherapy*, 1964, *14*, 107-116.

Ribner, Neil G. *The effects of an explicit group contract on self-disclosure and group cohesiveness.* Unpublished doctoral dissertation, University of Cincinnati, 1971. *Dissertation Abstracts International*, 1972, *32* (7-B), 4226.

Ribner, Neil G. Effects of an explicit group contract on self-disclosure and group cohesiveness. *Journal of Counseling Psychology*, 1974, *21*, 116-120.

Rivenbark, Wilburn H. III. *Self-disclosure and sociometric choice in the adolescent period.* Unpublished doctoral dissertation, University of Florida, 1966. *Dissertation Abstracts International*, 1967, *28* (5-B), 2147.

Rivenbark, Wilburn H. III. Self-disclosure patterns among adolescents. *Psychological Reports*, 1971, *28*, 35-42.

Robison, Joan Tucker. *The role of self-disclosure, interpersonal attraction, and physical attractiveness in the initial stages of relationship development within single-sex female dyads.* Unpublished doctoral dissertation, University of Georgia, 1975. *Dissertation Abstracts International*, 1976, *36* (9-B), 4760.

Smith, Samuel C. *The effects of feedback on self-disclosure in a dyadic interaction.* Unpublished doctoral dissertation, University of Wisconsin, Madison, 1974. *Dissertation Abstracts International*, 1974, *35* (3-B), 1418.

Sote, Gbade A. and Good, Larence R. Similarity of self-disclosure and interpersonal attraction. *Psychological Reports*, 1974, *34*, 491-494.

Weigel, Richard; Dinges, Norman; Dyer, Robert; and Straumfjord, A. A. Perceived self-disclosure, mental health, and who is liked in group treatment. *Journal of Counseling Psychology*, 1972, *19*, 47-52.

Weigel, Richard G. and Warnath, Charles F. The effects of group therapy on reported self-disclosure. *International Journal of Group Psychotherapy*, 1968, *18*, 31-41.

E2.2 Interpersonal Dimensions

Willingham, Mary E. *The relationship between self-concept, self-disclosure, and peer selection.* Unpublished doctoral dissertation, George Washington University, 1971. *Dissertation Abstracts International,* 1972, *32* (8-A), 4365.

Worthy, Morgan; Gary, Albert L.; and Kahn, Gay M. Self-disclosure as an exchange process. *Journal of Personality and Social Psychology,* 1969, *13,* 59-63.

Wortman, Camille B.; Adesman, Peter; Herman, Elliot; and Greenberg, Richard. Self-disclosure: An attributional perspective. *Journal of Personality and Social Psychology,* 1976, *33,* 184-191.

Young, Taylor S. *The effects of cooperative and competitive interaction on self-disclosure.* Unpublished doctoral dissertation, Arizona State University, 1976. *Dissertation Abstracts International,* 1976, *37* (5-A), 2655.

E2.3   *Avoidance and conflict*

Horenstein, David and Gilbert, Shirley.   Anxiety, likeability, and avoidance as responses to self-disclosing communication. *Small Group Behavior,* 1976, *7,* 423-432.

E2.4   *Trust (see also C3.4.6 Rotter's Internal-External Locus of Control)*

Benedict, Barbara A. *The effects of self-disclosure on the development of trust.* Unpublished doctoral dissertation, Columbia University, 1970. *Dissertation Abstracts International,* 1971, *31* (9-B), 5601.

Cash, Thomas F.; Stack, James J.; and Luna, Gloria C. Convergent and discriminate behavioral aspects of interpersonal trust. *Psychological Reports,* 1975, *37,* 983-986.

Egan, Gerald. *Encounter: Group processes for interpersonal growth.* Belmont, California: Brooks/Cole Publishing Company, 1970.

Ellison, Craig W. *The development of interpersonal trust as a function of self-esteem, status, and style.* Unpublished doctoral dissertation, Wayne State University, 1972. *Dissertation Abstracts International,* 1972, *33* (5-B), 2319-2320.

Ellison, Craig W. and Firestone, Ira J. Development of interpersonal trust as a function of self-esteem, target status, and target style. *Journal of Personality and Social Psychology,* 1974, *29,* 655-663.

Fuller, James B. *An investigation of self-disclosing behavior and the affective response within a T-group setting.* Unpublished doctoral dissertation, West Virginia University, 1971. *Dissertation Abstracts International,* 1971, *32* (4-A), 1852.

Gilbert, Shirley J. *A study of the effects of self-disclosure on interpersonal attraction and trust as a function of situational appropriateness and the self-esteem of the recipient.* Unpublished doctoral dissertation, University of Kansas, 1972. *Dissertation Abstracts International,* 1973, *33* (8-A), 4566.

Johnson, David W. and Noonan, M. Patricia. Effects of acceptance and reciprocation of self-disclosures on the development of trust. *Journal of Counseling Psychology,* 1972, *19,* 411-416.

Jongsma, Arthur E. Jr. *The effects of experimenter trust and trustworthiness on subject's reciprocal self-disclosure.* Unpublished doctoral dissertation, Northern Illinois University, 1973. *Dissertation Abstracts International,* 1973, *34* (3-B), 1277.

Kessel, Elizabeth V. *Interpersonal trust and attitude toward the expression of positive and negative affect within the T-group.* Unpublished doctoral dissertation, West Virginia University, 1971. *Dissertation Abstracts International,* 1971, *32* (4-A), 1855-1856.

Luft, Joseph. *Of human interaction.* Palo Alto: National Press Books, 1969.

Luft, Joseph. The Johari Window and self-disclosure. In Gerald Egan (Ed.), *Encounter groups: Basic readings.* Belmont, California: Brooks/Cole Publishing Company, 1971.

MacDonald, A. P.; Kessel, Viki S.; and Fuller, James B. Self-disclosure and two kinds of trust. *Psychological Reports,* 1972, *30,* 143-148.

McAllister, Ann and Kiesler, Donald J. Interpersonal disclosure as a function of interpersonal trust, task modeling, and interviewer self-disclosure. *Journal of Consulting and Clinical Psychology,* 1975, *43,* 428.

Ollerman, Thomas E. *The effect of group counseling upon self-actualization, self-disclosure, and the development of interpersonal trust among prison inmates.* Unpublished doctoral dissertation, New Mexico State University, 1975. *Dissertation Abstracts International,* 1975, *36* (6-A), 3415.

Piper, William E. *Evaluation of the effects of sensitivity training and the effects of varying group composition according to interpersonal trust.* Unpublished doctoral dissertation, University of Connecticut, 1972. *Dissertation Abstracts International,* 1972, *33* (6-B), 2819.

Rubin, Zick. Lovers and other strangers: The development of intimacy in encounters and relationships. *American Scientist,* 1974, *62,* 182-190.

Rubin, Zick. Disclosing oneself to a stranger: Reciprocity and its limits. *Journal of Experimental Social Psychology,* 1975, *11,* 233-260.

Rubin, Zick. Naturalistic studies of self-disclosure. *Personality and Social Psychology Bulletin,* 1976, *2,* 260-263.

Schutte, Jerald G. *The effects of power and trust on self-disclosure in social interaction.* Unpublished doctoral dissertation, University of California, Los Angeles, 1974. *Dissertation Abstracts International,* 1974, *35* (5-B), 2484.

Sote, Gbade and Good, Larence R. Similarity of self-disclosure and interpersonal attraction. *Psychological Reports,* 1974, *34,* 491-494.

Tolor, Alexander; Cramer, Marie; D'Amico, Denis; and O'Marra, Margaret. The effects of self-concept, trust, and imagined positive or negative self-disclosures on psychological space. *Journal of Psychology,* 1975, *89,* 9-24.

Vondracek, Fred W. and Marshall, Marilyn J. Self-disclosure and interpersonal trust: An exploratory study. *Psychological Reports,* 1971, *28,* 235-240.

Wheeless, Lawrence R. and Grotz, Janis. *Self-disclosure and trust: Conceptualization, measurement, and interrelationships.* Paper presented at the Convention of the International Communication Association, Chicago, April, 1975.

Williams, Bertha M. *The effects of two models of counseling—peer and professional—on the levels of self-disclosure and trust of black college students.* Unpublished doctoral dissertation, Arizona State University, 1973. *Dissertation Abstracts International,* 1973, *34* (6-A), 3076.

Williams, Bertha M. Trust and self-disclosure among black college students. *Journal of Counseling Psychology,* 1974, *21,* 522-525.

Young, Taylor S. *The effects of cooperative and competitive interaction on self-disclosure.* Unpublished doctoral dissertation, Arizona State University, 1976. *Dissertation Abstracts International,* 1976, *37* (5-A), 2655.

E2.5 *Risk*

Anchor, Kenneth N. *High and low risk self-disclosure in group psychotherapy.* Paper presented at the Midwestern Psychological Association Meeting, Chicago, 1974. (ERIC Document Reproduction Service No. ED 099 746)

Bednar, Richard L.; Melnick, Joseph; and Kaul, Theodore J. Risk, responsibility, and structure: A conceptual framework for initiating group counseling and psychotherapy. *Journal of Counseling Psychology,* 1974, *21,* 31-37.

Culbert, Samuel A. The interpersonal process of self-disclosure: It takes two to see one. *Explorations in Applied Behavioral Science,* 1967, *3,* 2-31.

Egan, Gerald. *Encounter: Group processes for interpersonal growth.* Belmont, California: Brooks/Cole Publishing Company, 1970.

Fullerton, Wayne S. *Self-disclosure, self-esteem, and risk-taking: A study of their validity and discriminate validity in elementary school children.* Unpublished doctoral dissertation, University of California, Berkeley, 1972. *Dissertation Abstracts International,* 1973, *33* (10-B), 5014.

Horton, Susan W. *A cognitive processing approach to projective test behavior.* Unpublished doctoral dissertation, University of Rochester, 1972. *Dissertation Abstracts International,* 1972, *33* (5-B), 2347. [risk of self-disclosure in projective tests]

Norton, Robert; Feldman, Charles; and Tafoya, Dennis. Risk parameters across types of secrets. *Journal of Counseling Psychology,* 1974, *21,* 450-454.

Powell, John. *Why am I afraid to tell you who I am?* Chicago: Peacock, 1969.

Scott, Alvin G. *Self-disclosure as personalized risk-taking in sensitivity training.* Unpublished doctoral dissertation, Harvard University, 1970. [not abstracted in *Dissertation Abstracts*]

E2.6 Interpersonal Dimensions

E2.6 *Expectations, attributions, and perceived similarity (see also E1.2.-1.2.2 Expectations of the client)*

Altman, Irwin. Reciprocity of interpersonal exchange. *Journal for the Theory of Social Behavior*, 1973, *3*, 249-261.

Branch, Alvia Y. *Until we meet again: Anticipation of future interaction and self-disclosure.* Unpublished doctoral dissertation, Harvard University, 1974. [not abstracted in *Dissertation Abstracts International*]

Brockner, Joel B. and Swap, Walter C. Effects of repeated exposure and attitudinal similarity on self-disclosure and interpersonal attraction. *Journal of Personality and Social Psychology*, 1976, *33*, 531-540.

Culbert, Samuel A. The interpersonal process of self-disclosure: It takes two to see one. *Explorations in Applied Behavioral Science*, 1967, *3*, 2-31.

Gergen, Kenneth J. and Wishnov, Barbara. Others' self-evaluations and interaction anticipations. *Journal of Personality and Social Psychology*, 1965, *2*, 348-358.

Gitter, A. George. *Studies in "hypocrisy."* Paper presented at the 18th International Congress of Psychology, Moscow, 1966.

Gitter, A. George; Antonellis, Richard; and Cohen, Steven. *Candor of communication about self.* (CRC Report No. 69), Boston: Boston University, 1975.

Gitter, A. George and Blakely, L. *Veracity of self-disclosed information* (CRC Report No. 39), Boston: Boston University, 1968.

Gitter, A. George and Brown, Harvey. Is self-disclosure self-revealing? *Journal of Counseling Psychology*, 1976, *23*, 327-332.

Gitter, A. George and Frankfurt, Leslie P. *Self-disclosure: Expectations and gilding.* Paper presented at the Meeting of the Western Psychological Association, San Diego, 1968.

Green, Richard B. Self-disclosure, self-esteem, and perceived similarity. Unpublished doctoral dissertation, City University of New York, 1976. *Dissertation Abstracts International*, 1976, *37* (3-B), 1434.

Hall, Jon A. *The effect of interviewer expectation and level of self-disclosure on interviewee self-disclosure in a dyadic stiuation.* Unpublished doctoral dissertation, University of Arkansas, 1976. *Dissertation Abstracts International,* 1976, *37* (5-B), 2506.

Jourard, Sidney M. Self-disclosure and other-cathexis. *Journal of Abnormal Social Psychology,* 1959, *59,* 428-431.

Kent, Joan H. Relation of personality, expectancy, and situational variables to self-disclosing behavior. *Journal of Consulting and Clinical Psychology,* 1975, *43,* 120-121.

Kimble, Charles E. *The effects of acquaintanceship, disclosure level, and attributional variables on attraction and self-disclosure.* Unpublished doctoral dissertation, University of Texas, Austin, 1972. *Dissertation Abstracts International,* 1973, *34* (2-A), 862.

Marcus, Bette B. *Self-disclosure as a function of attitude similarity and physical attractiveness.* Unpublished doctoral dissertation, University of Maryland, 1976. *Dissertation Abstracts International,* 1976, *37* (6-B), 3155.

Nooney, James B. *Verbal accessibility as determined by perceived similarity and personality.* Unpublished doctoral dissertation, Western Reserve University, 1960. [not abstracted in *Dissertation Abstracts*]

Nooney, James B. and Polansky, Norman A. The influence of perceived similarity and personality on verbal accessibility. *Merrill-Palmer Quarterly,* 1962, *8,* 33-40.

Olberz, Paul D. and Steiner, Ivan D. Order of disclosure and the attribution of dispositional characteristics. *Journal of Social Psychology,* 1969, *79,* 287-288.

Stamm, Keith R. and Pearce, W. Barnett. Message locus and message content: Two studies in communication behavior and coorientational relations. *Communication Research,* 1974, *1,* 184-203.

Stein, Donald K. *Expectation and modeling in sensitivity groups.* Unpublished doctoral dissertation, University of Connecticut, 1971. *Dissertation Abstracts International,* 1971, *32,* (1-B), 571-572.

Stephan, Walter G.; Lucker, G. William; and Aronson, Elliot. The interpersonal consequences of self-disclosure and internal attributions for success. *Personality and Social Psychology Bulletin,* 1976, *2,* 252-255.

Taylor, Dalmas A. and Altman, Irwin. Self-disclosure as a function of reward-cost outcomes. *Sociometry*, 1975, *38*, 18-31.

Taylor, Dalmas A.; Altman, Irwin; and Sorrentino, Richard. Interpersonal exchange as a function of rewards and costs and situational factors: Expectancy confirmation-disconfirmation. *Journal of Experimental Social Psychology*, 1969, *5*, 324-339.

Tessler, R. C. and Plansky, Norman A. Perceived similarity: A paradox in interviewing. *Social Work*, 1975, *20*, 359-363.

Wortman, Camille G.; Adesman, Peter; Herman, Elliot; and Greenberg, Richard. Self-disclosure: An attributional perspective. *Journal of Personality and Social Psychology*, 1976, *33*, 184-191.

Young, Barbara A. *The effects of sex, assigned therapist or peer role, topic intimacy, and expectations of partner compatibility on dyadic communication patterns.* Unpublished doctoral dissertation, University of Southern California, 1969. *Dissertation Abstracts International*, 1969, *30* (2-B), 857.

E2.7   *Interpersonal distance (see also* E2.8 *Interpersonal Solidarity)*

E2.7.1   *Communication immediacy*

Dietlein, John R. *Self-disclosure in an interview situation as a function of self-esteem and immediacy.* Unpublished master's thesis, California State University, Long Beach, 1975. *Master's Abstracts*, 1975, *13*, 91.

Moss, Carolyn J. *Effects of leader behavior in personal growth groups: Self-disclosure and experiencing.* Unpublished doctoral dissertation, Southern Illinois University, Carbondale, 1975. *Dissertation Abstracts International*, 1976, *36* (12-B), 6361.

Moss, Carolyn J. and Harren, Vincent A. Effects of leader disclosure on member disclosure in personal growth groups. *Small Group Behavior*, in press.

Roth, Marvin and Kuiken, Don. Communication immediacy, cognitive compatibility, and immediacy of self-disclosure. *Journal of Counseling Psychology*, 1975, *22*, 102-107.

Wiener, Morton and Mehrabian, Albert. *Language within a language: Immediacy, a channel in verbal communication.* New York: Appleton-Century-Crofts, 1968. [theoretical background for immediacy]

E2.7.2 *Proxemics: physical distance, personal space, and body accessibility*

Braithwaite, Ronald L. *An analysis of proxemics and self-disclosing behavior of recidivist and non-recidivist adult social offenders from black, chicano, and white inmate populations.* Unpublished doctoral dissertation, Michigan State University, 1974. *Dissertation Abstracts International,* 1975, *35* (9-B), 4621.

Carr, Suzanne J. and Dabbs, James M. Jr. The effects of lighting, distance, and intimacy of topic on verbal and visual behavior. *Sociometry,* 1974, *37,* 592-600.

Delbam, Andrew R. *The effect of intragroup distance on self-disclosure.* Unpublished doctoral dissertation, Indiana University, 1974. *Dissertation Abstracts International,* 1975, *35* (7-B), 3645.

Dietch, James and House, James. Affiliative conflict and individual differences in self-disclosure. *Representative Research in Social Psychology,* 1975, *6,* 69-75.

Duke, Marshall P. and Nowicki, Stephen. A new measure and social learning model for interpersonal distance. *Journal of Experimental Research in Personality,* 1972, *6,* 119-132. [theoretical background on interpersonal distance and The Comfortable Interpersonal Distance Scale]

Fitzgerald, Maureen P. *Relationship between expressed self-esteem, assumed similarity, and self-disclosure.* Unpublished doctoral dissertation, Fordham University, 1961. *Dissertation Abstracts International,* 1962, *22* (12), 4402.

Fitzgerald, Maureen P. Self-disclosure and expressed self-esteem, social distance, and areas of the self revealed. *Journal of Social Psychology,* 1963, *56,* 405-412.

Fraum, Robert M. *The effect of interpersonal distance on self-disclosure in a dyadic interview.* Unpublished doctoral dissertation, Long Island University, 1975. *Dissertation Abstracts International,* 1975, *35* (8-B), 4170.

Janofsky, Annelies I. *A study of affective self-references in telephone vs. face to face interviews.* Unpublished doctoral dissertation, University of Oregon, 1970. *Dissertation Abstracts International,* 1971, *31* (10-B), 6258.

Janofsky, Annelies I. Affective self-disclosure in telephone vs. face-to-face interviews. *Journal of Humanistic Psychology*, 1971, *11*, 93-103.

Johnson, Carl F. and Dabbs, James M. Jr. Self-disclosure in dyads as a function of distance and the subject-experimenter relationship. *Sociometry*, 1976, *39*, 257-263.

Johnson, Patrick J. *Personal space as reaction to threat*. Unpublished doctoral dissertation, The Catholic University of America, 1973. *Dissertation Abstracts International*, 1973, *33* (11-B), 5495.

Jourard, Sidney M. and Friedman, Robert. Experimenter-subject "distance" and self-disclosure. *Journal of Personality and Social Psychology*, 1970, *15*, 278-282.

Kassover, Carletta J. *Self-disclosure, sex and the use of personal distance*. Unpublished doctoral dissertation, University of Texas, Austin, 1971. *Dissertation Abstracts International*, 1972, *33* (1-B), 442.

Kutner, David H. Jr. *Ecological aspects of immediacy and self-disclosure in an interview setting*. Unpublished doctoral dissertation, Yale University, 1975. *Dissertation Abstracts International*, 1976, *36* (12-B), 6447.

Lassen, Carol L. Effect of proximity on anxiety and communication in the initial psychiatric interview. *Journal of Abnormal Psychology*, 1973, *81*, 226-232.

Pedersen, Darhl M. Self-disclosure, body-accessibility, and personal space. *Psychological Reports*, 1973, *33*, 975-980.

Rogers, Richard. *The effects of interpersonal distance on perceived self-disclosure*. Unpublished doctoral dissertation, Utah State University, 1975. *Dissertation Abstracts International*, 1976, *36* (9-B), 4670.

Rogers, Richard and Wright, E. Wayne. Preliminary study of perceived self-disclosure. *Psychological Reports*, 1976, *38*, 1334.

Ronsvalle, John L. *The influence of perceptual presence on interpersonal disclosure*. Unpublished doctoral dissertation, University of Illinois, Urbana-Champaign, 1972. *Dissertation Abstracts International*, 1973, *34* (2-B), 883.

Savicki, Victor E. *Self-disclosure strategy and personal space proximity in intimacy development.* Unpublished doctoral dissertation, University of Massachusetts, 1971. *Dissertation Abstracts International*, 1971, *31* (8-B), 5008.

Sims, Gregory K. and Sims, Janet M. Does face-to-face contact reduce counselee responsiveness with emotionally insecure youth? *Psychotherapy: Theory, Research, and Practice*, 1973, *10*, 348-351.

Stein, Waltraut J. The myth of the transparent self. *Journal of Humanistic Psychology*, 1975, *15*, 71-77.

Stone, Gerald L. and Morden, Cathy J. Effect of distance on verbal productivity. *Journal of Counseling Psychology*, 1976, *23*, 486-488.

Switkin, Linda R. *Self-disclosure as a function of sex roles, experimenter-subject distance, sex of experimenter, and intimacy of topic.* Unpublished doctoral dissertation, St. Louis University, 1974. *Dissertation Abstracts International*, 1974, *35* (5-B), 2451.

Tolor, Alexander; Cramer, Marie; D'Amico, Denis; and O'Marra, Margaret. The effects of self-concept, trust, and imagined positive or negative self-disclosure on psychological space. *Journal of Psychology*, 1975, *89*, 9-24.

Weber, Judy W. *The effects of physical proximity and body boundary size on the self-disclosure interview.* Unpublished doctoral dissertation, University of Southern California, 1972. *Dissertation Abstracts International*, 1973, *33* (7-B), 3327.

E2.7.3 *Nonverbal encounter: eye contact, touching, and kinesics*

Canino-Stolberg, Glorisa. *The effects of physical contact exercises in marathon encounter leaderless groups on dimensions of self-concept, self-disclosure and touching behavior.* Unpublished doctoral dissertation, Temple University, 1975. *Dissertation Abstracts International*, 1976, *36* (7-B), 3592.

Carr, Suzanne J. and Dabbs, James M. Jr. The effects of lighting, distance, and intimacy of topic on verbal and visual behavior. *Sociomentry*, 1974, *37*, 592-600.

E2.7.3 Interpersonal Dimensions

Cooper, Cary L. and Bowles, David. Physical encounter and self-disclosure. *Psychological Reports,* 1973, *33,* 451-454.

Dawson, Carolyn. *Affect and self-disclosure as a function of touch in an interview between strangers.* Unpublished doctoral dissertation, Columbia University, 1973. *Dissertation Abstracts International,* 1973, *34* (6-B), 2925.

Derlega, Valerian J. *Social penetration processes: The effects of acquaintance, topic intimacy, and support on nonverbal behavior.* Unpublished doctoral dissertation, University of Maryland, 1971. *Dissertation Abstracts International,* 1972, *32* (10-B), 6025-6026.

Dietch, James and House, James. Affiliative conflict and individual differences in self-disclosure. *Representative Research in Social Psychology,* 1975, *6,* 69-75.

Ehrentheil, Otto F.; Chase, Stanley J.; and Hyde, Mary R. Revealing and body display. *Archives of General Psychiatry,* 1973, *29,* 363-367.

Ellsworth, Phoebe and Ross, Lee. Intimacy in response to direct gaze. *Journal of Experimental Social Psychology,* 1975, *11,* 592-613.

Exline, Ralph V.; Gray, David; and Schuette, Dorothy. Visual behavior in a dyad as affected by interview content and sex of respondent. *Journal of Personality and Social Psychology,* 1965, *1,* 201-209.

Friedman, Robert. *Eye-contact and self-disclosure.* Unpublished honors paper, University of Florida, 1968. [see summary in Charles D. Spielberger (Ed.), *Current topics in clinical and community psychology* (Vol. 1). New York: Academic Press, 1969, pp. 126-131]

Gardner, Joseph A. *The effects of body motion, sex of counselor, and sex of subject on counselor attractiveness and subject's self-disclosure.* Unpublished doctoral dissertation, University of Wyoming, 1973. *Dissertation Abstracts International,* 1973, *34* (5-B), 2337.

Jourard, Sidney M. An exploratory study of body accessibility. *British Journal of Clinical Psychology,* 1966, *5,* 221-223.

Jourard, Sidney. *Disclosing man to himself.* Princeton: D. Van Nostrand, 1968.

Jourard, Sidney M. *Self-disclosure: An experimental analysis of the transparent self.* New York: Wiley-Interscience, 1971.

Jourard, Sidney M. and Rubin, Jane E. Self-disclosure and touching: A study of two modes of interpersonal encounter and their inter-relation. *Journal of Humanistic Psychology,* 1968, *8,* 39-48.

Keiser, George J. and Altman, Irwin. The relationship of nonverbal behavior to the social penetration process. *Catalog of Selected Documents in Psychology,* 1974, *4,* 10-11.

Keiser, George J. and Altman, Irwin. Relationship of nonverbal behavior to the social penetration process. *Human Communication Research,* 1976, *2,* 147-161.

Lomranz, J. and Shapira, A. Communicative patterns of self-disclosure and touching behavior. *Journal of Psychology,* 1974, *88,* 223-227.

Paradis, Mark H. *The effects of eye contact on positive and negative self-disclosure.* Unpublished doctoral dissertation, Washington State University, 1972. *Dissertation Abstracts International,* 1972, *33* (6-B), 2795.

Sodikoff, Charles L.; Firestone, Ira J.; and Kaplan, Kalman J. Distance matching and distance equilibrium in the interview dyad. *Personality and Social Psychology Bulletin,* 1974, *1,* 243-245.

Sousa-Poza, Joaquin F.; Rohrberg, Robert; and Mercure, André. *Kinesic behavior accompanying person-oriented and non-person oriented verbal content: A preliminary report.* Paper presented at First International Symposium on Non-Verbal Aspects and Techniques of Psychotherapy, Vancouver, July, 1974.

Sundstrom, Eric D. *A study of crowding: Effects of intrusion, goal-blocking, and density on self-reported stress, self-disclosure, and nonverbal behavior.* Unpublished doctoral dissertation, University of Utah, 1973. *Dissertation Abstracts International,* 1974, *34* (7-A), 4412.

Sundstrom, Eric. Experimental study of crowding: Effects of room size, intrusion and goal-blocking on nonverbal behavior, self-disclosure, and self-reported stress. *Journal of Personality and Social Psychology,* 1975, *32,* 645-654.

E2.7.3 Interpersonal Dimensions

Vannote, Vance G. *An investigation of the effects of physical contact upon self-disclosure in marathon groups.* Unpublished doctoral dissertation, University of North Dakota, 1974. *Dissertation Abstracts International,* 1975, *35* (10-B), 5143.

E2.8 *Interpersonal solidarity: closeness (see also E2.6 Expectations, attributions, and perceived similarity and E2.7 Interpersonal distance)*

Wheeless, Lawrence R. Self-disclosure and interpersonal solidarity: Measurement, validation, and relationships. *Human Communication Research,* 1976, *3,* 47-61.

E2.9 *Therapeutic conditions: empathy, genuineness or congruency, and positive regard (see D3. Response style of the disclosee and E1.2.1-1.4.1 Facilitative conditions)*

E2.10 *Social accessibility, verbal accessibility, and willingness to disclose (see C3.5. Verbal accessibility, social accessibility, and willingness to disclose)*

F. SITUATIONAL DIMENSIONS: STRUCTURAL
AND ENVIRONMENTAL

(See also E1.2.1.4 *Situational dimensions)*

Altman, Irwin and Haythorn, William W. Interpersonal exchange in isolation. *Sociometry*, 1965, *28*, 411-426.

Bailey, Roger L. *The effects of temporal sequence variation on self-directed small groups in a college environment.* Unpublished doctoral dissertation, United States University, 1971. *Dissertation Abstracts International*, 1971, *32* (6-B), 3614.

Baum, Ronald C. *Self-disclosure in small groups as a function of group composition.* Unpublished doctoral dissertation, University of Cincinnati, 1971. *Dissertation Abstracts International*, 1972, *32* (7-B), 4200.

Bednar, Richard L.; Melnick, Joseph; and Kaul, Theodore J. Risk, responsibility, and structure: A conceptual framework for initiating group counseling and psychotherapy. *Journal of Counseling Psychology*, 1974, *21*, 31-37.

Bloom, Melanie M. *A study of self-disclosing communication in two different approaches to the basic speech course.* Unpublished doctoral dissertation, Ohio University, 1975. *Dissertation Abstracts International*, 1976, *36* (10-A), 6364.

Carr, Suzanne J. and Dabbs, James M. Jr. The effects of lighting, distance, and intimacy of topic on verbal and visual behavior. *Sociometry*, 1974, *37*, 592-600.

Chaikin, Alan L.; Derlega, Valerian J.; and Miller, Sarah J. Effects of room environment on self-disclosure in a counseling analogue. *Journal of Counseling Psychology,* 1976, *23,* 479-481.

Cogan, James M. *The effect of the presence or absence of another person on the verbalizations of schizophrenics under a demand for intimate self-disclosure.* Unpublished doctoral dissertation, University of Missouri, Columbia, 1975. *Dissertation Abstracts International,* 1976, *36* (7-B), 3594.

Conyne, Robert K. Effects of facilitator-directed and self-directed group experiences. *Counselor Education and Supervision,* 1974, *13,* 184-189.

Crews, Catherine Y. and Melnick, Joseph. Use of initial and delayed structure in facilitating group development. *Journal of Counseling Psychology,* 1976, *23,* 92-98.

D'Augelli, Anthony R. *The effects of interpersonal skills and pretraining on group interaction.* Unpublished doctoral dissertation, University of Connecticut, 1973. *Dissertation Abstracts International,* 1973, *33* (10-B), 5010. (a)

D'Augelli, Anthony R. Group composition using interpersonal skills: An analogue study on the effects of members interpersonal skills on peer ratings and group cohesiveness. *Journal of Counseling Psychology,* 1973, *20,* 531-534. (b)

D'Augelli, Anthony R. and Chinsky, Jack M. Interpersonal skills and pretraining: Implications for the use of group procedures for interpersonal learning and for the selection of nonprofessional mental health workers. *Journal of Consulting and Clinical Psychology,* 1974, *42,* 65-72.

D'Augelli, Anthony R.; Chinsky, Jack M.; and Getter, Herbert. The effect of group composition and duration on sensitivity training. *Small Group Behavior,* 1974, *5,* 56-64.

Drag, Richard M. *Experimenter behavior and group size as variables influencing self-disclosure.* Unpublished doctoral dissertation, University of Florida, 1968. *Dissertation Abstracts International,* 1969, *30* (5-B), 2416.

Haythorn, William W. and Altman, Irwin. Together in isolation. In Dalmas A. Taylor (Ed.), *Small groups.* Chicago: Markham, 1971.

Hurley, Shirley J. *Self-disclosure in counseling groups as influenced by structured confrontation and interpersonal process recall.* Unpublished doctoral dissertation, Michigan State University, 1967. *Dissertation Abstracts International,* 1968, *29* (1-A), 123.

Kaplan, Kalman J.; Firestone, Ira J.; Degnore, Roberta; and Moore, Michael. Gradiants of attraction as a function of disclosure probe intimacy and setting formality: On distinguishing attitude oscillation from attitude change—study one. *Journal of Personality and Social Psychology,* 1974, *30,* 638-646.

Kinder, Billy N. *The relationship of pre-therapy self-disclosure, the structure of group therapy and locus-of-control on therapeutic outcome.* Unpublished doctoral dissertation, University of South Carolina, 1975. *Dissertation Abstracts International,* 1976, *37* (1-B), 465.

Kopfstein, Joan H. *Need for approval, expectancy for consequences, and behavior in Gestalt experiments.* Unpublished doctoral dissertation, Georgia State University, 1972. *Dissertation Abstracts International,* 1974, *34* (8-B), 4048.

Kutner, David H. Jr. *Ecological aspects of immediacy and self-disclosure in an interview setting.* Unpublished doctoral dissertation, Yale University, 1975. *Dissertation Abstracts International,* 1976, *36* (12-B), 6447.

Query, William T. Jr. *An experimental investigation of self-disclosure and its effect upon some properties of psychotherapeutic groups.* Unpublished doctoral dissertation, University of Kentucky, 1961. *Dissertation Abstracts International,* 1970, *31* (4-B), 2263.

Query, William T. Jr. Self-disclosure as a variable in group psychotherapy. *The International Journal of Group Psychotherapy,* 1964, *14,* 107-116.

Ribner, Neil G. *The effects of an explicit group contract on self-disclosure and group cohesiveness.* Unpublished doctoral dissertation, University of Cincinnati, 1971. *Dissertation Abstracts International,* 1972, *32* (7-B), 4226.

Ribner, Neil G. Effects of an explicit group contract on self-disclosure and group cohesiveness. *Journal of Counseling Psychology,* 1974, *21,* 116-120.

Robbins, Ronald B. *The effects of cohesiveness and anxiety on self-disclosure under threatening conditions.* Unpublished doctoral dissertation, University of Missouri, Columbia, 1965. *Dissertation Abstracts International,* 1965, *27* (6-B), 2145.

Schwartz, Robert I. *An experimental study of massed and spaced encounter.* Unpublished doctoral dissertation, State University of New York, Albany, 1971. *Dissertation Abstracts International,* 1972, *33* (6-A), 2723.

Sundstrom, Eric D. *A study of crowding: Effects of intrusion, goal-blocking, and density on self-reported stress, self-disclosure, and nonverbal behavior.* Unpublished doctoral dissertation, University of Utah, 1973. *Dissertation Abstracts International,* 1974, *34* (7-A), 4412.

Sundstrom, Eric D. Experimental study of crowding: Effects of room size, intrusion, and goal-blocking on nonverbal behavior, self-disclosure, and self-reported stress. *Journal of Personality and Social Psychology,* 1975, *32,* 645-654.

G. MODIFICATION OF SELF-DISCLOSING BEHAVIOR: PRETRAINING, TRAINING, AND CONDITIONING

(See also E1.2.1.2.3 Pretherapy training and E2.1.1. Modeling)

Ashcraft, Carolyn. *Effects of laboratory training on self-concept, self-disclosure, and locus of control.* Paper presented at the Meeting of the Southeastern Psychological Association, New Orleans, 1969. [*see* A1. Breed and Jourard, 1970, p. 1]

Bednar, Richard L.; Melnick, Joseph; and Kaul, Theodore J. Risk, responsibility, and structure: A conceptual framework for initiating group counseling and psychotherapy. *Journal of Counseling Psychology,* 1974, *21,* 31-37.

Boyum, Richard K. *Improving self-disclosure in an educational setting through self-help methods.* Unpublished doctoral dissertation, University of Northern Colorado, 1972. *Dissertation Abstracts International,* 1973, *33* (7-A), 3368.

Brasfield, Charles R. and Cubitt, Anne. Changes in self-disclosure behavior following an intensive "encounter" group experience. *Canadian Counselor,* 1974, *8,* 12-21.

Braukmann, Curtis J.; Fixsen, Dean L.; Phillips, Elery L.; Wolf, Montrose M.; and Maloney, Dennis M. An analysis of a selection interview training package for predelinquents at Achievement Place. *Criminal Justice and Behavior,* 1974, *1,* 30-42.

Campbell, Edson E. *The effects of couple communication training on married couples in the child rearing years: A field experiment.*

G. Modification of self-disclosing behavior: pretraining, training, and conditioning

Unpublished doctoral dissertation, Arizona State University, 1974. *Dissertation Abstracts International,* 1974, *35* (4-A), 1942-1943.

Canino-Stolberg, Glorisa. *The effects of physical contact exercises in marathon encounter leaderless groups on dimensions of self-concept, self-disclosure and touching behavior.* Unpublished doctoral dissertation, Temple University, 1975. *Dissertation Abstracts International,* 1976, *36* (7-B), 3592.

Coven, Betty E. *The effects of self-disclosure training on counselor trainees.* Unpublished doctoral dissertation, Wayne State University, 1975. *Dissertation Abstracts International,* 1975, *36* (5-A), 2624.

Crowley, Thomas J. *The conditionability of positive and negative self-reference emotional affect statements in a counseling type interview.* Unpublished doctoral dissertation, University of Massachusetts, 1970. *Dissertation Abstracts International,* 1970, *31* (5-A), 2100.

Crowley, Thomas J. and Ivey, Allen E. Dimensions of effective interpersonal communications: Specifying behavioral components. *Journal of Counseling Psychology,* 1976, *23,* 267-271.

D'Augelli, Anthony R. *The effects of interpersonal skills and pretraining on group interaction.* Unpublished doctoral dissertation, University of Connecticut, 1973. *Dissertation Abstracts International,* 1973, *33* (10-B), 5010.

D'Augelli, Anthony R. and Chinsky, Jack M. Interpersonal skills and pretraining: Implications for the use of group procedures for interpersonal learning and for the selection of nonprofessional mental health workers. *Journal of Consulting and Clinical Psychology,* 1974, *42,* 65-72.

D'Augelli, Anthony R.; Deyss, Christine; Guerney, Bernard G., Jr.; Hersenberg, Bernard; and Sborofsky, Sandra. Interpersonal skill training for dating couples: An evaluation of an educational mental health service. *Journal of Counseling Psychology,* 1974, *21,* 385-389.

Diethelm, Daniel R. *Changes in levels of self-disclosure and perceived self-disclosure between partners following participation in a weekend encounter group for couples.* Unpublished doctoral dissertation, University of Connecticut, 1974. *Dissertation Abstracts International,* 1974, *34* (9-A), 5622.

Fantasia, Saverio C.; Lombardo, John P.; and Wolf, Thomas M. Modification of self-disclosing behaviors through modeling and vicarious reinforcement. *Journal of General Psychology,* 1976, *95,* 209-218.

Modification of self-disclosing behavior: pretraining, training, and conditioning G.

Fuller, James B. *An investigation of self-disclosing behavior and the affective response within a T-group setting.* Unpublished doctoral dissertation, West Virginia University, 1971. *Dissertation Abstracts International,* 1971, *32* (4-A), 1852.

Gottlieb, Marvin R. *The effects of laboratory training methods on highly stable variables such as self-esteem and self-disclosure.* Paper presented at the Annual Meeting of the International Communication Association, Montreal, 1973. (ERIC Document Reproduction Service No. ED 085 788)

Harren, Vincent A. *Videotape pretraining program for encounter group members: A training manual for encounter group co-facilitators.* Unpublished manuscript, Southern Illinois University, Carbondale, 1975.

Hrubetz, Joan. *Measurement of changes in nursing students' levels of empathy, self-disclosure, and confrontation as outcomes of systematic human relations training.* Unpublished doctoral dissertation, St. Louis University, 1975. *Dissertation Abstracts International,* 1975, *36* (6-B), 2725.

Juarez, Shirlee J. *An experimental analysis of a counseling procedure emphasizing peer self-help in a prison setting.* Unpublished doctoral dissertation, University of California, Riverside, 1973. *Dissertation Abstracts International,* 1974, *34* (7-B), 3467.

Kelber, Sister Mary B. *Exploration of group sessions with rehabilitating post-myocardial infarction males regarding self-disclosure and cardiac adjustment with objective and subjective evaluations of group sessions.* Unpublished doctoral dissertation, The Catholic University of America, 1976. *Dissertation Abstracts International,* 1976, *37* (3-B), 1408.

Linville, Malcolm E. Jr. *The effects of training in self-disclosing behaviors on students preparing to become teachers.* Unpublished doctoral dissertation, University of Missouri, Kansas City, 1974. *Dissertation Abstracts International,* 1974, *35* (5-A), 2826.

Lovett, Jerry A. *Self-disclosure: An inservice training process for volunteers in helping roles.* Unpublished doctoral dissertation, Memphis State University, 1975. *Dissertation Abstracts International,* 1976, *36* (11-A), 7212.

Marlatt, G. Alan. *Vicarious and direct reinforcement control of verbal behavior in an interview situation.* Unpublished doctoral dissertation,

G. Modification of self-disclosing behavior: pretraining, training, and conditioning

Indiana University, 1968. *Dissertation Abstracts International,* 1968, *29* (5-B), 1845-1846.

Marlatt, G. Alan. Comparison of vicarious and direct reinforcement control of verbal behavior in an interview setting. *Journal of Personality and Social Psychology,* 1970, *16,* 695-703.

Marlatt, G. Alan; Jacobson, Edward A.; Johnson, Donald L.; and Morrice, D. James. Effects of exposure to a model receiving evaluative feedback upon subsequent behavior in an interview. *Journal of Consulting and Clinical Psychology,* 1970, *34,* 104-112.

Miller, Sherod L. *The effects of communication training in small groups upon self-disclosure and openness in engaged couples' systems of interaction: A field experiment.* Unpublished doctoral dissertation, University of Minnesota, 1971. *Dissertation Abstracts International,* 1971, *32* (5-A), 2819.

Milliren, Alan P. *The training of counselor self-disclosure utilizing microcounseling techniques.* Unpublished doctoral dissertation, Univeristy of Illinois, Urbana-Champaign, 1971. *Dissertation Abstracts International,* 1972, *32* (8-A), 4355.

Ollerman, Thomas E. *The effects of group counseling upon self-actualization, self-disclosure, and the development of interpersonal trust among prison inmates.* Unpublished doctoral dissertation, New Mexico State University, 1975. *Dissertation Abstracts International,* 1975, *36* (6-A), 3415.

Pfeiffer, J. William and Jones, John E. *A handbook of structured experiences for human relations training* (Vol. 1). Iowa City: University Associates Press, 1969.

Pheterson, Gail I. *A field experimental study of the effects of re-evaluation counseling training.* Unpublished doctoral dissertation, University of California, Riverside, 1974. *Dissertation Abstracts International,* 1974, *35* (6-B), 3030-3031.

Pino, Christopher J. Relation of a trainability index to T-group outcomes. *Journal of Applied Psychology,* 1971, *55,* 439-442.

Resnick, Jaquelyn L. *The effectiveness of a brief communications skills program involving facilitative responding and self-disclosure training for student volunteers in college residence halls.* Unpublished doctoral dissertation, University of Florida, 1972. *Dissertation Abstracts International,* 1973, *34* (6-A), 3069.

Schlein, Stephen P. *Training dating couples in empathic and open communication: An experimental evaluation of a potential preventive
mental health program.* Unpublished doctoral dissertation, Pennsylvania State University, 1971. *Dissertation Abstracts International,*
1972, *32* (11-B), 6487.

Schwartz, Robert I. *An experimental study of massed and spaced encounter.* Unpublished doctoral dissertation, State University of New
York, Albany, 1971. *Dissertation Abstracts International,* 1972, *33*
(6-A), 2723.

Tittler, Bennett I.; Anchor, Kenneth N.; and Weitz, Lawrence J. Measuring change in openness: Behavioral assessment techniques and the
problem of the examiner. *Journal of Counseling Psychology,* 1976,
23, 473-478.

Voight, Nancy L. *The effects of self-management strategies as initial
training and as secondary training for affective self-disclosure of
undergraduate males.* Unpublished doctoral dissertation, Michigan
State University, 1975. *Dissertation Abstracts International,* 1976,
36 (9-A), 5842.

Wagner, Stephen C. *The effects of pretraining and intimacy level of
topic and depth of self-disclosure.* Unpublished doctoral dissertation,
Ohio State University, 1976. *Dissertation Abstracts International,*
1976, *37* (6-B), 3101.

189

H. SELF-DISCLOSURE IN SPECIAL POPULATIONS

H1. *Children and Preadolescents*

Beaven, Mary H. Beyond language arts and reading: Self-disclosure. *Elementary English,* 1974, *51,* 437-439.

Bliss, Beverly. *The effect of modeling and behavior rehearsal upon the modification of self-disclosing behavior in children.* Unpublished doctoral dissertation, University of Wisconsin, Madison, 1973. *Dissertation Abstracts International,* 1974, *34* (10-B), 5182.

Blum, Arthur. Peer-group structure and a child's verbal accessibility in a treatment institution. *Social Service Review,* 1962, *36,* 385-395.

Blum, Arthur and Plansky, Norman A. Effect of staff role on children's verbal accessibility. *Social Work,* 1961, *6,* 29-37.

Fullerton, Wayne S. *Self-disclosure, self-esteem, and risk-taking: A study of their convergent and discriminate validity in elementary school children.* Unpublished doctoral dissertation, University of California, Berkeley, 1972. *Dissertation Abstracts International,* 1973, *33* (10-B), 5014.

Ganter, Grace and Polansky, Norman A. Predicting a child's accessibility to individual treatment from diagnostic groups. *Social Work,* 1964, *9,* 56-63.

Ganter, Grace; Yeakel, Margaret; and Polansky, Norman A. Intermediary group treatment of inaccessible children. *American Journal of Orthopsychiatry,* 1965, *35,* 739-746.

191

Polansky, Norman A. and Weiss, Erwin S. Determinants of accessibility to treatment in a children's institution. *Journal of Jewish Communal Service*, 1959, *36*, 130-137.

Polansky, Norman A.; Weiss, Erwin S.; and Blum, Arthur. Children's verbal accessibility as a function of content and personality. *American Journal of Orthopsychiatry*, 1961, *31*, 153-169.

Post, Barbara J. *The effectiveness of modeling, vicarious reinforcement, behavior rehearsal and self-instruction in facilitating self-disclosure by pre-adolescent children.* Unpublished doctoral dissertation, University of Wisconsin, Madison, 1975. *Dissertation Abstracts International*, 1975, *36* (3-B), 1452.

Skypeck, G. *Self-disclosure in children, ages six through twelve.* Unpublished master's thesis, University of Florida, 1967. [*see* A1. Breed and Jourard, 1970, pp. 42-43]

Sussman, Gilbert. *The effects of writing about self on the self-esteem of fifth and sixth grade children.* Unpublished doctoral dissertation, Fordham University, 1973. *Dissertation Abstracts International*, 1973, *34* (1-A), 179.

Vondracek, Sarah I. *The measurement and correlates of self-disclosure in pre-adolescents.* Unpublished doctoral dissertation, Pennsylvania State University, 1969. *Dissertation Abstracts International*, 1970, *30* (11-B), 5230.

Vondracek, Sarah I. and Vondracek, Fred W. The manipulation and measurement of self-disclosure in pre-adolescents. *Merrill-Palmer Quarterly*, 1971, *17*, 51-58.

Weber, Ruth. *Children's verbal accessibility as a predictor of treatment outcome.* Unpublished doctoral dissertation, Western Reserve University, 1963. [not abstracted in *Dissertation Abstracts*]

Wildman, Laura L. *The effect of dyadic exercises in self-disclosure on the self-concept and social acceptability of pre-adolescents.* Unpublished doctoral dissertation, University of Maryland, 1972. *Dissertation Abstracts International*, 1973, *33* (8-B), 3968.

Woolfolk, Anita E. and Woolfolk, Robert L. Student self-disclosure in response to teacher verbal and nonverbal behavior. *Journal of Experimental Education*, 1975, *44*, 36-40.

H2. *Adolescents*

Appelberg, Esther. *Verbal accessibility of adolescents.* Unpublished doctoral dissertation, Western Reserve University, 1961. [not abstracted in *Dissertation Abstracts*]

Appelberg, Esther. Verbal accessibility of adolescents. *Child Welfare,* 1964, *43,* 86-90.

Daluiso, Victor E. *Self-disclosure and perception of that self-disclosure between parents and their teen-age children.* Unpublished doctoral dissertation, United States International University, 1972. *Dissertation Abstracts International,* 1972, *33* (1-B), 420.

Davis, Wesley A. *Academic achievement and self-disclosure of high school students and their parents.* Unpublished doctoral dissertation, University of Florida, 1969. *Dissertation Abstracts International,* 1970, *31* (1-A), 144.

Dimond, Richard E. and Hellcamp, David T. Race, sex, ordinal position of birth, and self-disclosure of high school students. *Psychological Reports,* 1969, *25,* 235-238.

Dimond, Richard E. and Munz, David C. Ordinal position of birth and self-disclosure in high school students. *Psychological Reports,* 1967, *21,* 829-833.

Jaffee, Lester D. and Polansky, Norman A. Verbal inaccessibility in young adolescents showing delinquent trends. *Journal of Health and Human Behavior,* 1962, *3,* 105-111.

Jones, Mary G. *Self-disclosure among deaf adolescents and its relationship to social sensitivity and personality.* Unpublished doctoral dissertation, The Catholic University of America, 1975. *Dissertation Abstracts International,* 1975, *36* (3-B), 1437.

Kim, Jee-Il. *The effect of self-disclosure on emotion perception and social adjustment.* Unpublished doctoral dissertation, University of Toronto, Canada, 1973. *Dissertation Abstracts International,* 1975, *35* (7-B), 3647.

Kraft, Lee W. and Vraa, Calvin W. Sex composition of groups and patterns of self-disclosure by high school females. *Psychological Reports,* 1975, *37,* 733-734.

Littlefield, Robert P. *An analysis of the self-disclosure patterns of ninth grade public school students in three selected subcultural groups.* Unpublished doctoral dissertation, Florida State University, 1968. *Dissertation Abstracts International,* 1969, *30* (2-A), 588.

Littlefield, Robert P. Self-disclosure among some negro, white, and Mexican-American adolescents. *Journal of Counseling Psychology,* 1974, *21,* 133-136.

McLeod, Michael A. *Orienting ninth-grade students to counseling services: A study of counselor self-disclosure.* Unpublished doctoral dissertation, St. Louis University, 1973. *Dissertation Abstracts International,* 1974, *34* (8-A), 234.

McRae, Stuart D. *A study of the relationship between self-disclosure and predictive accuracy for a sample of adolescent subjects.* Unpublished master's thesis, University of Calgary, Canada, 1974.

Mulcahy, Gloria A. Sex differences in patterns of self-disclosure among adolescents: A developmental perspective. *Journal of Youth and Adolescence,* 1973, *2,* 343-356.

Liske, Carol. *Self-disclosure and similarity of values among adolescents.* Unpublished master's thesis, University of Calgary, Canada, 1975.

Paulson, Marguerite J. *Differences in self-disclosure patterns between a group of maladjusted and a group of adjusted male adolescents.* Unpublished master's thesis, University of Calgary, Canada, 1976.

Ramsey, Gene A. *Self-disclosure patterns among selected black and white high school students.* Unpublished doctoral dissertation, Auburn University, 1972. *Dissertation Abstracts International,* 1972, *33* (3-A), 9750.

Rivenbark, Wilburn H. III. *Self-disclosure and sociometric choice in the adolescent period.* Unpublished doctoral dissertation, University of Florida, 1966. *Dissertation Abstracts International,* 1967, *28* (5-B), 2147.

Rivenbark, Wilburn H. III. Self-disclosure patterns among adolescents. *Psychological Reports,* 1971, *28,* 35-42.

Solberg, Oskar. *An analysis of Norwegian and American high school students' real and ideal self-disclosure in school as related to selected demographic and school variables.* Unpublished doctoral dissertation, Purdue University, 1973. *Dissertation Abstracts International,* 1974, *35* (1-A), 200.

Sparks, Dennis C. *Self-disclosure and its relationship to self-concept among students in a selected high school.* Unpublished doctoral dissertation, University of Michigan, 1976. *Dissertation Abstracts International,* 1976, *37* (3-A), 1412.

Tiwari, J. G. and Singh, Sultan. Self-disclosure in urban and rural students. *Journal of Psychological Researches,* 1967, *11,* 7-12.

West, Lloyd W. *Patterns of self-disclosure for a sample of adolescents and the relationship of disclosure style to anxiety and psychological differentiation.* Unpublished doctoral dissertation, University of Alberta, Canada, 1968. [not abstracted in *Dissertation Abstracts*]

West, Lloyd W. Sex differences in the exercise of circumspection in self-disclosure among adolescents. *Psychological Reports,* 1970, *26,* 226. (a)

West, Lloyd W. Some implications of self-disclosure studies for group counseling with adolescents. *Canadian Counselor,* 1970, *4,* 57-62. (b)

West, Lloyd W. A study of the validity of the Self-Disclosure Inventory for Adolescents. *Perceptual and Motor Skills,* 1971, *33,* 91-100.

West, Lloyd W. Mapping the communication patterns of adolescents. *Canadian Counselor,* 1974, *8,* 54-65.

West, Lloyd W. and Zingle, Harvey W. A self-disclosure inventory for adolescents. *Psychological Reports,* 1969, *24,* 439-445.

White, Roger L. *Adolescent and pubescent self-disclosure patterns: Phenomenal ratings of the privacy and importance of topics.* Unpublished doctoral dissertation, Claremont Graduate School, 1974. *Dissertation Abstracts International,* 1975, *35* (8-A), 5045.

Wiebe, Bernhard. *Self-disclosure and perceived relationships of Mennonite adolescents in senior high school.* Unpublished doctoral dissertation, University of North Dakota, 1974. *Dissertation Abstracts International,* 1975, *35* (10-A), 6472.

Wiebe, Bernhard and Scott, Thomas B. Self-disclosure patterns of Mennonite adolescents to parents and their perceived relationships. *Psychological Reports,* 1976, *39,* 355-358.

Wiebe, Bernhard and Williams, John D. Self-disclosure to parents by high school seniors. *Psychological Reports,* 1972, *31,* 690.

H3. Self-disclosure in special populations

H3. *College Students*

Brodsky, Stanley L. Self-disclosure in dormitory residents who seek counseling. *Psychology,* 1964, *1,* 12-14.

Cleland, Robert S. and Carnes, G. Derwood. Emotional vs. ideational emphasis during group counseling with student nurses. *Journal of Counseling Psychology,* 1965, *12,* 282-286.

Hrubetz, Joan. *Measurement of changes in nursing students' levels of empathy, self-disclosure, and confrontation as outcomes of systematic human relations training.* Unpublished doctoral dissertation, St. Louis University, 1975. *Dissertation Abstracts International,* 1975, *36* (6-B), 2725.

Jourard, Sidney M. Self-disclosure patterns in British and American college females. *Journal of Social Psychology,* 1961, *54,* 315-320. (a)

Jourard, Sidney M. Self-disclosure scores and grades in nursing college. *Journal of Applied Psychology,* 1961, *45,* 244-247. (b)

Komarovsky, Mirra. Patterns of self-disclosure of male undergraduates. *Journal of Marriage and the Family,* 1974, *36,* 677-686.

Lee, La Mont R. *The effect of modeling on the persistence of change in self-disclosure among ministerial students.* Unpublished doctoral dissertation, Fuller Theological Seminary, 1974. *Dissertation Abstracts International,* 1975, *36* (1-B), 448.

Lee, Robert E. *Some effects of a protestant clergy stereotype on counselor preference, self-disclosure readiness, and desire for counseling among junior college students.* Unpublished doctoral dissertation, University of Florida, 1969. *Dissertation Abstracts International,* 1970, *31* (3-A), 1015.

Melikian, Levon H. Self-disclosure among university students in the Middle East. *Journal of Social Psychology,* 1962, *57,* 257-263.

Mesch, Joyce C. *Interpersonal attraction and self-disclosure in interaction between orthopedically disabled and non-disabled male college students.* Unpublished doctoral dissertation, New York University, 1974. *Dissertation Abstracts International,* 1974, *35* (2-A), 894.

Pasternack, Thomas L. and Van Landingham, Martha. A comparison of the self-disclosure behavior of female undergraduates and married women. *Journal of Psychology,* 1972, *82,* 233-240.

Petersen, Dwight J. *The relationship between self-concept and self-disclosure of underachieving college students in group counseling.* Unpublished doctoral dissertation, Brigham Young University, 1972. *Dissertation Abstracts International,* 1972, *33* (5-B), 2354.

Powell, W. James and Jourard, Sidney M. Some objective evidence of immaturity in underachieving college students. *Journal of Counseling Psychology,* 1963, *10,* 276-282.

Rickers-Ovsiankina, Maria A. Social accessibility in three age groups. *Psychological Reports,* 1956, *2,* 283-294. [freshmen, seniors, and alumnae]

Rivenbark, Wilburn H. III. *Self-disclosure target choice preferences in female college students.* Paper presented at the Meeting of the Southeastern Psychological Association, New Orleans, 1969. [*see* A1. Breed and Jourard, 1970, p. 38]

H4. *Professional Groups*

Brown, Delindus R. *Self-disclosure and identification: Dyadic communications of the new assistant black professor on a white campus.* Paper presented at the Annual Meeting of the Speech Communication Association, Chicago, 1974. (ERIC Document Reproduction Service No. ED 102 630)

Gorman, John R. *Adjustment and self-disclosing behavior of Roman Catholic priests.* Unpublished doctoral dissertation, Loyola University of Chicago, 1973. *Dissertation Abstracts International,* 1973, *34* (1-B), 413.

Jourard, Sidney M. and Shain, E. K. *The status of nurses and self-disclosure.* Unpublished manuscript, 1968. [*see* A1. Breed and Jourard, 1970, p. 25]

Slobin, Dan I.; Miller, Stephen H.; and Porter, Lyman W. Forms of address and social relations in a business organization. *Journal of Personality and Social Psychology,* 1968, *8,* 289-293.

South, L. L. *A study of the relationship of nurses' self-disclosure to the importance they assign to supportive emotional care of patients.* Unpublished master's thesis, University of Pittsburgh, 1962. [see A1. Breed and Jourard, 1970, pp. 43-44]

Taylor, Dalmas A. *Self-disclosure and communication processes and recruitment of ethnic minorities for graduate psychology.* Paper

H4. Self-disclosure in special populations

presented at Colloquium, Bell Telephone Laboratories, Murray Hill, New Jersey, March, 1976.

H5. *Medical Patients and the Physically Impaired*

Feldman, Ronald L. *Self-disclosure patterns in the parents of stuttering children.* Unpublished doctoral dissertation, New York University, 1970. *Dissertation Abstracts International,* 1971, *32* (6-B), 3688.

Jones, Mary G. *Self-disclosure among deaf adolescents and its relationship to social sensitivity and personality.* Unpublished doctoral dissertation, The Catholic University of America, 1975. *Dissertation Abstracts International,* 1975, *36* (3-B), 1437.

Kelber, Sister Mary B. *Exploration of group sessions with rehabilitating post-myocardial infarction males regarding self-disclosure and cardiac adjustment with objective and subjective evaluations of group sessions.* Unpublished doctoral dissertation, The Catholic University of America, 1976. *Dissertation Abstracts International,* 1976, *37* (3-B), 1408.

Kleck, Robert E. Self-disclosure patterns of the non-obviously stigmatized. *Psychological Reports,* 1968, *23,* 1239-1248. [epileptics]

Mesch, Joyce C. *Interpersonal attraction and self-disclosure in interaction between orthopedically disabled and nondisabled male college students.* Unpublished doctoral dissertation, New York University, 1974. *Dissertation Abstracts International,* 1974, *35* (2-A), 894.

Prophit, Sister Penny. *The relationship of the psychological construct of self-disclosure to post-coronary adjustment.* Unpublished doctoral dissertation, The Catholic University of America, 1974. *Dissertation Abstracts International,* 1975, *36* (1-B), 163.

Wharton, Mary C. *Some personality characteristics of frequent and infrequent visitors to a university infirmary.* Unpublished doctoral dissertation, University of Florida, 1962. *Dissertation Abstracts International,* 1962, *23* (9), 3483.

H6. *Psychiatric Patients and the Emotionally Disturbed*

H6.1 *Psychiatric patients*

Anchor, Kenneth N. *High and low risk self-disclosure in group psychotherapy.* Paper presented at the Meeting of the Midwestern

Psychological Association, Chicago, 1974. (ERIC Document Reproduction Service No. ED 099 746)

Anchor, Kenneth N.; Vojtisek, John E.; and Berger, Stephen E. Social desirability as a predictor of self-disclosure in groups. *Psychotherapy: Theory, Research, and Practice*, 1972, *9*, 262-264.

Anchor, Kenneth N.; Vojtisek, John E.; and Patterson, Roger L. Trait anxiety, initial structuring, and self-disclosure in groups of schizophrenic patients. *Psychotherapy: Theory, Research, and Practice*, 1973, *10*, 155-158.

Carlson, Christopher R. *The relationship of anxiety, openness, and group psychotherapy experience with perceptions of therapist self-disclosure among psychiatric patients.* Unpublished doctoral dissertation, University of Texas, Austin, 1975. *Dissertation Abstracts International*, 1976, *37* (1-B), 453.

Dirks, Stanley J. and Kuldan, John M. Validity of self-report by psychiatric patients of employment earnings and hospitalization. *Journal of Consulting and Clinical Psychology*, 1974, *42*, 738.

Formica, Richard F. *The influence of self-disclosure with schizophrenic outpatients.* Unpublished doctoral dissertation, Columbia University, 1972. *Dissertation Abstracts International*, 1973, *33* (10-B), 5012.

Mayo, P. R. Self-disclosure and neurosis. *British Journal of Social and Clinical Psychology*, 1968, *7*, 140-148.

Rogers, Carl R.; Gendlin, Eugene T.; Kiesler, Donald J.; and Truax, Charles B. (Eds.). *The therapeutic relationship and its impact: A study of psychotherapy with schizophrenics.* Madison: University of Wisconsin Press, 1967.

Shimkunas, Algimantas M. Demand for intimate self-disclosure and pathological verbalization in schizophrenia. *Journal of Abnormal Psychology*, 1972, *80*, 197-205.

Smallwood, Ronney E. *Group modification of affective and self-disclosing verbalizations in a psychiatric population.* Unpublished doctoral dissertation, Oklahoma State University, 1975. *Dissertation Abstracts International*, 1976, *36* (11-B), 5817.

Tucker, Gregory E. *A study of verbal accessibility in hospitalized paranoid schizophrenics in response to two styles of interviewing.* Unpublished doctoral dissertation, Western Reserve University, 1961. [not abstracted in *Dissertation Abstracts*]

H6.2 Self-disclosure in special populations

H6.2 *Emotionally disturbed*

Appelberg, Esther. *Verbal accessibility of adolescents.* Unpublished doctoral dissertation, Western Reserve University, 1961. [not abstracted in *Dissertation Abstracts*]

Appelberg, Esther. Verbal accessibility of adolescents. *Child Welfare,* 1964, *43,* 86-90.

Blum, Arthur. Peer-group structure and a child's verbal accessibility in a treatment institution. *Social Service Review,* 1962, *36,* 385-395.

Blum, Arthur and Polansky, Norman A. Effect of staff role on children's verbal accessibility. *Social Work,* 1961, *6,* 29-37.

Ganter, Grace and Plansky, Norman A. Predicting a child's accessibility to individual treatment from diagnostic groups. *Social Work,* 1964, *9,* 56-63.

Ganter, Grace; Yeakel, Margaret; and Polansky, Norman A. Intermediary group treatment of inaccessible children. *American Journal of Orthopsychiatry,* 1965, *35,* 739-746.

Garrigan, James J. *Effects of modeling on self-disclosure of emotionally disturbed preadolescent boys.* Unpublished doctoral dissertation, Lehigh University, 1975. *Dissertation Abstracts International,* 1975, *36* (5-B), 2467.

Polansky, Norman A. and Weiss, Erwin S. Determinants of accessibility to treatment in a children's institution. *Journal of Jewish Communal Service,* 1959, *36,* 130-137.

Polansky, Norman A.; Weiss, Erwin S.; and Blum, Arthur. Children's verbal accessibility as a function of content and personality. *American Journal of Orthopsychiatry,* 1961, *31,* 153-169.

Weber, Ruth. *Children's verbal accessibility as a predictor of treatment outcome.* Unpublished doctoral dissertation, Western Reserve University, 1963. [not abstracted in *Dissertation Abstracts*]

H7. *Alcoholics and Drug Addicts*

Ball, J. C. The reliability and validity of interview data obtained from 59 narcotic addicts. *American Journal of Sociology,* 1967, *72,* 650-654.

Gary, A. L. and Hammond, R. Self-disclosures of alcoholics and drug addicts. *Psychotherapy: Theory, Research, and Practice*, 1970, 7, 142-143.

Guze, Samuel B.; Tuason, Vicente B.; Stewart, Mark A.; and Picken, Bruce. The drinking history: A comparison of reports by subjects and their relatives. *Quarterly Journal of Studies on Alcohol*, 1963, 24, 249-260.

Liberman, Bernard L. *The effect of modeling procedures on attraction and disclosure in a psychotherapy analogue.* Unpublished doctoral dissertation, Syracuse University, 1970. *Dissertation Abstracts International*, 1970, 32 (1-B), 564. [alcoholic inpatients]

Sobell, Linda C. and Sobell, Mark B. Outpatient alcoholics give valid self-reports. *Journal of Nervous and Mental Disease*, 1975, 161, 32-42.

Sobell, Mark B.; Sobell, Linda C.; and Samuels, Fred H. Validity of self-reports of alcohol-related arrests by alcoholics. *Quarterly Journal of Studies on Alcohol*, 1974, 35, 276-280.

Stephens, Richard. The truthfulness of addict respondents in research projects. *International Journal of the Addictions*, 1972, 7, 549-558.

Summers, Trudy. Validity of alcoholics' self-reported drinking history. *Quarterly Journal of Studies on Alcohol*, 1970, 31, 972-974.

H8. *Criminals, Delinquents, and Recidivists*

Braithwaite, Ronald. A paired study of self-disclosure of black and white inmates. *Journal of Non-White Concerns in Personnel and Guidance*, 1973, 1, 86-94.

Braithwaite, Ronald L. *An analysis of proxemics and self-disclosing behavior of recidivist and non-recidivist adult social offenders from black, chicano, and white inmate populations.* Unpublished doctoral dissertation, Michigan State University, 1974. *Dissertation Abstracts International*, 1975, 35 (9-B), 4621.

Braukmann, Curtis J.; Fixsen, Dean L.; Phillips, Elery L.; Wolf, Montrose M.; and Maloney, Dennis M. An analysis of a selection interview training package for predelinquents at Achievement Place. *Criminal Justice and Behavior*, 1974, 1, 30-42.

Brodsky, Stanley L. An inventory for measuring prisoner disclosure of institutionally related events. *Correctional Psychologist*, 1968, 3, 18-20.

H8. Self-disclosure in special populations

Brodsky, Stanley L. and Komaridis, George V. Military prisonization. *Military Police Journal,* July, 1966, 8-9.

Brodsky, Stanley L. and Komaridis, George V. Self-disclosure in prisoners. *Psychological Reports,* 1968, *23,* 403-407.

Jaffee, Lester D. and Plansky, Norman A. Verbal inaccessibility in young adolescents showing delinquent trends. *Journal of Health and Human Behavior,* 1962, *3,* 105-111.

Juarez, Shirlee J. *An experimental analysis of a counseling procedure emphasizing peer self-help in a prison setting.* Unpublished doctoral dissertation, University of California, Riverside, 1973. *Dissertation Abstracts International,* 1974, *34* (7-B), 3467.

Ollerman, Thomas E. *The effect of group counseling upon self-atualization, self-disclosure, and the development of interpersonal trust among prison inmates.* Unpublished doctoral dissertation, New Mexico State University, 1975. *Dissertation Abstracts International,* 1975, *36* (6-A), 3415.

Persons, Roy W. Jr. *Interpersonal intimacy with recidivists.* Unpublished doctoral dissertation, Ohio State University, 1969. *Dissertation Abstracts International,* 1969, *30* (4-B), 1905.

Persons, Roy W. and Marks, Philip A. Self-disclosure with recidivists: Optimum interviewer-interviewee matching. *Journal of Abnormal Psychology,* 1970, *76,* 387-391.

Rothenberg, Eugenia. *The effect of self-disclosure and pseudo-self-disclosure on social adjustment of institutionalized delinquent girls.* Unpublished doctoral dissertation, University of New Mexico, 1969. *Dissertation Abstracts International,* 1970, *30* (12-A), 5246.

AUTHOR INDEX

AUTHOR INDEX

AUTHOR INDEX

AUTHOR INDEX

Haymes, M., 47
Hays, Charles F., 121
Haythorn, William W., 13, 32, 71, 72, 103, 106, 181, 182
Hayward, Richard H., 47, 121, 128
Heifitz, M. L., 43, 135
Heilbrun, Alfred B., Jr., 97, 118, 126
Hellcamp, David T., 54, 57, 61, 193
Heller, Kenneth, 122, 131, 159
Hendry, Derek, 20
Herman, Elliot, 22, 34, 112, 168, 174
Herndon, James, 15, 134, 153
Hershenberg, Bernard, 105, 186
Hick, Kenneth W., 7, 16, 154
Higbee, Kenneth L., 38, 40, 56, 81, 83, 85, 87, 97, 108, 146
Highlen, Pamela S., 23, 159
Hill, Clara E., 40, 55, 113, 131
Hill, James A., 40
Himelstein, Philip, 33, 36, 42, 75, 81, 151, 152, 154
Hines, David A., 30, 31, 112
Hodge, M. B., 139
Homans, George C., 154
Hood, Thomas C., 135
Hope, G. M., 106
Horenstein, David, 20, 47, 99, 164, 168
Horner, Beverly M., 10, 122, 128
Horton, Susan W., 171
House, James, 15, 72, 175, 178
Howard, Kenneth I., 40
Howard, Lydia R., 58
Hoyt, Michael F., 90
Hrubetz, Joan, 146, 187, 196
Huesmann, L. Rowell, 106, 154
Hurley, John R., 37, 42
Hurley, Shirley J., 37, 42, 146, 183
Hutchins, Trova K., 122
Hyde, Mary R., 145, 178
Hyink, Paul W., 16, 26, 55, 65, 114, 126

Isaza, Judith L., 8, 12, 40, 58
Iversen, Craig A., 63
Ivey, Allen E., 23, 158, 186
Ivie, Robert L., 13, 104

Jackson, Russel H., 114
Jackson, Ted, 9, 82, 162
Jacobson, Edward A., 119, 160, 188
Jaffe, Peggy E., 16, 120, 122, 159
Jaffee, Lester D., 84, 193, 202
James, Charles R., 65, 122, 131, 159
Janis, Irving L., 90
Janofsky, Annelies I., 7, 23, 133, 134, 175, 176
Jennings, Floyd L., 60
Johannesen, Richard L., 97
Johnson, Carl F., 135, 176
Johnson, David L., 146
Johnson, David W., 106, 154, 169
Johnson, Donald L., 119, 160, 188
Johnson, Patrick J., 176
Jones, Edward E., 20, 33, 94, 154, 164
Jones, John E., 188
Jones, Lawrence K., 60, 68, 159
Jones, Mary G., 16, 75, 82, 193, 198
Jongsma, Arthur E., Jr., 135, 169
Jourard, Sidney M., 1, 4, 6, 9, 10, 16, 28, 35, 37, 39, 47, 48, 51, 53, 59, 60, 61, 65, 68, 69, 70, 83, 85, 90, 91, 94, 96, 102, 106, 120, 122, 131, 132, 135, 136, 154, 162, 165, 173, 176, 178, 179, 196, 197
Joure, Sylvia, 75, 141
Juarez, Shirlee J., 187, 202

Kahn, Gay M., 12, 44, 75, 112,

AUTHOR INDEX

AUTHOR INDEX

AUTHOR INDEX

SUBJECT INDEX

This Subject Index consists of six major rubrics, as follows:

DISCLOSEE
DISCLOSER
DISCLOSURE

INTERPERSONAL DIMENSIONS
METHODOLOGY
REVIEWS OF SELF-DISCLO-
SURE LITERATURE

DISCLOSEE:
  characteristics of, 95-97
  choice of, 93-95
  effect of disclosure on, 99
  experiencing of, 88-89
  leader of group as, 137-140
  relationship of to discloser, 93-95
  response style of, 97-99, 115-124
  therapist, counselor, and inter-
    viewer as, 112-119, 124-125

DISCLOSER:
  achievement of, 89-90
  adolescent as, 193-195
  age of, 53
  alcoholic as, 200-201
  attitudes of, 86-87
  attributions of, 172-174
  authenticity of, 5-6
  behavior modification of, 115,
    129-130, 185-189
  beliefs of, 86-87
  birth order of, 61-62
  child as, 191-192
  client and interviewee as, 125-130
  college student as, 196-197

congruency of, 5-6
criminal and delinquentas, 201-
  202
drug addict as, 200-201
educational level of, 191-197
emotionally disturbed, 200
employee as, 152
ethnic group of, 58-60
expectations of, 127-129, 172-
  174
experiencing of, 88-89
family of, 61-64
flexibility of, 31-32
genuineness of, 5-6
group member as, 140-142
leader of group as, 137-140
medical patient as, 198
nationality of, 58-60
perceptions of, 87-88, 172-
  174
performance of, 89-90
personality inventory assessments
  of, 78-83
personality of, 64-78
physical appearance of, 90-91
physically impaired, 198

217